2014

YOUTH ENGAGEMENT: THE CIVIC-POLITICAL LIVES OF CHILDREN AND YOUTH

SOCIOLOGICAL STUDIES OF CHILDREN AND YOUTH

Series Editor: David A. Kinney (from 1999)

Series Editors: David A. Kinney and Katherine Brown Rosier (2004–2010)

Series Editors: David A. Kinney and Loretta E. Bass (from 2011)

Series Editor: Loretta E. Bass (from 2012)

Recent Volumes:

SOCIOLOGICAL STUDIES OF CHILDREN AND YOUTH
VOLUME 16

YOUTH ENGAGEMENT: THE CIVIC-POLITICAL LIVES OF CHILDREN AND YOUTH

EDITED BY

SANDI KAWECKA NENGA

Southwestern University, Georgetown, TX, USA

JESSICA K. TAFT

Davidson College, Davidson, NC, USA

Emerald

United Kingdom – North America – Japan
India – Malaysia – China

Emerald Group Publishing Limited
Howard House, Wagon Lane, Bingley BD16 1WA, UK

First edition 2013

Copyright © 2013 Emerald Group Publishing Limited

Reprints and permission service
Contact: permissions@emeraldinsight.com

British Library Cataloguing in Publication Data
A catalogue record for this book is available from the British Library

ISBN: 978-1-78190-543-2
ISSN: 1537-4661 (Series)

ISOQAR certified
Management System,
awarded to Emerald
for adherence to
Environmental
standard
ISO 14001:2004.

Certificate Number 1985
ISO 14001

INVESTOR IN PEOPLE

CONTENTS

LIST OF CONTRIBUTORS

Lucia Alcalá — Department of Psychology, University of California, Santa Cruz, CA, USA

Lily Appoh — Department of Psychology, Norwegian University of Science and Technology, Trondheim, Norway

Emily Bent — Women's and Gender Studies Department, The College of New Jersey, Ewing, NJ, USA

Rebecca M. Callahan — Department of Curriculum and Instruction, Population Research Center, University of Texas at Austin, Austin, TX, USA

William A. Corsaro — Department of Sociology, Indiana University, Bloomington, IN, USA

Shira Eve Epstein — Department of Secondary Education, School of Education, The City College of New York (CUNY), New York, NY, USA

Jesica Siham Fernández — Department of Psychology, University of California, Santa Cruz, CA, USA

Berit O. Johannesen — Department of Psychology, Norwegian University of Science and Technology, Trondheim, Norway

Rachel Kulick — Department of Sociology, Anthropology, Crime and Justice Studies, University of Massachusetts, Dartmouth, MA, USA

Stuart Lester — School of Leisure, University of Gloucestershire, Gloucester, UK

L. Alison Molina-Girón   Part-time professor, Faculty of
                              Education, University of Ottawa,
                              Ottawa, ON, Canada

Shauna A. Morimoto   Department of Sociology and Criminal
                              Justice, University of Arkansas,
                              Fayetteville, AR, USA

Christopher D. O'Connor   Department of Human Behavior,
                              Justice & Diversity, University of
                              Wisconsin, Superior, WI, USA

Kathryn M. Obenchain   Department of Curriculum and
                              Instruction, Purdue University,
                              West Lafayette, IN, USA

*Jocelyn Solís (Dr. Solís   School of Education, CUNY-Brooklyn
passed away in 2004)*   College, New York, NY, USA

ACKNOWLEDGMENTS

Ultimately, any published volume represents the hard work of a large group of people. Working on this volume has given us a new appreciation for reviewers and their generous gift of their intellectual critiques. We wish to thank all of the anonymous reviewers for their supportive and insightful reviews. In addition, we are grateful to the series editor, Loretta E. Bass, for her unwavering support and timely advice. We also wish to express our thanks to the extraordinarily competent editorial team at Emerald Insight.

EDITORIAL BOARD

SERIES BACKGROUND

This series was originally conceived and edited by sociologists Patricia Adler and Peter Adler. The first volume was published in 1986 and the Adlers aptly noted at that time that "the study of children and child development is empirically and theoretically central to the discipline of sociology." This fact is even more apparent today and is due in part to the efforts of the Adlers, associate and guest editors, and contributors to the volume over the past 20 years.

It is important to note that during the same time span, the American Sociological Association developed the Section on Sociology of Children and Youth and the International Sociological Association started the thematic group "Sociology of Childhood." The series provides an outlet for social scientists whose reports on their work with children or youth may not "fit" in traditional academic journals due to the length of their pieces or for other reasons. Some volumes will emphasize specific themes, while others will include a range of chapters on diverse topics. Contributions from all methodological and theoretical orientations are welcome and are peer-reviewed by the series editor, members of the editorial board, and other researchers. Finally, the volume has a history of publishing work by international scholars and continues to welcome contributions from around the world.

INTRODUCTION: CONCEPTUALIZING YOUTH ENGAGEMENT

Since we began work on this volume in 2011, images of youth who are politically and civically engaged have populated news stories. Youth activists played key roles in the social movements that sparked and spread through Africa and the Middle East in the "Arab Spring" of 2011 and 2012. In Norway, politically engaged youth attending a summer camp run by the ruling Labour Party became the victims of a mass shooting in July of 2011. Students in Chile, Mexico City, and Quebec took to the streets in order to challenge the rising costs of education and to organize for improvements to their colleges and universities. Undocumented youth in the United States publicly shared their stories and lobbied for passage of the DREAM Act. And local newspapers throughout the United States continued to celebrate youth who were honored for their volunteer service with awards and scholarships.

Yet for decades politicians, scholars, and members of the general public have expressed concern about young people's low levels of civic and political engagement (Pfaff, 2009; Putnam, 2000; Youniss et al., 2002). Cultural narratives of youth as unruly, hormone-driven actors with the potential to threaten the social order (Lesko, 2001) may partially motivate this concern with youth's low levels of civic and political engagement. For those subscribing to a developmental approach, the concern is that youth who are not properly socialized to become competent civic and political actors will not be able to take their place as productive citizens in adulthood.

To ensure that youth are able to practice civic and political engagement, governments and universities have invested considerable resources in youth's civic and political activities. In the United Kingdom, the Crick Report led to the establishment of compulsory citizenship education in England's secondary schools in 2002 (Weller, 2007). In 2009, the United States Congress funded the Edward M. Kennedy Serve America Act which extended and expanded national service programs; this included funding for Learn and Serve America which promotes service learning in schools. In addition, universities have fostered youth engagement by hiring service-learning coordinators, encouraging professors to use community-based learning as a pedagogical method, and praising students' volunteer efforts.

References to the desirability of youth engagement can be found in a wide range of government and academic documents. However, the meaning of "youth engagement" is not necessarily identical in each document. Youth engagement is used to refer to a diverse array of activities including – but not limited to – volunteer work, charity projects, youth councils, youth media projects, voting, work on political campaigns, and social movement activity. The questions and concerns of scholars studying these different forms of youth engagement have been quite similar: What gets people involved? Or on the flip side, what fosters apathy? What keeps people coming back to an organization? How do people construct and understand social problems? What benefits do people derive from participation in the group? And how do individuals create social change? Despite sharing these basic questions, scholars of social movements and voluntary organizations rarely collaborate. They tend to use different vocabulary to tease out aspects of the social phenomena they scrutinize. Social movement scholars tend to focus on framing, collective identity, recruitment, and mobilization (Benford & Snow, 2000; Clay, 2006; McAdam, 1986; Van Dyke, 1998). Scholars of volunteer organizations focus on volunteer demographics, organizational philosophy, social capital, caring, and the development of a moral self (Allahyari, 2000; Rhoads, 1997; Wilson, 2000; Youniss & Yates, 1997). While the vocabulary may be distinct, there is substantial potential for the productive cross-germination of findings and concepts.

One of our aims in this volume is to bring together scholarly examinations of a variety of youth engagement forms. In order to explore and analyze the implications of divergent approaches to youth engagement, we find it useful to offer here an initial definition of the boundaries of the concept. Youth engagement, as it is understood in this volume, refers to those activities in which children and youth enact a public-spirited commitment in pursuit of the common good (Lichterman, 1996). Volunteerism, service-learning, community organizing, activism, military service, youth councils, youth advisory boards, and youth media production among others all qualify as forms of youth engagement. All of these activities offer youth the potential to influence collective social life and, in turn, to be influenced by civic and/or political groups. However, while there may be similarities between various forms of engagement, these should not distract us from significant differences between types of youth engagement. For example, some important ways to distinguish and compare youth engagement activities include assessing and analyzing their varying degrees of collectivity, their tactics for social action, their relationship to governmental institutions, the scale of their goals for change or intervention, and the extent to which they are organized and led by young people or by adults.

Examining a range of youth engagement activities side by side allows us to investigate these critical variations in engagement activities and to explore different visions of ideal youth citizenship. By reading these types of youth engagement alongside one another, we highlight the multiplicity of ways that young people's civic and political identities, capabilities, and rights are envisioned and articulated both by institutions socializing youth for civic and political life and, of course, by young people themselves. It is our contention that these various forms of youth engagement exist in relationship to one another, rather than as isolated or separate practices.

Indeed, when we look to the lives of young people themselves, we find empirical evidence that the divisions between civic and political spheres, between volunteerism and activism, are often not clear-cut. For example, Andrew (17, white) first got involved with Habitat for Humanity through his high school. After working with the group to raise funds to build a house in his hometown, he spent his summers attending blitz builds in other parts of the country. His continuing education at Habitat for Humanity helped him to understand how mortgages work, how zoning and urban planning affect housing, and to see how politics shaped these larger policies. Andrew said he could not wait to turn 18 so that he could vote. He also said that he wanted to attend college in Washington, DC so he could protest on the White House lawn (Nenga, 2010). In another example, Clare (17, multiracial) spent many years as an active member of the girls' advisory board for an organization that aims to empower girls through outdoor activities. When she was in middle school, Clare also attended many anti-war rallies and participated in several walk-outs opposing the invasion of Iraq. However, by the time she was a senior in high school, she was less interested in these visible forms of protest and was spending more and more of her free time working with the girls' organization, developing leadership training programs and strengthening the advisory board's role in the organization's decision-making structure. Clare self-identified as an activist, and she spoke extensively about her own changing ideas about what it means to be an activist (Taft, 2011). When we consider the lives of youth like Andrew and Clare, the division between voluntary organizations and social movements seems artificial and arbitrary. Many youth who volunteer are simultaneously involved in activism. Many youth engaged in activist work also do volunteer work. As they move through volunteer organizations and activist groups, youth participate in both civic and political socialization.

In addition to this empirical rationale for a more comprehensive approach to the study of youth engagement, there are also several important theoretical benefits. First, a more inclusive approach to the study of youth engagement draws our attention to the diversity of models emphasizing how *youth engagement does not have a fixed meaning.* Just within this volume, authors consider models of youth engagement that focus on fundraising (Bent; Callahan and Obenchain), volunteer work (Callahan and Obenchain; Morimoto), youth councils (O'Connor), play (Lester), classroom service projects (Epstein; Molina-Girón), youth media projects (Kulick), national holidays (Corsaro, Johannesen, and Appoh), and rallies and protests (Solís, Fernández, and Alcalá).

By examining these various forms of youth engagement, it becomes clear that *youth engagement is a multifaceted concept with contested social and political goals.* For example, Emily Bent's chapter "A Different Girl Effect: Producing Political Girlhoods in the 'Invest in Girls' Climate," demonstrates how a group of foundations and their viral internet videos promote a vision of youth engagement in which affluent Western girls donate time and money to save their Nonwestern sisters from illiteracy, early childbearing, and poverty. Drawing heavily on discourses of charity and neoliberalism, the model of youth engagement constructed by the Girl Effect discourages Western girls from thinking critically about colonialism, racism, and global relations. Stuart Lester's chapter, "Rethinking Children's Participation in Democratic Processes: A Right to Play," points out that the modernist and developmental discourses informing the United Nations Convention on the Rights of the Child produce a paradoxical vision of children as both dependent objects of care and active agents capable of participating in the social world. By highlighting children's agency, Lester argues that play can become an important arena for children's political engagement. Different stakeholders work to produce a variety of developmental, civic, and political outcomes in various youth engagement models.

The papers in this volume also underline the many ways that *adults both expand and contract young people's civic and political participation.* In "Bridging Worlds in the Social Studies Classroom: Teachers' Practices and Latino Immigrant Youths' Civic and Political Development," Rebecca M. Callahan and Kathryn M. Obenchain document the ways that nationally board-certified social studies teachers helped to strengthen the civic engagement of immigrant students in their US classrooms. By bringing immigrant students' experiences into the curriculum and nurturing students' ability to argue and persuade, the teachers helped to expand youths' capacity for civic engagement and leadership. In contrast, Christopher D.

O'Connor's chapter, "Engaging Young People? The Experiences, Challenges, and Successes of Canadian Youth Advisory Councils," gives voice to the frustration felt by youth in Canadian youth councils when adults underestimated their capacities and limited their ability to make decisions. Shira Eve Epstein's chapter, "'They Have Their Hands on the Pulse of the City': Teachers' Constructions of Students' Civic Knowledge in an Urban Middle School Classroom," demonstrated that teachers initially assumed their students were ignorant of community issues and in need of information from adults. By conceptualizing youth as unable to participate, the teachers nearly blocked youths' ability to become engaged. However, once teachers afforded youth agency, youth were able to demonstrate their knowledge of local issues and actively develop solutions adults had not considered. When adults make space for youth to exercise agency, they generally expand the possibilities for youth engagement.

Considering different forms of youth engagement simultaneously *reveals a set of beliefs adults hold about what kinds of citizenship actions are ideal for citizens of any age and which should be promoted specifically for youth citizens.* Models of citizenship and assumptions about youth capacity undergird visions of "youth engagement" and thus can be the subject of significant critical scholarly analysis across the civic–political divide. In "Educating Active Citizens: What Roles Are Students Expected to Play in Public Life," L. Alison Molina-Girón delineates the different models of citizenship shaping types of youth engagement in three civics classrooms in Ottawa. Teachers structured civics classes to emphasize understandings of citizenship either as a legal status endowed by the state and carrying with it certain rights and benefits; as behavioral practices which support the common good and reaffirm a commitment to the local community; or as a set of political practices emphasizing participation in decision making and linked to values of plurality and justice. Arguing against a theoretical conceptualization of youth as "citizens in the making" which reserves citizenship for adults, Rachel Kulick's chapter "Learning From Each Other: Collective Practices in Making Independent Youth Media," reveals the ways that young adult staff members in youth media projects promote a vision of "actualizing citizenship," in which young people collectively and artistically challenge oppression while working toward social justice. Thus, while adults working with youth typically agree on the value of citizenship, there is a great deal of variation in the meaning of citizenship.

Finally, examining youths' experiences in different kinds of engagement projects allows us to understand the ways that *youth themselves construct and challenge meanings of youth citizenship.* Some children and youth are clearly aware of – and resistant to – adults' understandings of citizenship. Shauna A. Morimoto's contribution to this volume, "Civic Engagement and the Emergence of Race: American Youth Negotiate Citizenship," carefully teases apart the meanings white youth and youth of color attribute to the identity of "US citizen." Morimoto argues that white youth see citizenship as a privilege which they must repay by engaging in volunteer work, while youth of color see volunteering as a way of distancing themselves from violent stereotypes and proving that they are good citizens. Jocelyn Solís, Jesica Siham Fernández, and Lucia Alcalá's chapter "Mexican Immigrant Children and Youth's Contributions to a Community *Centro*: Exploring Civic Engagement and Citizen Constructions" documents the ways Mexican immigrant children at a center for immigrants' rights challenge the idea that citizenship only refers to a legal status and expand the notion to include residency and participation. In the context of a highly nationalistic holiday in Norway, William A. Corsaro, Berit O. Johannesen, and Lily Appoh elicited narratives from immigrant youth in Norway. Their chapter, "'My Mother and Father Are African, But I'm Norwegian': Immigrant Children's Participation in Civic Society in Norway," points to the way immigrant youth actively expand the boundaries of Norwegian citizenship to include their own bicultural, immigrant experiences.

All of the chapters in this volume raise similar critical questions about models of youth engagement and the visions of citizenship linked to them. Looking forward, we argue that more inclusive approaches to the study of youth engagement will illuminate how different forms of youth engagement relate to one another. For example, by examining youth activism alongside youth volunteerism, we are able to consider if these two sets of opportunities offered to youth are seen by young people and adults as part of a singular project (i.e., "making a difference"), or if they are seen as distinct kinds of practices (i.e., "giving back" vs. "changing the world"). Or, by considering them together, we might also be able to better understand how youth move between different forms of engagement. Further, we could ask what kinds of contexts and conditions facilitate one form of engagement over another? Which young people are offered which kinds of engagement opportunities? How do different groups of youth respond to these different forms of engagement? Or, what happens when youth experience conflicting narratives about their rights and capacities, as when one engagement opportunity implies that they are simply practicing for future citizenship and another encourages them to see themselves as agents of change in the present?

In short, by examining the broader field of youth engagement, we can gain a more complex picture of the institutional and individual dynamics of this terrain.

Sandi Kawecka Nenga
Jessica K. Taft
Co-Editors

REFERENCES

Allahyari, R. A. (2000). *Visions of charity: Volunteer workers and moral community.* Berkeley, CA: University of California Press.

Benford, R. D., & Snow, D. A. (2000). Framing processes and social movements: An overview and assessment. *Annual Review of Sociology, 26,* 611–639.

Clay, A. (2006). All I need is one mic: Mobilizing youth for social change in the post-civil rights era. *Social Justice, 33*(2), 105–121.

Lesko, N. (2001). *Act your age! A cultural construction of adolescence.* New York, NY: Routledge.

Lichterman, P. (1996). *The search for political community: American activists reinventing commitment.* Cambridge, UK: Cambridge University Press.

McAdam, D. (1986). Recruitment to high-risk activism: The case of freedom summer. *The American Journal of Sociology, 92*(1), 64–90.

Nenga, S. K. (2010). The value of volunteering: Comparing youths' experiences to popular claims. In H. B. Johnson (Ed.), *Sociological studies of children and youth: Children and youth speak for themselves* (Vol. 13, pp. 295–318). Bingley, UK: Emerald.

Pfaff, N. (2009). Youth culture as a context of political learning: How young people politicize amongst each other. *Young: Nordic Journal of Youth Research, 17*(2), 167–189.

Putnam, R. D. (2000). *Bowling alone: The collapse and revival of American community.* New York, NY: Touchstone.

Rhoads, R. A. (1997). *Community service and higher learning: Explorations of the caring self.* Albany, NY: State University of New York Press.

Taft, J. K. (2011). *Rebel girls: Youth activism and social change across the Americas.* New York, NY: New York University Press.

Van Dyke, N. (1998). Hotbeds of activism: Locations of student protest. *Social Problems, 45*(2), 205–220.

Weller, S. (2007). *Teenagers' citizenship: Experiences and education.* New York, NY: Routledge.

Wilson, J. (2000). Volunteering. *Annual Review of Sociology, 26,* 215–240.

Youniss, J, Bales, S., Christmas-Best, V., Diversi, M., McLaughlin, M., & Silbereisen, R. (2002). Youth civic engagement in the twenty-first century. *Journal of Research on Adolescence, 12*(1), 121–148.

Youniss, J., & Yates, M. (1997). *Community service and social responsibility in youth.* Chicago, IL: University of Chicago Press.

PART I
FRAMING THE CIVIC-POLITICAL
LIVES OF CHILDREN AND YOUTH

A DIFFERENT GIRL EFFECT: PRODUCING POLITICAL GIRLHOODS IN THE "INVEST IN GIRLS" CLIMATE

Emily Bent

ABSTRACT

Purpose – *This article critically (re)examines the Girl Effect narrative in order to problematize the ways that this discursive paradigm shapes the forms and possibilities for girls' political subjectivity and agency.*

Approach – *Based on a close, textual reading of the first Girl Effect video, the study adopts the tools of deconstruction to reveal the discursive (im)possibilities for differently situated girls. It draws from contemporary girls' studies scholarship and postcolonial feminist theory to identify the production of oppositional girlhoods and neoliberal girl power, while further considering how these disciplinary effects inform girls' political practices.*

Findings – *The author suggests that the Girl Effect paradigm offers limited understandings of girls' political subjectivity: prompting Western girls to become agents of missionary girl power and positioning Third World girls as perpetual victims waiting for rescue.*

Youth Engagement: The Civic-Political Lives of Children and Youth
Sociological Studies of Children and Youth, Volume 16, 3–20
ISSN: 1537-4661/doi:10.1108/S1537-4661(2013)0000016005

Originality/value – *By exploring the* effects *of the Girl Effect logic, this article troubles the political ideologies framing the "invest in girls" message and contributes original research to the growing field of girls' studies.*

Keywords: Girl Effect; girlhood; political subjectivity; neoliberalism

INTRODUCTION

Over the last several years, international development policy has increasingly focused on the power of adolescent girls (Carella, 2011; Harris, 2004; Hayhurst, 2011). From Plan International's *Because I am a Girl* campaign to the United Nations Foundation's *Girl Up* program, proponents suggest girls are the key to breaking the cycle of intergenerational poverty and advancing the modernity of Third World nations. Among these recent marketing initiatives, *the Girl Effect* is likely the most widely recognized. According to the New York Times journalist Kristof (2010), the Girl Effect videos have been viewed well over 10 million times and boast a following of over 300,000 friends on social media sites. The Girl Effect has also played a prominent role at the Clinton Global Initiative, Davos, and the World Bank (Eitel, 2009) and has been featured throughout mainstream Western media. Yet despite the growing popularity of this viral movement, the Girl Effect campaign has received limited scholarly attention and little is known about how the Girl Effect "works" in the everyday lives of girls (Provost, 2012).

    This article examines what is made (im)possible for differently situated girls vis-à-vis the Girl Effect paradigm. It investigates how the logic of the Girl Effect shapes girls' political selves, and draws from postcolonial and poststructuralist feminist theory to deconstruct the Girl Effect narrative. The Girl Effect, I propose, problematically (re)inscribes colonialist divides between Western and Third World girlhoods[1] that reify the dichotomies of Western empowerment and Third World vulnerability. This article correspondingly considers three interrelated practices: the production of oppositional girlhoods, (re)vitalization of neoliberal girl power, and the concealed logic of *missionary girl power* (Sensoy & Marshall, 2010). Taken together, I suggest the Girl Effect paradigm functions to constrain girls' political subjectivity and agency – prompting girls in the Global North to maintain colonialist power structures and divides, and to advocate for *other* girls' rights and concerns, as different from their own.

THE GIRL EFFECT

The Girl Effect is a marketing campaign created by the Nike and NoVo Foundations to generate funding for girls economic development in the Global South. Gender and development scholar Hayhurst (2011) characterizes this initiative as "a growing but understudied movement that assumes girls are catalysts capable of bringing social and economic change for their families, communities and countries" (p. 531). The Girl Effect contends that girls' education delays early marriage, reduces infant and maternal mortality, slows down population growth, and improves local and global economies. Since its launch in 2008, Nike and NoVo have committed over $90 million dollars to support the advancement of the Girl Effect within the human rights and international development communities, and similarly to promote its "invest in girls" message to governments, civil society actors, and philanthropists (Roberts, 2010).

The Girl Effect brand features two viral videos[2] that explore the untapped economic potential of adolescent girls living in the Global South. The first self-titled video, *The Girl Effect*, suggests with the right investments girls can transform their local and global communities. It includes 2:23 minutes of stylized graphics and rhetorical text that guides viewers through Third World poverty and gender inequality, but concludes with the feel good message of girls' economic empowerment. In the first video, viewers witness the broader impacts of Western intervention in the Global South; the video illustrates how adolescent girls can inspire change within their families and communities when they are educated and employed. The first Girl Effect closes with the simple, yet powerful, message "invest in a girl and she will do the rest" (Girl Effect, 2008, screen 2: 06).

The second video titled *The Clock is Ticking* demonstrates the dangers of delaying such investments in Third World girls and presses viewers to consider that "a 12-year-old girl could be the solution the world needs right now" (Girl Effect, 2010, para. 1). Following the format of the first Girl Effect video, the second incorporates self-narrated text with graphic illustrations of girl children, adolescent girls, and adult women. Running at 3:04 minutes, this video exposes issues of sex trafficking, forced and early marriage, teen pregnancy, and HIV/AIDS. The second video, like the first, focuses on adolescent girls' economic potentials and concludes with the statement, "50 million 12-year-old girls in poverty, equals 50 million solutions" (Girl Effect, 2010, screens 2:37–2:38).

Certainly, the Girl Effect campaign draws critical attention to the needs and concerns of adolescent girls in the Global South; the videos present an uplifting story of possibility and transformation sparked by the ethos of girl power. But the Girl Effect also constructs Western and Third World girlhoods in politically limiting ways – mediating the forms and possibilities for girls' political subjectivity and agency. Girls' studies scholar Gonick (2003) asserts, "girls become girls by participating within available sets of social meanings and practices, the discourses which define them as girls" (p. 5). In this article, I focus on how the first Girl Effect video regulates what is (im)possible for Western and Third World girls to *become* in the context of the Girl Effect paradigm. I employ the tools of poststructuralist deconstruction to identify the types of subjectivities made available to girls, and then consider how these subject positions inform girls' political practices and political selves.

THE NEOLIBERAL MOMENT

In order to understand the political significance of the Girl Effect logic, it is first necessary to take into account the ways that its "invest in girls" message reflects neoliberal ideals. Neoliberalism is characterized by a decentralized government; the privatization of social programs, education systems, and other services; increased consumer power; free market strategies; global competition; and the erasure of sociocultural identities and differences. Collectively, neoliberal ideologies have unique implications for adolescent girls in the (re)production of their respective girlhood(s).

According to Giddens (1991, 1994) and Beck (1992), neoliberal ideology necessitates the construction of self-reflexive actors invested in notions of choice, individuality, and autonomy. The neoliberal order, Rose and Miller (1992) attest, demands that "each individual must render his or her life meaningful, as if it were the outcome of individual choices made in the furtherance of a biographical project of self-realization" and not regulated by forces of structuralized difference (p. 185). It is in this way that the personal liberties associated with neoliberal ideology function as regulatory illusions, making the ideals of autonomy and choice, seem not only plausible but also desirable for all neoliberal subjects. Indeed for adolescent girls, this neoliberal project of ambitious and continuous self-(re)production parallels the normative construction of their everyday girlhoods as well.

Neoliberalism favors a direct relationship between the global marketplace and the autonomous consuming subject. This ideology obscures the ways that deeply entrenched power structures make difficult the project of autonomy and choice for differently situated subjects. Neoliberal discourse rather inspires choice biographies that encourage girls to take personal responsibility for their successes and failures, often at the expense of their political selves (Taft, 2010). And because free market strategies have come to replace governmental oversight and infrastructure, the globalized labor market demands the production of feminized citizen subjects able to independently succeed despite the dismantling of state structures. Within these neoliberal parameters, Walkerdine (2003) concludes, girls "come to understand themselves as responsible for their own regulation" because structural inequalities and differences are "taken to have melted away" (p. 239). As a result, Ringrose (2007) suggests, girls "come to represent both the dire problem and fantastical possibility" of personal success in an unstable global economy (p. 483).

Neoliberal ideologies further prompt girls to privatize and depoliticize their everyday experiences, making them less likely to challenge the very same structures and institutions that determine their differential status. In the absence of state-based social protection strategies, generational hierarchies and other structural inequalities alternatively determine the extent to which girls *can* claim political subjectivity and agency. The Girl Effect, I contend, mobilizes neoliberal discourses of autonomy, individuality, and choice in the global economy to position girls differently with respect to their political practices and selves. This article thinks critically about the types of subject positions made available to girls, as well as troubles the political ideologies informing the "invest in girls" message. In the next section, I investigate the production of oppositional girlhoods vis-à-vis the Girl Effect paradigm.

OPPOSITIONAL GIRLHOODS

The Girl Effect is marketed as a campaign about Third World girls and *not* girls in the Global North. Operating under the auspices of the "invest in girls" message, the Girl Effect recycles colonized narratives of the Western rescuer versus the Third World victim, and reinforces the ideological boundaries between "*us and them.*" It is my contention that the Girl Effect paradigm works to universalize and position particular types of Western and Third World girlhoods in opposition to one another. This production of oppositional girlhoods in turn fosters colonized notions of privilege and pity, while simultaneously encouraging Western girls to associate poverty, gender discrimination, and violence with the Global South. It is in this way that the Girl Effect prompts Western girls to dismiss the role of gender inequality, structuralized difference, and power in their daily lives, while further confining Third World girls to simplistic characterizations of their imagined girlhoods. Together, the oppositional production of Western and Third World girlhoods serves to limit the forms and possibilities for girls' political subjectivity and agency.

For the purposes of this article, I approach the West/Third World distinction as predominantly about girls' physical locations residing in either the Global North/South, and not necessarily about their racial or ethnic identities, or relative socioeconomic status. The production of oppositional girlhoods rather ensures that Western girls always appear economically, socially, and politically empowered when poised in comparison to the colonized image of Third World vulnerability. According to Hayhurst (2011), the Girl Effect promotes the idea that Third World girls require "their counterparts in the global North" to rescue and liberate them (p. 534). It is in this way that the oppositional production of Third World girlhood makes possible the problematic signification of Third World girls as little more than vulnerable figures waiting for Western rescue and empowerment, and that of Western girls as *already* empowered subjects with little need for human rights or engaged political resistance.

Postcolonial feminist theory affords much to the analysis of the Girl Effect and its relational construction of Western and Third World girlhoods. At its most basic level, postcolonial feminist theory reverses the colonizing gaze of the West to reveal the prescriptive forces of colonial power and discursive signification. Building off the work of Said (1978), this form of feminist theorizing infuses orientalism with the concepts of gender and sexuality. Said (1978) famously argued, orientalism is "fundamentally a political doctrine willed over the Orient" in which representations of the *other* serve to legitimize Western colonization and reaffirm Western power (p. 204). Feminist theorist Yegenoglu (1998) adds that Western representations of non-Western subjectivity also rely upon "a network of codes, imageries, [and] signs" that not only reflect colonized desires and power, but sexualized differences as well (p. 22).

The discourses of the colonizer work to solidify the Western subject as the dominant and desirable subject position. This relational structure allows for the Western subject to definitively articulate the differences between self and other, and to erase existing connections and interdependencies among differential subjects. In her classic essay *Under Western Eyes: Revisited,* Mohanty (2003) notes that the practice of discursive colonization produces composite images of the feminine *other* as universally defined by experiences of gender inequality and patriarchal oppression. This practice of "discursive homogenization" in turn requires that the colonized takes on the identity of the *other* in order to be recognized as "real" or "true" in the eyes of the Western colonizer (Mohanty, 2003, p. 374). As a result, Yegenoglu (1998) attests, the non-Western *other* is always little more than a discursive effect "already entangled with its representation, always articulated within a political field of signification," and forever made true by and for Western subjectivity and agency (p. 22).

The Girl Effect is quite clearly framed from the perspective of the Western viewer; it presupposes a literate, English-speaking audience and relies upon the viewer's own voice and imagination to narrate the Girl Effect story. Ironically because the video is captured almost entirely in text-based images and marketable slogans, it acts to privilege the voice and agency of the Western viewer over that of Third World girls themselves. The Girl Effect indeed allows viewers to unquestioningly determine the present, past, and future of girls living in the Global South.

For example, the first Girl Effect video begins by asking the viewer to "imagine a girl living in poverty" (Girl Effect, 2008, screen 0:36) and then in anticipation of some respective resistance, repeats the request stating, "No, go ahead. Really, imagine her" (Girl Effect, 2008, screens 0:37–0:39). Immediately following this sentiment of reassurance, the word "girl" appears in the center of a blank screen and the viewer is assisted in "seeing" Third World girlhood with words like baby, husband, HIV, and hunger, while several word "flies" buzz around "girl." These loaded terms recall mainstream media depictions of poverty in the Global South, and they (re)inscribe colonized images of difference and power. The viewer is made to bear witness to the devastating impacts of Third World patriarchy, dominance, and inequality, while simultaneously experiencing the benevolent rescue of Third World girls by the Western subject. It is in this way that the Western viewer is transformed from passive observer to proactive investor who can "pretend [to] fix this picture" (Girl Effect, 2008, screen 0:49).

The Girl Effect video also lacks the voices and experiences of *actual* Third World girls. Without the images and dialogue of *real* girls in the Global South, viewers learn virtually nothing about the realities of their daily lives, nor do they gain a more complex understanding of their girlhoods, families, communities, or nations. The girls of the Girl Effect are rather singularly defined by their experiences with poverty, gender inequality, and patriarchy: they remain fixed victims and *become* whatever the viewer imagines them to be. At the same time, the logic of the Girl Effect precludes the colonized *other* from speaking or representing herself as anything other than what the colonizer has constructed. Third World girlhood is instead predetermined by the parameters of their own colonized signification. Based on the critical logic of postcolonial feminist theory, the discursive production of non-Western girlhoods can also therefore be read as working to stabilize Western girlhoods as the preferred norm.

The Girl Effect, I have argued, problematically (re)inscribes colonialist power structures that simplistically position Western and Third World girls in opposition to one another. This approach universalizes a very particular set of Western and non-Western girlhoods that reinforce the ideological boundaries between "*us and them*" and obscure the ways that structural inequalities continue to shape girls' lives all over the world. Moreover, the Girl Effect constructs a dangerous image of Third World vulnerability that universally denies Third World girls' agency and power, while likewise framing Western girls as having little to no need for the *Girl Effect*. This oppositional positioning negates the experiences of poor, vulnerable, or disempowered girls in the West as well as those of affluent or empowered girls in the Global South. The Girl Effect instead encourages Western girls to associate poverty, gender discrimination, and violence with the Global South; to silence their own experiences and struggles; and to confine Third World girls to their colonized and victimized status.

NEOLIBERAL GIRL POWER

The Girl Effect also espouses neoliberal principals throughout the entirety of its narrative, but particularly in the portrayal of girls' economic empowerment as the key to solving gross global inequities. Epitomized by the message of investing in girls, the Girl Effect evokes ideals of hard work, autonomous agency, and making the right decisions in a free market economy as producing personal success, upward mobility, and, above all, the modernity of Third World nations. Previously, I have proposed that the Girl Effect operates as the latest manifestation of neoliberal ideologies personified in the colonized images of Third World girlhood. In this section, I explore how the Girl Effect mobilizes the discourse of neoliberal girl power to dismiss the forces of structuralized difference and to alternatively encourage girls to take personal responsibility for their successes and failures. Utilizing my previous identification of oppositional girlhoods, I reveal the ways in which the Girl Effect problematically equates girls' economic capacities with their political empowerment.

The Girl Effect discourse traces a direct causal relationship between the autonomous neoliberal agent and the global marketplace, claiming because she chooses to

> Use the profits from the milk to help her family ... she becomes the business owner who brings clean water to the village, which makes the men respect her good sense and invite her to the village council, where she convinces everyone that all girls are valuable. Soon, more girls have a chance and the village is thriving (Girl Effect, 2008, screens 1:00–1:24).

Without the interference (or support) of her government, the "girl" of the Girl Effect leads herself through a series of never-ending achievements in her school and workplace, and within her family and local community. In fact, the Girl Effect explains that it is not "the internet. It's not science. It's not the government. It's not money. It's (dramatic pause) A Girl" (Girl Effect, 2008, screens 0:24–0:33) that brings, "Food. Peace. Lower HIV. Healthier Babies. Education. Commerce. Sanitation. Stability" (Girl Effect, 2008, screens 1:25–1:30) to her country and the rest of the world. She is thus in every sense the neoliberal biographer of her own life story.

My concern with this account is not only about its narrative revival of girl power, but rather also how the Girl Effect makes invisible and unnecessary girls familial, geopolitical, and sociocultural support systems. The Girl Effect positions Third World girls as "the new poster boy for neoliberal dreams of winning, and 'just doing it' against the odds" (Ringrose, 2007, p. 484). According to this discursive logic, Third World girls are only successful when they are completely and utterly alone. Indeed, when the Girl Effect first introduces "a girl," the viewer watches, as she is trapped by daunting black capital letters: hunger, HIV, poverty, husband, and baby. These terms collectively dominate, crush, and force her into the background of her own life story, and it is only when she is "freed" from the burdens of her husband, child, hunger, community, and the flies of poverty that she emerges an empowered neoliberal agent with infinite possibilities and choices. Within a matter of seconds, the girl is literally stripped of her sociocultural, geopolitical, and historical "baggage" and left to embark on a solitary journey of economic development and personal empowerment. Indeed, it is at this stage of the Girl Effect text – when *girl* emerges without her family, community, and culture – that the viewer is told, "Now, she has a chance" (Girl Effect, 2008, screen 0:55).

The Girl Effect's promotion of neoliberal girl power encourages girls to become subjects "capable of bearing the burdens of liberty" (Rose, 1999, p. ix). Taft (2004) notes, this new understanding of girl power frequently "excludes girls' political selves" in favor of individualist, postfeminist, and consumer-driven notions of political power, which "define girls as noncritical and nonactive subjects" outside of the global marketplace (pp. 69–70). Neoliberal girl power prompts girls to divorce their girlhoods "from any serious relationship to structural systems" and to instead more securely attach themselves to notions of individualized choice and responsibility as consumers, but not political subjects (Gonick, 2007, p. 439). The Girl Effect paradigm, I concurrently suggest, builds off of this neoliberal ideology to dismiss the ways that structural inequalities and difference inform girls' everyday lives.

Throughout the entirety of the first Girl Effect video, *girl* does not encounter any limitations or constraints based on her gender, age, ethnicity, or socioeconomic status. She never experiences resistance, violence, or inequitable treatment in her pursuit of economic power and gender equality; and once she *becomes* an empowered neoliberal agent, she *alone* resolves her country's systemic issues of poverty, inadequate education, poor food and water supply, HIV/AIDS, and gender inequality. In the end, viewers learn that apart from a cow and invitation to speak with the village council, neoliberal girl power allows Third World girls to "turn this sinking ship around" (Girl Effect, 2008, screens 0:15–0:18).

At the same time, the Girl Effect walks viewers through the disciplinary processes of continuous self-management and self-production in the new neoliberal order. It sequentially moves Third World girls from school to "Cow. $. Business. Clean H2O. Stronger Economy. Better World" in a series of nonstop textual frames that seem to illustrate the apparent ease with which this neoliberal success story can be accomplished (Girl Effect, 2008, screens 1:43–1:48). The Girl Effect indeed presents the quintessential girl power story where economic prosperity "naturally" occurs once girls "choose" to be successful. Despite ample evidence to the contrary,[3] the Girl Effect identifies school as the first "safe" and depoliticized space where girls are free to construct their choice biographies and make possible the Girl Effect's central message: "invest in a girl and she *will* do the rest" (my emphasis, Girl Effect, 2008, screen 2:06).

The Girl Effect characterizes Third World girls as "untapped 'natural resources' ready to be harnessed and dispatched for their society's good" (Sensoy & Marshall, 2010, p. 301). It ties girls' political empowerment to the needs of the global marketplace and in doing so, reifies the oppositional production of Western and Third World girlhoods. On the other hand, this practice instrumentalizes girls' consumer power without giving equitable attention to girls' human rights and political agency. Neoliberal girl power instead works to mask the value of collective social justice movements, putting the onus "on the girls to change their behaviors, actions, and attitudes in order to achieve gender equality" (Hayhurst, 2011, p. 534). It is in this way that I propose the practice of neoliberal girl power acts to dismiss the sociocultural, geopolitical, and historical complexities of girls' everyday lives, while further pressuring girls to take sole responsibility for their successes and failures. In the end, the demand for neoliberal autonomy produces depoliticized girlhood subjects who *may* be able to successfully traverse gender inequality, poverty, and discrimination as individual economic agents, but not as empowered political subjects.

In this section, I have drawn attention to the ways that the Girl Effect logic (re)vitalizes neoliberal girl power to promote the "invest in girls" message. It is my contention that this discursive practice problematically limits the possibilities for girls' political subjectivity and agency by aligning girls' political selves with the needs of the global marketplace and prompting girls to rely on individual choices rather than more collective means for sociopolitical change or economic justice. I have also suggested that the Girl Effect paradigm positions Western and Third World girls in opposition to one another. In the next section, I connect the concepts of neoliberal girl power and oppositional girlhoods to reveal the underlying and centralized logic of *missionary girl power* at play within the Girl Effect discourse (Sensoy & Marshall, 2010).

MISSIONARY GIRL POWER

After reviewing post-9/11 children's books distributed in the Global North, literary scholars Sensoy and Marshall (2010) coined the phrase *missionary girl power* to describe the textual representation of Western girls relationship to Third World girls. They propose missionary girl power recycles neocolonial characterizations of the *East* vs. *West* to "position 'First World' girls as the saviours or caretakers of 'Third World' girls" (Sensoy & Marshall, 2010, p. 296). In this article, I employ Sensoy and Marshall's (2010) concept of missionary girl power to manage the discursive function of neoliberal girl power and oppositional girlhoods vis-à-vis the Girl Effect paradigm. This section investigates how the missionary girl power logic mediates girls' global relationships with one another, as well as how it informs girls' political subjectivity and agency. I maintain the logic of missionary girl power encourages Western girls to identify themselves as privileged consumers with the ability to "invest" in vulnerable Third World girls.

Missionary girl power is perhaps best understood as an assemblage of discursive practices that shape girls' experiences as political subjects. Sensoy and Marshall (2010) conclude that "in this discursive project, non-Western girls are cast as the most vulnerable citizens" whose political and economic capacities wait to be "harnessed" by compassionate Westerners (p. 301). The Girl Effect campaign, they contend, appeals to "adult Western women and other 'feminists' to do the right thing [and] break the cycle of backwardness to free the non-Western girl from the conditions that do not recognize her potential" (Sensoy & Marshall, 2010, p. 301). By focusing on Third World girls' lost talents, the Girl Effect suggests the West "need only harness latent 'girl power'" to address the injustices experienced by Third World girls (Sensoy & Marshall, 2010, p. 301).

The logic of missionary girl power additionally draws upon contemporary discourses of neoliberal girl power in order to root humanitarian aid efforts to situations and contexts that exist outside of Western girls presumed geopolitical, sociocultural, and historical lives. The Girl Effect in turn prompts Western girls to "ingest a pedagogy that positions the project of feminism and social action as helping less fortunate others, all the while ignoring the ways in which masculinist institutional domination impacts their lives as girls and women in the West" (Sensoy & Marshall, 2010, p. 308). This discursive logic functions to continuously mask more complex genealogies of Third World girlhoods, while likewise encouraging Western girls to construct their political selves and girlhoods against the signified *other* of the Third World. In the end, missionary girl power ensures that Western girls come to understand that their role in the Girl Effect is to save and invest in *other* girls – not in themselves or in other girls from the Global North.

The launch of the United Nations Foundation's *Girl Up* program illustrates the problematic function of the missionary girl power logic in the "invest in girls" climate. In February 2010, Girl Up announced its mission to give "American girls the opportunity to become global leaders and channel their energy and compassion to raise awareness and funds for United Nations programs that help some of the world's hardest-to-reach adolescent girls" (Girl Up, 2010, sec. Learn). According to Executive Director Elizabeth Gore (2011), Girl Up mobilizes a "surprising army" of *philanthro-teens* dedicated to "rescuing girls [because] it is the right thing to do" (Gibbs, 2011, para. 6). This generation of American girls, Gore (2011) states, "are all givers ... they gave after Katrina. They gave after the tsunami and Haiti. More than any earlier generation, they feel they know girls around the world" (Gibbs, 2011, para. 6). The Girl Up program thus provides North American girls with a "place" to invest their funds and "untapped" consumer power.

The identification of Western girls as philanthro-teens very clearly identifies "Western girls as 'good girls' who participate in the patriarchal salvation of non-White oppressed women/girls" (Sensoy & Marshall, 2010, p. 302). But it also (re)inscribes colonialist discourses that affirm a set of predetermined differences between Western and Third World girls. These differences include the idea that Third World girls experience oppression by "men in the East, but not by Western masculinities or patriarchal policies of the West" and that Western girls do not experience patriarchal oppression in their everyday lives (Sensoy & Marshall, 2010, p. 302). The logic of missionary girl power thereby prompts Western girls to identify themselves as empowered neoliberal "investors" in their so-called Third World sisters.

A recent PBS report on the Girl Up campaign provides a similar example of the missionary girl power logic. In this report, correspondent Ray Suarez (2011) interviews a group of American girls involved in the Girl Up initiative. He focuses the majority of the newscast on a conversation with Isabella, a Vietnamese girl adopted by an American family whose twin sister still lives in Vietnam. Isabella says of her work with Girl Up:

> I just wanted to help, not just her, but other adolescent girls around the world. There's a huge difference between our lives. I go to school. I play with my friends. I hang out with my friends. She doesn't get to hang with her friends. She gets to do chores and she's got to work 24/7. It's not what a normal teenager would do (Suarez, 2011, para. 33).

This particular interview clip, I suggest, captures how the missionary girl power logic works to mediate the discursive relationship between Western and Third World girls – solidifying colonized images of Western benevolence and Third World oppression, and embedding them within notions of normalcy, difference, and liberation. In this way, missionary girl power requires Isabella to "become an agent of missionary girl power, saving wounded children (rather than critiquing US policy), 'pulling oneself up by the bootstraps' (rather than organizing together), and fighting against all odds – ideas firmly rooted in mainstream US ideals ... and Western values of individuality" (Sensoy & Marshall, 2010, p. 307). By focusing on the (imagined and "real") differences between Isabella's daily life and that of her sister, this discursive logic prevents viewers from asking more complex and difficult questions; questions that postcolonial feminist theorist Abu-Lughod (2002) comments "lead to the exploration of global interconnections" which challenge the artificial divides between the Global North and South (p. 789). The missionary girl power logic instead solidifies the assumed differences between Western and Third World girls and in doing so, limits the forms and possibilities for their political subjectivity and agency.

The Girl Effect remains one of the most popular viral campaigns to date; however, it problematically employs the logic missionary girl power to literally call upon Western girls to save their Third World sisters. This discursive logic teaches Western girls that experiences of patriarchal oppression overwhelmingly (if not exclusively) occur in the Global South, prompting girls in the North to identify themselves as empowered neoliberal agents or philanthro-teens with the ability to invest in *other* girls, but not themselves. Sensoy and Marshall (2010) additionally state that in identifying "Third World girls as the most in need, those in the 'West' pass up a rich opportunity to engage in complex questions about [how] oppression, patriarchy, war, families, displacement, and the role of values" shape girls' lives all over the world – not just in the Global South (p. 309). It is in this way, I maintain, the Girl Effect logic brings certain political subjectivities and agencies into focus for Western and Third World girls, while foreclosing others. This section has considered the ways in which the missionary girl power logic integrates oppositional girlhoods and neoliberal girl power to shape girls global relationships to one another.

CONCLUDING THOUGHTS

This essay deconstructed the narrative of the Girl Effect campaign in order to problematize the conceptualization of girls' political subjectivity and agency in the current "invest in girls" climate. The Girl Effect paradigm, I have proposed, (re)inscribes a neocolonial and oppositional relationship between the Global North and South, (re)vitalizes the ethos of neoliberal girl power, and employs the logic of missionary girl power to promote the "invest in girls" agenda. Taken together, these discursive practices make difficult a more complex and nuanced understanding of Western and Third World girlhoods, and of girls' political selves. The Girl Effect logic rather imagines Western girls to be decidedly more empowered than their counterparts in the Global South and, in turn, encourages Western girls to focus their energy and money on helping *other* girls – but not themselves.

On the other hand, the Girl Effect confines Third World girls to colonizing images of poverty and victimization. Berman and Jiwani (2001) note:

> Third World girls are [often portrayed as] the desperate and reluctant victim of female genital mutilation in Africa; the poverty-stricken child laborer and child-bride in India; the child prostitute in Thailand; the undeserving victim of honour killing in the Middle East; the illiterate, uneducated, exploited and uncared for child in Latin American; or the unwanted girl child in China (p. 1).

In the Girl Effect, this simplistic and homogenized depiction does not leave room for Third World girls to *become* political agents without the aid of the West or the global marketplace. It is this troubling approach that I call attention to in this article.

Because of the discursive production of oppositional girlhoods, neoliberal girl power, and the logic of missionary girl power, I, lastly, mean to suggest that the Girl Effect tells us more about the normative construction of Western girlhood(s) than it does anything about Western or Third World girls' everyday lives. Toward that end, I offer the following summation of the troubling discursive *Girl Effects* of this contemporary paradigm:

- Dismissal of the ways that sociocultural and geopolitical power structures inform girls everyday lives;
- Negation of the political similarities, linkages, and connections among girls living in the Global North and South;
- Privatization of girls experiences with discrimination, violence, and inequality;
- Signification of Western and Third World girlhoods as oppositional subject positions defined by colonized images of privilege versus vulnerability;
- Individualization of girls economic potentials and successes based on the needs of the global marketplace;
- Replacement of human rights discourse with neoliberal ideology; and
- Erasure of the transformative possibilities of girls' human rights.

Collectively, these discursive effects make projects of solidarity exceedingly difficult for different girlhood subjects. However, in revealing the tensions produced by the Girl Effect logic, this essay endeavors to make possible a *different* kind of Girl Effect message – one that takes seriously the voices and experiences of girls as complex political subjects, and that which seeks to build an authentic relationship (rather than homogenized distance) among girls in the Two-Thirds and One-Thirds World.

NOTES

1. In this essay, I adopt the terms Western/Third World and Global North/Global South. These terms, Mohanty (2003) suggests, "retain a political and explanatory value in a world that appropriates and assimilates multiculturalism and "difference" through commodification and consumption" (p. 226). I use them interchangeably to distinguish between nations of economic and political privilege and disadvantage.

2. Prior to the branding of the Girl Effect, the Nike Foundation (2008) produced another video titled "I Dare You." This video did not go viral in the same way as the Girl Effect, nor is it part of the official Girl Effect brand; however, Switzer (2011) proposes that it might reflect the testing phase of the foundation's work to develop their marketing strategy around the Girl Effect message.

3. See Plan International's annual reports on the State of the World's Girls beginning in 2007 to the present (Plan International, 2007, 2008a, 2008b, 2009, 2010a, 2010b).

ACKNOWLEDGMENTS

This article is derived from my doctoral research entitled (Re)Thinking the Girl Effect: A Critical Analysis of Girls' Political Subjectivity and Agency at the United Nations 54th Session of the Commission on the Status of Women (CSW54), which was funded by the Galway Fellowship Programme at the National University of Ireland, Galway (NUIG). An earlier version of this article was presented at the SUNY Cortland College Girls' Studies Conference – Reimagining Girlhood: Communities, Identities, Self-Portrayals in 2010 – and the National Women's Studies Association Conference – Feminist Transformations in 2011. I would like to acknowledge my Ph.D. supervisor Dr. Niamh Reilly at NUIG Global Women's Studies Programme for her ongoing support. I thank the anonymous reviewers for their constructive comments on earlier drafts, and special thanks to Dr. Heather Switzer for her invaluable insight on this work.

REFERENCES

Abu-Lughod, L. (2002). Do Muslim women really need saving? Anthropological reflections on cultural relativism and its others. *American Anthropologist New Series, 104*(3), 783–790.

Beck, U. (1992). *Risk society: Towards a new modernity*. London: Sage.

Berman, H., & Jiwani, Y. (2001). *In the best interests of the girl child: Phase II report*. Retrieved from http://www.nnvawi.org/pdfs/alo/Berman.pdf

Carella, A. (2011, January 4). So now we have to save ourselves and the world, too? A critique of "the girl effect". [Web log post]. Retrieved from http://aidwatchers.com/2011/01/

Eitel, M. (2009, February 3). Girls' session steals the show at Davos. *Huffington Post*. Retrieved from http://www.huffingtonpost.com/marie-eitel/girls-session-steals-the_b_163633.html

Gibbs, N. (2011, February 14). To fight poverty: Invest in girls. *TIME Magazine*. Retrieved from http://www.time.com/time/magazine/article/0,9171,2046045,00.html

Giddens, A. (1991). *Modernity and self-identity: Self and society in the Late Modern Age*. Cambridge, UK: Polity Press.

Giddens, A. (1994). *Beyond left and right – The future of radical politics*. Cambridge, UK: Polity Press.

Girl Effect. (2008). Retrieved from http://www.girleffect.org. Accessed on November 15, 2008.

Girl Effect. (2010). *The clock is ticking*. Retrieved from http://www.girleffect.org. Accessed on April 5, 2010.

Girl Up. (2010). Retrieved from http://www.girlup.org. Accessed on October 10, 2010.

Gonick, M. (2003). *Between femininities: Ambivalence, identity and the education of girls*. Albany, NY: State University of New York Press.

Gonick, M. (2007). Girl number 20 revisited: Feminist literacies in new hard times. *Gender & Education, 19*(4), 433–454.

Harris, A. (Ed.). (2004). *All about the girl: Culture, power and identity*. New York, NY: Routledge.

Hayhurst, L. M. C. (2011). Corporatizing sport, gender and development: Postcolonial IR feminisms, transnational private governance and global corporate social engagement. *Third World Quarterly, 32*(3), 531–549.

Kristof, N. (2010, September 23). Boast, build, and sell. *The New York Times*. Retrieved from http://www.nytimes.com/2010/09/23/opinion/23kristof.html

Mohanty, C. T. (2003). *Feminism without borders: Decolonizing theory, practicing solidarity*. Durham, NC: Duke University Press.

Nike Foundation. (2008). Retrieved from http://www.nikefoundation.org. Accessed on October 1, 2010.

PLAN International. (2007). *Because I am a girl: The state of the world's girls 2007*. Italy: Amadeus.

PLAN International. (2008a). *Because I am a girl: In the shadow of war*. Italy: Amadeus.

PLAN International. (2008b). *The economic cost of failing to educate girls*. Italy: Amadeus.

PLAN International. (2009). *Because I am a girl: Girls in the global economy*. Italy: Amadeus.

PLAN International. (2010a). Retrieved from http://plan-international.org/girls/. Accessed on December 5, 2010.

PLAN International. (2010b). *Because I am a girl: Digital and urban frontiers*. Italy: Amadeus.

Provost, C. (2012, March 23). *Watchdog raises questions over impact of Nike's Girl Hub*. [Web log post]. Retrieved from www.guardian.co.uk/global-development/poverty-matters/2012/mar/23/girl-hub-strength-weaknesses

Ringrose, J. (2007). Successful girls? Complicating post-feminist, neoliberal discourses of educational achievement and gender equality. *Gender & Education, 19*(4), 471–489.

Roberts, K. (2010, July 23). Save a girl, save the world. *Oprah*. Retrieved from http://www.oprah.com/world/PSI-interviews-Jennifer-Buffet-and-Maria-Eitel

Rose, N. (1999). *Governing the soul: The shaping of the private self*. New York, NY: Free Association Books.

Rose, N., & Miller, P. (1992). Political power beyond the State: Problematics of government. *British Journal of Sociology, 43*(2), 173–205.

Said, E. (1978). *Orientalism*. New York, NY: Random House Inc.

20 EMILY BENT

Sensoy, O., & Marshall, E. (2010). Missionary girl power: Saving the 'Third World' one girl at a time. *Gender & Education, 22*(3), 295–311.

Suarez, R. (2011, August 9). Girl Up campaign helps teens empower peers around the globe. *PBS News.* Retrieved from http://www.pbs.org/newshour/bb/social_issues/july-dec11/girlup_08-09.html

Switzer, H. (2011). Girl "effects": Feminist fables or cautionary tales? *National Women's Studies Association Conference,* Atlanta, GA.

Taft, J. K. (2010). Girlhood in action: Contemporary U.S. girls' organizations and the public sphere. *Girlhood Studies, 3*(2), 11–29.

Taft, J. K. (2004). Girl power politics: Pop-culture barriers and organizational resistance. In A. Harris (Ed.), *All about the girl* (pp. 69–78). New York, NY: Routledge.

Walkerdine, V. (2003). Reclassifying upward mobility: Femininity and the neoliberal subject. *Gender & Education, 15*(3), 237–248.

Yegenoglu, M. (1998). *Colonial fantasies: Towards a feminist reading of orientalism.* New York, NY: Cambridge University Press.

RETHINKING CHILDREN'S PARTICIPATION IN DEMOCRATIC PROCESSES: A RIGHT TO PLAY

Stuart Lester

ABSTRACT

Purpose – *This paper presents a critical exploration of the concept of children's 'participation' by looking in more detail at children's right to play and the possibilities this presents for a different understanding of children as political actors.*

Design/methodology/approach – *The paper applies a range of concepts, largely drawn from Deleuzian philosophy and children's geographies, to produce an account of playing that unsettles traditional ways of valuing this behaviour. In doing so, it also extends current approaches to children's participation rights by presenting play as a primary way in which children actively participate in their everyday worlds. Observations of children's play are utilised to illustrate the multiple ways in which moments of playfulness enliven the spaces and routines of children's lives.*

Findings – *Playing may be viewed as micro-political expressions in which children collectively participate to establish temporary control over their immediate environment in order to make things different/better. These everyday acts are largely unnoticed by adults and represent a markedly*

Youth Engagement: The Civic-Political Lives of Children and Youth
Sociological Studies of Children and Youth, Volume 16, 21–43
Copyright © 2013 by Emerald Group Publishing Limited
All rights of reproduction in any form reserved
ISSN: 1537-4661/doi:10.1108/S1537-4661(2013)0000016006

different form of political engagement from the ways in which children are brought into adult-led political realms. Yet playful moments are a vital expression of children's power and ability to influence the conditions of their lives.

Originality/value – *Thinking differently about playing offers an opportunity to revitalise the very notion of participation. Such a move marks a line of flight which opens up the possibility for everyday collective acts to disturb dominant ways of accounting for adult–child relationships and by doing so establish moments of hope that people can get on and go on together by co-creating more just and participative spaces of childhood.*

Keywords: Participation; playing; children's politics; assemblage; rights

INTRODUCTION

Two young children, a boy and a girl, are sitting playing with some 'gooey' like stuff, when the following conversation occurred:

Boy: What about if everything was made out of gooey?

Girl: Well, hmm, we would actually have all goo on our bums and stuff and we'd be all gooey and pooey and booey

The boy laughs

Boy: What if everything was made out of pooeugh!

Girl: Err, we would all have poo on our bums

Boy: And what about poo people?

Girl: Yuck

Boy: And what about poo willy's!

Girl: No [boys name], no

Boy: What about poo trees

Girl: Yuck

Boy: What about, this is the worsest thing, what about poo leaves!

Girl: Why would you want to make poo leaves?

Boy: What if everything was made out of poo?

Girl: I dunno

This paper presents a critical exploration of the nature of 'participation' as currently used in adult agendas and political arenas. While great progress has been made in establishing the principle of children's right to be consulted and actively participate in decision-making processes that affect their lives, as enshrined in Article 12 of the United Nations Convention on the Rights of the Child (UNCRC), the discussion that follows suggests that this right is often applied in an exclusive manner, at the expense of the 'cluster' of other participation rights, including Articles 13, 14, 15 and importantly Article 31 often referred to as 'children's right to play'.

The ideas developed here revolve around an appreciation that moments of playing, as illustrated by the opening observation, may be a vital and vibrant expression of children's full participation in their everyday spaces. Given that children's worlds are generally a production of powerful (adult) forces that operate from global to local levels, paying attention to children's playful moments releases a new possibility of understanding children's politics as subjective expressions that bring the conditions of their lives under scrutiny. Participation may be seen as everyday encounters through which children can collectively express their power to act and momentarily feel, imagine and create a different world. These moments matter for all children; they signify children acting to be in a better state. They also matter for adults: the very conditions in which children's playfulness thrives are also ones in which adults can realise that minor everyday collective acts can disturb dominant economic–political forces and offer moments of hope that people can get on and go on together, fully participating in creating more just and participative spaces of childhood.

CHILDREN'S RIGHTS

The United Nations (1989) 'Convention on the Rights of the Child' (CRC) obliges signatory States to enshrine the 54 Articles of the Convention into legislation, policy and practice in regards to children. As Jupp (1990) observes, the innovative aspect of the Convention is that States are held accountable for realising children's rights, and, in the optimistic spirit of the launch, declares that 'it will unite people everywhere, mobilising them for action in a worldwide movement' (Jupp, 1990, p. 136). The founding principles of the CRC are expressed in Article 2 (non-discrimination), Article 3 (the best interests of the child as a primary consideration), Article 6 (the right to life, maximum survival and development) and Article 12 (respect for the views of the child). Whilst recognising the indivisibility of the Articles, they are often grouped into three broad categories, referred to as the 'three P's': rights to *protection* from adverse conditions and protection of basic rights such as identity; rights to *provision* to support the survival and full development of the child; and rights of *participation* and self-determination. Looking across the three P's, it is evident that the Convention explicitly and somewhat paradoxically recognises the immaturity and dependency of children while at the same time acknowledges that they are active agents in the creation of their worlds.

At the outset, there is no doubt that the desire of the Convention to improve the conditions of children's lives is a worthwhile project and the recognition of children as politically active subjects is a crucial theme in this. The point of divergence presented here is that the dominant CRC discourse of the 'child' as a rational being who, as they acquire the necessary competences, can participate in adult political arenas may diminish ways of thinking more critically about adult–child relationships and different ways of looking at children's participation. As such, the paper adopts a stance that is critical of hegemonic power relations which in this context primarily concerns common-sense accounts of what it is to be an 'adult'(competent and charged with the transmission of generational cultural values) and a 'child' (growing-up competent in adult ways of the world). But this is not simply an exercise in abstraction; the intention here is to think differently by looking at children's right to play in relation to the cluster of participation rights in order to produce a more sophisticated and critical understanding.

CRC protection and provision rights are relatively un-contentious, and imply a particular role for adults in children's lives, surrounding the child to ward off dangers and provide resources they could not obtain for themselves (Lee, 2005). This would appear to be a reasonable argument given that millions of children live under conditions of material poverty and political instability which invariably impacts on their experiences of childhood (Rehfeld, 2011). Claims made on behalf of children from the poorest regions of the majority world highlight the multiple and profound ways in which children's survival is severely compromised, and that protection and provision rights are seen to be of prime importance. This may suggest an implicit hierarchy of rights, with the claims of Articles 2, 3 and 6 establishing precedence over Article 12; protection and provision are deemed to be more important than the minority world's seemingly trivial preoccupation with children's participation (James, 2010) and any claims to participation or political rights can only be addressed when children's basic protection and welfare rights are secured (Rehfeld, 2011). Such a distinction perpetuates the essentialist production of the 'needy' child, where participation assumes secondary significance and is used to reinforce the supremacy of care and protection rights; children participate in adult decision-making processes to reaffirm the structures and processes designed in their best interests to protect and care for them. There is a danger in claiming the primacy of protection and provision over participation rights in that it potentially detracts from a position which sees childhood as a social participatory space that is produced through multiple encounters between adults, children, symbols, materials, discourse, histories and technologies (James, 2010). Without this, there is a tendency to replicate the increasingly outworn binaries of structure (the preserve of protection and provision rights) and agency (participation) alongside adult–child, mature–immature and so on, and by doing so mask the underlying ways in which childhood and adulthood are continually and dynamically produced and reproduced.

CHILDREN'S PARTICIPATION

The ways in which children's rights, and in particular rights of participation, are translated from policy to local practices (and *vice versa*) are highly complex. Participation rights potentially offer a contrasting but complementary role for adults, namely that of *being with* children (which paradoxically may also imply at times being away from them) rather than surrounding them; children are 'accompanied rather than possessed' (Lee, 2005, p. 18). It marks the hard-won recognition within the broad field of the social studies of childhood to recover 'children's agency and their socio-political contribution to society' (De Castro, 2011, p. 53). The rise of the 'participative child' is evident not only in the public sphere of politics and civil law but also in the institutional domains of families and schools (De Castro, 2011; Smith, 2012), supported by a range of participation articles: Article 15 promotes children's right for free association and peaceful assembly; Article 14 is the requirement to respect children's freedom of thought; Article 13 promotes children's freedom of expression; and Article 12 'assures to the child who is capable of forming his or her own views the right to express those views freely in all matters affecting the child, the views of the child being given due weight in accordance with the age and maturity of the child' (CRC, 1989).

Undoubtedly, the issue of the competent child has attracted great academic interest and contributed to the success of the CRC (Smith, 2012). The broad children's participation movement offers an alternative discourse which challenges and deregulates 'the normative framework which positioned [children] as objects of adult attention' (De Castro, 2011, p. 53). It

seeks to de-naturalise childhood by challenging the deterministic biological
and psychological accounts that present children as incompetent adults-in-
the-making by emphasising the capabilities and competences of children
as children (Prout, 2005). Accompanying this, the field has developed
innovative and valuable ways of creating conditions for children to express
their views (see, e.g. Clark & Moss, 2001; Hart, 1997; Johnson, 2010).

However, parallel to such developments are increasing concerns over
the conceptual and practical foundations of children's participation (Percy-
Smith & Thomas, 2010). Participation legitimises and perpetuates a
particular form of adult–child relationship in which children are positioned
by what they lack and therefore by definition are in perpetual need.
Adulthood represents everything that childhood is not: adults are mature,
children immature; adults are rational, children irrational; adults work,
children play (Johansson, 2012). The child's right to express their views
freely in all matters affecting them generally assumes that children need to
be 'supported, empowered and educated by adults to learn how to act as
political agents (Kallio & Hakli, 2011a, p. 99). Essentially, the notion of
participation assumes an autonomous child who can represent and
articulate their desires and opinions in ways that fit with adult political
processes; 'to act rationally, to express oneself through dialogue and
decentred communication, to act with emotional independence, self-control
and subjective autonomy' (De Castro, 2011, p. 54). Children's participation
becomes a form of consumerism (Sinclair, 2004) that resonates 'strongly
with the idea of the self-maximising, entrepreneurial subject of neoliberal
and advanced liberal thought' (Smith, 2012, p. 30). But a rights focused
discourse situated in a consumerist framework is conceptually ill equipped
to work with the on-going collective and caring relationships that mark the
interdependence of adults and children (Arneil, 2002; Bae, 2009).

At a somewhat more practical level, there have been a number of
objections and growing concerns about the effectiveness of attempts to
include children in adult decision-making processes (De Castro, 2011;
Kallio & Hakli, 2011a; Reynaert, Bouverne-de-Bie, & Vandevelde, 2009).
Children's involvement largely follows adult-determined policy streams and
tends to avoid any politically contentious or controversial issues. Venn
(2007), cited in Kallio and Hakli (2011a, p. 102) comments 'the
responsibilization of children by the representative system strips their voices
from dissidence and instead recruits them in stabilising the norms of good
conduct'. There are doubts raised as to whether the efforts to include
children in adult agendas have been matched by any real evidence of
changes in services and children's everyday experiences (De Castro, 2011;

Kallio & Hakli, 2011a; Matthews & Limb, 1998). The requirements to perform in adult arenas and follow adult-designed conventions runs counter to the ways in which children's carry out their everyday transactions. Children and young people's involvement is often tokenistic (Wyness, Harrison, & Buchanan, 2004) and 'unrepresentative in membership, adult-led in process and ineffective in acting upon what children want' (Davis & Hill, 2006, p. 9, cited in Graham & Fitzgerald, 2010).

PLAYING AS POLITICAL ACTION

Adults exercise power across micro and macro levels of organisation to structure children's routines and spatial practices. The primary purpose is to protect and provide for children; the idea of children's participation is easily overshadowed by the focus given to the potential harmful outcomes of such forces as social exclusion, risks and marginalisation (Strandell, 2010). Children spend their days moving through a range of bordered institutional spaces, each in their own way protecting and progressing the child towards the state of becoming self-reliant, autonomous, responsible and mature (Aitken & Plows, 2010). The Convention has instilled the importance of consultation and participation with children across these bordered spaces, but as noted above, this is often used merely to ratify adult decisions and give credibility to paternalistic actions rather than contribute to any transformation of provision and spaces. Bordered spaces not only seek to create and maintain a specific version of childhood but also inevitably shape the roles of adults. Childhood and adulthood are held by common sense and habitual practices to be the opposite of each other (Lee, 2005) and even when adults are not directly present they are an implicit reference point (White, 2002). On this basis, the production of space and associated spatial practices subjugate the identities of both children and adults in an un-reflexive manner (Mozere, 2006). The Convention, through a 'hegemonic, official discourse of legal constructs' (Tarulli & Skott-Myhre, 2006, p. 187), presents children as individuals or a social group in their own right, separated from the rest of humanity and brought in as clients or beneficiaries of adult largesse (White, 2002). Rights are attributed to children based on the fact that they are excluded and disempowered. The judicial nature of the Convention is based on a molar logic that operates to fix or identify a 'self' in time and space, and as such privileges sameness over difference.

What is largely missing from the participation debate is an exploration of the multiple, messy and mundane ways in which children actively engage in negotiating, contesting and changing everyday spaces, relationships and practices (Kallio, 2009). Children have their own desires, or a productive force, that finds expression through creative acts that disturb the order of things, or what is referred to here as 'play'. Such a rendition of play places it as a fundamental democratic process, a subtraction from the sovereignty of adults (Hardt & Negri, 2004). Katz (2004, p. 98) wonderfully captures this through the study of Howa children's lives and the ways they play with their identities 'wildly imagining themselves otherwise or just tweaking the details ... able to imagine, enact and transmogrify "becoming other" with fluidity and grace'. While definitions of play continue to be elusive (Burghardt, 2005), playing can be distinguished by being spontaneous, unpredictable, pleasurable, 'as if' behaviour in which children can exercise collective control of being out of control (Lester & Russell, 2008). It is an embodied performance that engages sensations, emotions and actions in novel formations. Such behaviours may be presented as 'political' in that they produce moments that reconfigure the existing order of the world to satisfy their own urges; moments in which children 'resist, conform and negotiate on their own terms, even if these struggles and negotiations do not and cannot be carried out in official political arenas or follow conventional political modes' (Kallio, 2009, p. 6).

Political acts are not pre-formed but context specific and ever-changing; any definition of politics must inevitably be relational and political acts can be found anywhere and everywhere (Kallio & Hakli, 2011b). Playing, as a dominant and highly desirable mode of activity, may be presented as a form of *minor* politics in which children momentarily take control over the conditions of their lives (Corsaro, 2003). These minor moments are 'concerned with the here and now, not with some fantasized future, with small concerns, petty details, the everyday and not the transcendental' (Rose, 1999, p. 279). Rather than being programmed politics, children's playful disposition and imaginings continually question and problematise the given order of things by asking 'what if ...' and find expression through 'as if ...' actions that acknowledges a different world is always possible, even a world made of poo! By playing, children subject the taken-for-granted to scrutiny, injecting a critique of their subordinate position, while at the same time hiding away from, or playing with their assumed innocence in the company of adults, the *'infrapolitics'* of the powerless (Scott, 1990; cited in Sutton-Smith, 1997). These 'secondary adjustments' (Goffman, 1974) enable children to distance themselves from adult demands and rework limitations to their own advantage, nicely illustrated by Corsaro's (2003) observations of the ways in which three pre-school boys appropriate the play box, which is forbidden to children due to a previous minor accident, and create a unique 'travelling bank' in the playground. Gallacher's (2005) study of toddlers in a nursery setting also reveals the 'underlife' of secondary adjustments that permeates the controlling practices of the nursery staff citing, for example, the ways in which children would run across the room and jump on the sleep mats in the storybook area squashing and pushing each other on the mats and by doing so subvert adult inscriptions and expectations of this space. Equally Thomson's (2007) study of primary school playgrounds in the United Kingdom uncovers the ways in which children make secondary adjustments to the playtime rule of 'not playing on the grass' through a range of playful actions, for example, by throwing an object onto the grass as a pretext for running onto the area to recover it. Here, we can see that even young children are active political agents, but these 'irruptive events' (Bennett, 2004) are far removed and disassociated from the formal participatory systems established by adults.

Playful moments transform bordered space into participatory spaces; children are no longer caught up in adult constructed spatial demands. They demonstrate that subjects who are at the same time produced and constrained can also act with intent in the diverse spaces in which they are positioned and 'engage in a performative politics of re-inscription' (Youdell & Armstrong, 2011, p. 145). No matter how far institutions seek to construct borders and limits to children's desires, they are always porous and open to children's playful inversions and subversions; 'people cross these borders bringing with them conflicting ideas, experiences, ideals, values and visions (all the things that make up discourses) and different material resources' (Prout, 2005, p. 82). The collective power that children hold over bodies at play may be presented as participatory political 'mo(ve)ments', a dynamic process of 'negotiations, challenges and re-constitutions' (Curti & Moreno, 2010, p. 414) of adult attempts to contain children's bodies. Such mo(ve)ments matter for children. They constitute the ways in which children simply go about their daily lives and denote a political sensitivity and sophistication that is largely unrecognised and unnoticed in discussions around participation. They appear as ordinary events, but as Lester and Russell (2008) drawing on the work of Masten (2001) comment, they contain potentially magical properties; through playing, children enhance biological and social systems that support their capability to look after themselves and cope with the demands of an uncertain world. Such moments are vital and offer the possibility that not only can things be different but also there is the possibility of more of these moments to come. Thus, acts of playing span the protection/participation divide discussed earlier; through playful participation, children are making their own provision by appropriating the materials at hand and by doing so are engaged in self-protection (Lester & Russell, 2010). Playing produces moments which are pleasurable and for the time of playing children get a sense that life is better and maintain a sense of optimism that things can simply go on (Kraftl, 2008).

This reading offers a different position with regards to the nature and value of play that currently prevails in the minority world and which is increasingly re-shaping childhoods in the majority world. Dominant accounts find representation in the phrase 'play and learning' and the taken-for-granted assumption that playing serves a purpose in developing skills that will be valuable later in life. The right to play is subsumed into adult-planned purposeful activity and spaces, hence the close association between Article 31 and Article 28 in State reporting procedures. What is suggested here is that there is more to playing than this: acts of playing are a sign that children are fully engaging in the creation of their everyday worlds. Participation, in this sense, is an affective state; the use of the term affective here is not simply referring to emotions, but marks the ability to affect and be affected. Affects are forces that arise in encounters and dispose a body to engage with the world in a certain style: every moment of an encounter shapes and orientates a body's affective disposition either by enhancing or diminishing the power to act. The power to affect and be affected is increased as one establishes affirming connections with other bodies, space and materials in novel formations (Deleuze, 1988). Play is a symbolic representation, an identity given to a novel assemblage of disparate materials in which bodies are disposed to act in a certain intensive affirmative manner. Such active forces are involved in the production of temporary spaces or milieus. This can be illustrated by the following observation of children's play in an after-school club in the United Kingdom (Lester, 2011). A small group of children aged between 5 and 8 years congregated around a CD player that had been used for adult-structured activities (musical chairs, statues, etc.) and then abandoned as the adult's prepared snacks. A child asked one of the adults 'what can we do now' and the adult responded 'I don't know' and walked away. At this point, one of the children tentatively suggested to the others they play 'musical worms'; it was fairly apparent that the child was responding spontaneously and creatively, and when other children looked interested and asked 'how do you play it', the notion developed into a concrete idea as the child responded 'you wriggle around on the floor like worms, and when the music stops you have to flip over on to your back and the last one over is out'. Following this explanation, another child asked if he could provide the music rather than use the CD player, and the other children all agreed to this. And so the game began – the child humming a tune, while the worms wriggled on the floor (with much laughter). As the child stopped humming, the worms flipped over and a decision was made about who was the slowest. Under conventional game rules, the last person is generally 'out', but in this game the children negotiated that the person who was last should provide the music for the next round and so all continued to participate in the game. After a short period, it became apparent that the real attraction for the children was in providing the music and the worms became increasingly reluctant to turn over when the music stopped, everyone wanted to be last and there was a period of worms gracefully turning in slow motion. In unspoken recognition that the game was changing, one child suggested that the first worm to flip over should provide the music for the next round and so the whole process started again with the worms energetically throwing themselves over as they attempted to 'win'. Of course, this is not the reality of play; the children's movements changed rapidly, far quicker than could be noted. But what it serves to illustrate is that the spaces of childhood are not mere containers for action but are fluid spaces constructed from heterogeneous materials and forces (Prout, 2005); musical worms is an assemblage in which each part is capable of acting and affecting others and so 'order' is emergent, continually reworked and re-shaped (Bennett, 2010). Here bodies, materials and affects combine together in a dynamic manner; there is no central organising system, but biological and social forces weave novel, unpredictable and complex networks of relationships that cannot be accounted for in traditional ways (Hengst, 2005; Lee & Motzkau, 2011).

While the forces that assemble musical worms are constituted from everyday, micro or molecular levels of organisation (Deleuze & Guattari, 1988), they are not independent of the macro or molar forces which shape spaces and spatial practices. Moments of playfulness are not simply random events or negations of everyday routines but are 'organically connected to it and intensify the vital productivity of daily life' (Gardiner, 2004, p. 242; cited in Kraftl, 2008, p. 89). The terms molar and molecular do not merely represent scale, but are an expression of force and flows (Deleuze & Guattari, 1988). Molar forces seek to stabilise and order within a normalising plane of organisation and in doing so impose a particular meaning on desires by capturing and feeding off them for their own purposes, shaping them into normal patterns (Mozere, 2006). Thus, the current focus for the implementation of participation rights is to over-code or by-pass children's everyday expressions by bringing children into adult designed processes. Equally, a play and learning discourse values children's acts of creativity and imagination as long as they remain consistent with the overall force and direction of this plane; children are encouraged to 'play properly' in order to create the independent, problem-solving, emotionally regulated, social self. In both examples, adults contribute to fixing the identity of the 'child-becoming-adult'. But molecular forces are interspersed into molar structures and are potentially disruptive as they arise from bottom-up, experimental processes (Saldhana, 2010). As suggested earlier, a plane of organisation cannot close off all desire and children's playful urges will seek to find improper expression between the cracks and crevices of ordered space, producing 'lines of flight' (Deleuze & Guattari, 1988) that delimit the constraints seeking to enclose creativity and different ways of becoming a child.

And just as children may temporarily disturb order through playing, adults can also overcome molar, commonsense and habitual constraints of being adult by creating and joining forces with improper acts to disrupt molar accounts of adult–child relationships. This can be illustrated by the following extract from Hannikainen's (2001, p. 127) study of the ways in which children's playful acts permeate the relationships, routines and practices in a kindergarten school. This particular observation concerns circle time, a common feature in early years and primary education that serves as an adult educative production of space/time to encourage children's emotional and social development. But in this case, children's clandestine acts produce a momentary dissolution of adult order:

> The kindergarten teacher, Sara, begins the roll call: 'Magnus?'
>
> Magnus replies: 'Yes, [here]'.
>
> Sara: 'Peter?'
>
> Peter: 'No, [not here], I am down inside Magnus'.
>
> Peter, Magnus, Tine, Natalia and several other children nearly split their sides laughing. Peter, too, smiles at his success.
>
> Sara asks, with a twinkle: 'Are you down inside Magnus?'
>
> Peter asks: 'Yes, isn't that a rather silly thing to say?'
>
> Sara: 'Frankly, yes.'
>
> When the roll call reaches Katrine she says that she, too, is down inside Magnus. The children laugh.

Sara points out in a surprised voice: 'Now there are two children down inside Magnus'.

Nadja: 'Then he must give birth'.

Tine: 'Two in his belly, no, two in his ears (the other children laugh) ... no, two in his nose

(all the children giggle and laugh) ... no, two in his little peter (meaning: penis) ...'

Peter continues: 'No, two in his bum'.

Peter and Magnus laugh so much that they almost fall off their chairs.

Both children and teacher share the play, 'the atmosphere is cheerful and all participants enjoy being together' (Hannikainen, 2001, p. 128); for a brief period, a normalising account of being adult and child is disturbed by a shared moment of nonsense and later on the roll call continues. But re-establishing order is not a return to the same. The shared act of disturbance redistributes bodies, time and space, allowing for an intensity of becoming different while creating the extensive possibility that things can go on becoming different. As Hannikainen's study notes, these moments appear throughout the day and there are many occasions when the boundaries established between teacher and pupil become blurred. Such everyday encounters are crucial in countering and resisting hegemonic forces that seek to fix adult and child identities (Katz, 2004). Indeed, this small act of shared affect may make more of a difference than adult grand politics (Bennett, 2010). Playing, as a practice of resistance and resilience, creates moments of hope by imaginatively reworking the constraints on children's daily lives, and by doing so realise that life can go on and there will be other opportunities for disturbance. Such processes are also evident in adult responses to the apparent constraints presented through dominant and habitual spatial practices. For children to exercise their 'right to play' as an expression of their participation and protection rights requires changes to totalising accounts of adult–child relationships and critically exploring ideas about what children are, what they can do and how adults and children are constructed and situated within society (James, 2010).

CHILDREN'S RIGHT TO PARTICIPATE AND PLAY

The discussion to date suggests a different perspective than is currently in circulation when talking about children as political actors. The focus here is on the expressions of children in mundane everyday contexts rather than the ways in which children may be brought into adult political arenas. That is not to deny the importance of these systems and processes, but such a narrow interpretation of participation and engagement is limited in terms of representing the body of childhood. Just as with adult politics, only certain types of children, such as older children, those with an interest in politics or from a wealthy background, may desire or have the opportunity to engage in adult political arenas (Wall, 2011). But all children must inevitably have a 'political self' by being a child in a unique environment in space and history (Kallio & Hakli, 2011b). Seeing play as an expression of children's political agency extends dominant accounts of children's right to participate by paying attention to the ways in which children can find time/space to express their desires and establish momentary control over the conditions of their daily lives, to fully and actively participate in the construction of their worlds. At the time of writing, the UNCRC is engaged in developing a general comment about Article 31. The intention of this is to elaborate on the meanings of this specific Article and increase State accountability for the ways in which children's play (and leisure, rest and the cultural arts) is promoted and supported. It provides an opportunity to bring play to the centre of thinking about children's rights and not as a luxury, something to be considered after basic provision and protection rights have been assured. State reporting, however, largely and somewhat inevitably deals with molar systems, seeking to present causal claims about the impact of government legislation, policies and adult practices in providing 'play spaces' or 'play opportunities', often incorporating children's voices into this accounting system. The intensity of children's and adult's shared moments is invisible in the technical application of the Convention in which the primary focus is on setting standards and monitoring their implementation rather than a critical dialogue about the notion and interpretation of rights themselves (Reynaert et al., 2009). Outcomes-driven accounting systems do not capture the messiness, spontaneity and contingency of playing. Much of children's political lives, or what Kallio and Hakli (2011c) refer to as the '*voiceless politics*' of childhood, cannot be readily brought into the political arena. Capturing the everyday, mundane and largely un-reflexive political acts of children is somewhat problematic. These embodied encounters resist becoming known and 'cannot be exhaustively understood through analysing its capture in language' (Saldhana, 2010, p. 284).

When children are asked to talk about play, it gets reduced to naming activities or certain play things. This is presented as a 'child's voice', which grants 'autonomy, rationality and intention to the speaking child while simultaneously divorcing the production of the child's voice from its inter-actional context' (Komulainen, 2007, p. 25). Equally, adults, while having played as children, now apply rational and literal meanings to this form of behaviour.

The politicising of children's embodied and dynamic relationship with space demands different conceptual tools to better understand the (contested) nature of childhood (Kallio, 2007). Rather than analysing the world into discrete components and reducing their manyness by categorising, ranking and ordering, the world may be perceived as the formation, maintenance and fracture of multiple and complex assemblages. It replaces seeing children as independent, or adult-in-the-making, to recognising that children can see, feel and act in the world differently and create political spaces in which they can 'express their own distinctive and submerged points of view ... to assert one's own difference against others' (Wall, 2011, pp. 7/8). This perspective disturbs commonsense ways of thinking about children, adults and space, by de-centring the human subject as an individual-fixed 'identity' that unfolds through a universal and teleological process to consider human development as an emergent, creative and 'discontinuous record of affective encounters' (Duff, 2010, p. 629). Rather than the 'becoming-adult' child of developmentalism, there is a minor discourse emerging here that offers the possibility of a different sensibility towards the concept of children's rights, one that is deeply rooted in Negri's (2004) assertion that the metaphysics of individuality 'constitutes a dreadful mystification of the multitude of bodies'. Bodies are not alone and autonomous but 'blended, mongrel, hybrid, transformed; they are like sea waves, in perennial movement and reciprocal transformation'. When one considers humans to be a source of rights, they are made alone (Negri, 2004). Development is a process of continuous variation that occurs through dynamic transformations in the myriad encounters of bodies and things that form the spaces of such encounters (Deleuze & Guattari, 1988; Duff, 2010). The contours and content of what happens in these spaces continually changes; there is no stable human experience because bodies are constantly reinvented as things happen (Thrift, 2008). From this perspective, development may be understood as a thoroughly relational and affective phenomenon, suggesting that the body contains no advance notice of what it can become (Ansell-Pearson, 1997). This immediately throws a different light on the notion of the competent child: no longer can a child be identified by a store or lack of competence, there is no pre-determined map of individual development by which one can measure progress. It also suggests a different perspective on agency, which can no longer be seen as individual freedom to make choices and act on these, but rather the 'locus of agency is always a human-nonhuman working group' (Bennett, 2010, p. xvii). The idea of the child as 'perpetually becoming and not being defined once and for all' (Olsson, 2009, p. 14) replaces the emphasis from what is happening inside individual children's mind's to what is happening within and between children's bodies and everything else that constitutes the spaces of their childhoods.

If we approach children's play as an assemblage of desire, or will to power, to simply join forces with human and nonhuman things in a joyous manner, focus shifts from treating play as a separate text apart from everyday life (Sutton-Smith, 1997) that requires segregated provision to seeing play as the formation of a peculiar space, that is, a space where the intense collective and affective power of bodies and materials disturbs order by producing a momentarily strange space in which things are different. Spaces may have certain material, relational and affective properties which enable or reduce the possibility of play emerging (Duff, 2011), but this cannot be predicted; spaces are always produced through an active process of assembly and encounter, and at any given moment there is always much happening in space at multiple levels of operation and organisation (Horton & Kraftl, 2006b). A turn towards play as an *event* offers a different way of thinking about this. An event arises from a combination of particular forces that stands alone as a unique sign of the emergent and chaotic nature of the world (Deleuze, 1992). The observation of 'what if', 'musical worms' and 'circle-time' can be seen as everyday encounters between child and adult bodies, affects, materials, symbols and so on. These occasions are made an 'event' through representation. But this is not a truthful account, nor can it ever fully capture the dynamic and intangible messiness of life. But paying closer attention to the minor, everyday activities of children starts to reveal the multiple ways in children and adults are intimately connected in 'small, banal, low-key, daft, happenstance things, moments, events, practices, experiences, emotions, complexities, quirks, details and who-knows-what-else in and of everyday lives' (Horton & Kraftl, 2005, p. 133). It is an attempt to interrogate the liveliness of these moments which 'although banal ... are key sites at which societal norms and expectations – including aged identities – are negotiated' (Kraftl, 2010, p. 105). Such events are inexhaustibly detailed and as they emerge produce little surprises that only come to life by engaging with the very specificity of the event (Laurier & Philo, 2006). They embody more than a material thing, a representation or a social practice but rather are a combination of chance encounters that produce singular assemblages that matter (Kraftl, 2010). Paying more *careful* attention to these embodied events questions commonsense productions of adult–child relationships, play and participation, and by doing so reveals a more vibrant account of the ways in which spaces are produced and reproduced. The use of the word careful is deliberate and important in that it denotes an expression of the care for such events and the promise they hold for becoming different for both adults and children. It does not mean that adults seek to understand, rationalise and usurp these events to progress children to grow up. Caring is a process of problematising dominant spatial patterns and positions, to leave room for the otherness of children and their affective dis-orderings that disturb the taken-for-granted. It implies witnessing these acts 'and just slow down, to wait and see what happens' (Horton & Kraftl, 2006a, p. 274). While each event stands alone and cannot be reduced to general classifications, it may be possible to infer from a collective of vibrant events some important 'resonances and discordances' (Horton and Kraftl, *ibid*) that occur in the everyday public and institutional spaces of childhood.

This also has implications for the very notion of children's rights and extends the indisputable importance of protection from life-threatening hazardous conditions of some childhoods and making provision to support healthy development to a broader consideration of the everyday experiences of all children. Children and adults are not autonomous but are caught up in a complex web of relationships. Rights cannot simply be held individually but are part of the solidarity of a multitude of diverse bodies and materials; they are in-common-with rather than apart. Attention is then drawn to the ways in which rights are held together and expressed in everyday contexts. A right to play marks the potential for children to *navigate* towards the spaces that will support their protection and participation (Ungar, 2008). The conventional sense of navigation implies a movement towards something and suggests an association with provision rights. But in the context of this paper and the relationship between playing and political agency, navigation would imply that children can appropriate available time/space within everyday routines to *move away* from adult provision and protection. Playful navigation, from this perspective, can be seen as full political participation by exercising embodied and embedded collective agency to creatively assemble bodies, time/space and materials for their desires. A second and interconnected principle from Ungar's (2008) analysis can be found in *negotiation* which in general terms implies that communities understand and negotiate time/space on behalf of children through their actions and attitudes. The process of negotiation, in this context, does not assume consultation with or provision for children, but more accurately represents the responsibility of local communities to adopt a holistic or caring approach to analyse and account for the ways in which micro and macro actions carried out by adults through the political, social, economic and cultural systems that shape the nature of everyday relationships may potentially impact on children's ability to navigate their own time/space for play. Negotiation is a process of questioning how adult responsibilities are enacted and how caring about children as others is mediated across space (Aitken, 2009).

The focus then is not simply on the physical conditions of space but the quality of the intersubjective relationships that contribute to producing a space of collective will to work out ways of living together and not apart. Respect for the otherness of children offers the possibility for unexpected encounters and mo(ve)ments under which the contradictions of social space are brought to life. Children's playful creation of 'spaces of hope' imagines a different world (Katz, 2004). Such imaginings are not simply the preserve of children's play but are present in everyday interactions between adults and children, minor moments of resilience, re-workings and resistance, a form of political imagination that may find expression in 'vigorous social movements' (Katz, 2004, p. 259) that may simply make the everyday more playful, and by doing so create democratic spaces that are fairer and more just.

CONCLUSION

This paper has sought to present children's play as a form of minor political activity in their everyday worlds. Playing is a universal feature of childhood that offers moments of simply being different, becoming a child rather than becoming adult and that such moments are highly important, not for some grand transcendental purpose but rather for simply enlivening the practicalities of everyday life. They are moments of hope that life can become better by venturing beyond the limits that the real world imposes and exercising collectively agency in a world that is generally beyond children's control. Playing is a belief and expression that the 'not-yet' can be actualised and as Sutton-Smith (2003) asserts, the opposite of play, so often assumed to be 'work', is depression and hopelessness. Playing necessarily invokes adults; the playful observations cited in this piece are just a few examples of the innumerable moments that occur in everyday life in which the commonsense distinction between child and adult is playfully problematised in spaces of encounter. They offer a reminder that 'becoming' is not an individual trait of children but is a shared process that draws on everyone and everything;

'nobody (and nothing) is completed or finished; we are always transforming and connecting to other humans and non-humans (Johansson, 2012, p. 104). Such vibrant and hopeful moments invite adults to rethink ideas about what constitutes a 'good life' and the ways in which adults and children make efforts to 'spin webs of social justice and human well-being and emancipation out of the prevailing circumstances' (Amin, 2006, p. 1010).

Given children's positioning in minority world countries as largely subordinate and separate a change in their rights and status will only come about by challenging and re-working the structural positioning of children and adults. This becomes a political and ethical movement for both adult and children, an opportunity to challenge the ways in which adult–child relationships are constructed and maintained to the detriment of both groups (James, 2010). Focusing on play as an event opens up the broader conditions of children's lives to scrutiny and requires a critical shift that makes it possible for adults to pay attention to the 'voiceless politics' that are present in the micro-events of playing and bear witness to the ways in which conventional reality becomes blurred and momentarily open to other possibilities. This does not mean a further colonisation of children's lives but rather recognition that children are separable but not separate from adults (Lee, 2005). There will be occasions when adults and children can be different together, as in circle time, and by doing so unsettle dominant accounts and present different ways of being adult–child. There also needs to be occasions when adults and children are separable, time/spaces when they are apart, for children to continue with their experiments of being children without coming under direct adult gaze and supervision, co-creating worlds made from poo. Caring for time together and apart offers an alternative to commonsense productions in which, for the most part, children's everyday experiences are held to be unimportant unless directly involved in becoming future adult citizens. A re-working may lead to greater imagination of the possibilities contained within 'adult's-being-and-becoming-with-children' and for new forms of social, economic and political order to emerge.

ACKNOWLEDGEMENTS

Thanks to Emma-Louise Simpson for sharing the opening observation of 'what if'. Thanks also to the two anonymous referees who provided valuable and productive advice for the revision of this work.

REFERENCES

Aitken, S. (2009). Throwntogetherness: Encounters with difference and diversity. In D. DeLyser, L. McDowell, S. Herbert, S. Aitken & M. Crang (Eds.), *The sage handbook of qualitative geography.* London: Sage.
Aitken, S., & Plows, V. (2010). Overturning assumptions about young people, border spaces and revolutions. *Children's Geographies, 8*(4), 327–333.
Amin, A. (2006). The Good City. *Urban Studies, 43*, 1009–1023.
Ansell-Pearson, K. (1997). Deleuze outside/outside Deleuze: On the difference engineer. In K. Ansell-Pearson (Ed.), *Deleuze and philosophy.* London: Routledge.
Arneil, B. (2002). Becoming versus being: A critical analysis of the child in liberal theory. In D. Archard & C. Macleod (Eds.), *The moral and political status of children.* Oxford: Oxford University Press.
Bae, B. (2009). Children's right to participate – Challenges in everyday interactions. *European Early Childhood Education Research Journal, 17*(3), 391–406.
Bennett, J. (2004). The force of things: Steps toward and ecology of matter. *Political Theory, 32*, 347–372.
Bennett, J. (2010). *Vibrant matter.* London: Duke University Press.
Burghardt, G. (2005). *The genesis of animal play: Testing the limits.* Cambridge, MA. MIT Press.
Clark, A., & Moss, P. (2001). *Listening to young children. The mosaic approach.* London: NCB and Joseph Rowntree Foundation.
Corsaro, W. (2003). *We're friends, right? Inside kids culture.* Washington, DC: John Henry Press.
Curti, G., & Moreno, C. (2010). Institutional borders, revolutionary imaginings and the becoming-adult of the child. *Children's Geographies, 8*(4), 413–427.
Davis, J., & Hill, M. (2006). Introduction. In E. Tisdall, M. Kay, J. Davis, A. Prout & M. Hill (Eds.), *Children, young people and social inclusion: Participation for what?* Bristol: Policy Press. Cited in Graham, A., & Fitzgerald, R. (2010). Progressing children's participation: Exploring the potential of a dialogical turn. *Childhood, 17* (3), 343–359.
De Castro, L. (2011). The 'good enough society'. The 'good enough citizen' and the 'good enough student': Where is children's participation agenda moving to in Brazil? *Childhood, 18*(1), 52–68.
Deleuze, G. (1988). *Spinoza: Practical philosophy.* San Francisco, CA: City Lights.
Deleuze, G. (1992). *Expressionism in philosophy: Spinoza.* New York: Zone Books.
Deleuze, G., & Guattari, F. (1988). *A thousand plateaus.* London: Continuum.
Duff, C. (2010). Towards a developmental ethology exploring Deleuze's contribution to the study of health and human development. *Health, 14*(6), 619–634.
Duff, C. (2011). Networks, resources, agencies: On the character and production of enabling places. *Health and Place, 17*, 149–156.
Gallacher, L.-A. (2005). The terrible twos': Gaining control in the nursery? *Children's Geographies, 3*(2), 243–264.
Gardiner, M. (2004). Everyday utopianism: Lefebvre and his critics. *Cultural Studies, 18*, 228–254. Cited in Kraftl, P. (2008). Young people, hope and childhood hope. *Space and Culture, 11*(2), 81–92.
Goffman, E (1974). *Frame analysis.* New York: Harper and Row.
Graham, A., & Fitzgerald, R. (2010). Progressing children's participation: Exploring the potential of a dialogical turn. *Childhood, 17*(3), 343–359.

Hannikainen, M. (2001). Playful actions as a sign of togetherness in day care centres. *International Journal of Early Years Education, 9*(2), 125–134.

Hardt, M., & Negri, A. (2004). *Multitude.* New York: Penguin.

Hart, R. (1997). *Children's Participation: the theory and practice of involving young citizens in community development and environmental care.* London: Earthscan.

Hengst, H. (2005). Complex interconnections: The global and their local in children's minds and everyday worlds. In J. Qvortrup (Ed.), *Studies in modern childhood: Society, agency and culture.* Basingstoke: Palgrave.

Horton, J., & Kraftl, P. (2005). For more-than-usefulness: Six overlapping points about children's geographies. *Children's Geographies, 3*(3), 131–143.

Horton, J., & Kraftl, P. (2006a). Not just growing up, but going on: Materials, spacings, bodies, situations. *Children's Geographies, 4*(3), 259–276.

Horton, J., & Kraftl, P. (2006b). What else? Some more ways of thinking and doing 'children's geographies'. *Children's Geographies, 4*(1), 69–95.

James, A. (2010). Competition or integration? The next step in childhood studies? *Childhood, 17*(4), 485–499.

Johansson, B. (2012). Doing adulthood in childhood research. *Childhood, 19*(1), 101–114.

Johnson, V. (2010). Rights through evaluation and understanding children's realities. In B. Percy-Smith & N. Thomas (Eds.), *A handbook of children and young people's participation.* London: Routledge.

Jupp, M. (1990). The UN convention on the rights of the child: An opportunity for advocates. *Human Rights Quarterly, 12*(1), 247–256.

Kallio, K. (2007). Performative bodies, tactical agents and political selves: Rethinking the political geographies of childhood. *Space and Polity, 11*(2), 121–136.

Kallio, K. (2009). Between social and political: Children as political selves. *Childhoods Today, 3*(2), 1–22.

Kallio, K., & Hakli, J. (2011a). Tracing children's politics. *Political Geography, 30,* 99–109.

Kallio, K., & Hakli, J. (2011b). Are there politics in childhood? *Space and Polity, 15*(1), 21–34.

Kallio, K., & Hakli, J. (2011c). Young people's voiceless politics in the struggle over urban space. *GeoJournal, 76,* 63–75.

Katz, C. (2004). *Growing up global: Economic restructuring and children's everyday lives.* Minneapolis, MN: University of Minnesota Press.

Komulainen, S. (2007). The ambiguity of the child's 'voice' in social research. *Childhood, 14*(1), 11–28.

Kraftl, P. (2008). Young people, hope and childhood hope. *Space and Culture, 11*(2), 81–92.

Kraftl, P. (2010). Events of hope and events of crisis: Childhood, youth and hope in Britain. In J. Leaming & M. Worsching (Eds.), *Youth in Contemporary Europe.* London: Routledge.

Laurier, E., & Philo, C. (2006). Possible geographies: A passing encounter in a café. *Area, 38*(4), 353–363.

Lee, N. (2005). *Childhood and human value.* Maidenhead: Open University Press.

Lee, N., & Motzkau, J. (2011). Navigating the bio-politics of childhood. *Childhood, 18*(1), 7–19.

Lester, S. (2011). The pedagogy of play, space and learning. In A. Pihlgren (Ed.), *Fritidspedagogik.* Lund, Sweden: Studentlitteratur.

Lester, S., & Russell, W. (2008). *Play for a change – Play, policy and practice: A review of contemporary perspectives.* London: National Children's Bureau.

Lester, S., & Russell, W. (2010). *Children's right to play. An examination of the importance of play in the lives of children worldwide.* Working Paper No. 57, Bernard van Leer Foundation, The Hague, The Netherlands.

Masten, A. (2001). Ordinary magic: Resilience processes in development. *American Psychologist, 56*(3), 227–238. Cited in Lester, S., & Russell, W. (2008). *Play for a change. Play, policy and practice: A review of contemporary perspectives.* London: NCB.

Matthews, H., & Limb, M. (1998). The right to say: The development of youth councils/forums within the UK. *Area, 30*(1), 66–78.

Mozere, L. (2006). What's the trouble with identity? Practices and theories from France. *Contemporary Issues in Early Childhood, 7*(2), 109–118.

Negri, A. (2004). *Towards an ontological definition of multitude.* Paper 4, Available online at: http://www.makeworlds.org/book/view/104 [last access 26/08/2012].

Olsson, L. (2009). *Movement and experimentation in young children's learning.* London: Routledge.

Percy-Smith, B., & Thomas, N. (Eds.). (2010). *A handbook of children and young people's participation.* London: Routledge.

Prout, A. (2005). *The future of childhood.* Abingdon: RoutledgeFalmer.

Rehfeld, A. (2011). The child as democratic citizen. *Annals of the American Academy of Political and Social Science, 633*, 141–166.

Reynaert, D., Bouverne-de-Bie, M., & Vandevelde, S. (2009). A review of children's rights literature since the adoption of the United Nations Convention of the Rights of the Child. *Childhood, 16*(4), 518–534.

Rose, N. (1999). *Powers of freedom: Reframing political thought.* Cambridge: Cambridge University Press.

Saldhana, A. (2010). Politics and difference. In B. Anderson & P. Harrison (Eds.), *Taking place: Non-representational theories and geography.* Farnham, UK: Ashgate.

Scott, J. (1990). *Domination and the arts of resistance: Hidden transcripts.* New Haven, CT: Yale University Press. Cited in Sutton-Smith, B. (1997). *The ambiguity of play.* Cambridge: Harvard University Press.

Sinclair, R. (2004). Participation in practice: Making it meaningful, effective and sustainable. *Children and Society, 18*, 106–118.

Smith, K. (2012). Producing governable subjects: Images of childhood old and new. *Childhood, 19*(1), 24–37.

Strandell, H. (2010). From structure-action to politics of childhood: Sociological childhood research in Finland. *Current Sociology, 58*(2), 165–185.

Sutton-Smith, B. (1997). *The ambiguity of play.* Cambridge, MA: Harvard University Press.

Sutton-Smith, B. (2003). Play as a parody of emotional variability. In D. Lytle (Ed.), *Play and educational theory and practice, play and culture studies* (Vol. 5). Westport, CT: Praeger.

Tarulli, D., & Skott-Myhre, H. (2006). The immanent rights of the multitude: An ontological framework for conceptualizing the issue of child and youth rights. *The International Journal of Children's Rights, 14*, 187–201.

Thomson, S. (2007). Do's and don'ts: Children's experiences of the primary school playground. *Environmental Education Research, 13*(4), 487–500.

Thrift, N. (2008). *Non-representational theory.* London: Routledge.

Ungar, M. (2008). Resilience across cultures. *British Journal of Social Work, 38*, 218–235.

United Nations. (1989). Convention on the rights of the child. Available online at: http://www2.ohchr.org/english/law/crc.htm [last access 30/09/2012].

Venn, C. (2007). Cultural theory, biopolitics, and the question of power. *Theory, Culture and Society*, *38*, 111–124. Cited in Kallio, K., & Hakli, J. (2011a). Tracing children's politics. *Political Geography*, *30*, 99–109.

Wall, J. (2011). Can democracy represent children? Towards a politics of difference. Childhood, Online first article, available at: http://chd.sagepub.com/content/early/2011/09/06/0907568211406756 [last access 28/12/2011].

White, S. (2002). Being, becoming and relationship. Conceptual challenges of a child rights approach to development. *Journal of International Development*, *14*(8), 1095–1104.

Wyness, M., Harrison, H., & Buchanan, I. (2004). Childhood, politics and ambiguity: Towards an agenda for children's political inclusion. *Sociology*, *38*(1), 81–99.

Youdell, D., & Armstrong, F. (2011). A politics beyond subjects: The affective choreographies and smooth spaces of schooling. *Emotion, Space and Society*, *4*(3), 144–150.

PART II
INSTITUTIONAL CONTEXTS
OF YOUNG PEOPLE'S
CIVIC-POLITICAL LIVES

EDUCATING ACTIVE CITIZENS: WHAT ROLES ARE STUDENTS EXPECTED TO PLAY IN PUBLIC LIFE?

L. Alison Molina-Girón

ABSTRACT

Purpose – *Educating active citizens engaged in civic life is a critical goal of citizenship education. This study examines how citizenship education is practiced in three public high schools in the City of Ottawa, Canada, and how teachers through their instruction prepare their students for active citizenship.*

Design – *This investigation draws on citizenship theories and an examination of citizenship pedagogy through observations of class instruction and interviews with teachers and students.*

Findings – *The research shows that despite shared provincial guidelines, in practice, there are dramatic differences in the design and provision of citizenship instruction across classrooms, shaped largely by teachers' understandings of what constitutes active citizenship. I detail three distinct understandings of active citizenship that are advanced through class instruction: the duty-based, the make-a-difference, and the politically oriented active citizenship.*

Youth Engagement: The Civic-Political Lives of Children and Youth
Sociological Studies of Children and Youth, Volume 16, 47–72
Copyright © 2013 by Emerald Group Publishing Limited
All rights of reproduction in any form reserved
ISSN: 1537-4661/doi:10.1108/S1537-4661(2013)0000016007

48 L. ALISON MOLINA-GIRÓN

Value – *The article discusses important implications that these differing understandings and pedagogical approaches have as they delineate different expectations and paths for youth citizenship participation in public life.*

Keywords: Citizenship education; active citizenship; political education; civic engagement

Democracy depends on all of us; the price of liberty is not just 'eternal vigilance' as Abraham Lincoln said, but eternal activity.

Bernard Crick

INTRODUCTION

The 1990s witnessed a renewed interest in educating civically engaged citizens concerned with the future of their societies. In Canada and abroad, governments[1] developed citizenship education policies and programs, such as introducing civics as a school subject, character education programs, and completing hours of community service. In the province of Ontario, where this research takes place, the civics curriculum specifies that a critical goal is to educate an "informed and participating citizen in a democratic society" (Ontario Ministry of Education and Training [OMET], 2005, p. 64).

While citizenship participation in public affairs is desirable, the form it should take and its purposes are still matters of contentious debate (Barber, 2003; Boyte, 1994, 2004; Miller, 2000; Walker, 2002; Westheimer & Kahne, 2004). At the heart of this debate lies the wide and, sometimes, contradictory spectrum of ideas of what active citizenship is and what students as active citizens do. Is voting in general elections enough? What public issues should citizens be concerned about and involved in? What kinds of learning strategies promote students' civic and political engagement?

There is consensus that citizenship education is fundamental to the development of an effective citizenry for a strong democracy; however, there is not a unified vision of citizenship education. Rather, there is a long-standing debate between those who endorse teaching young people a more mainstream, knowledge-based citizenship education and those who advocate for a more progressive, participatory-based citizenship education (Parker, 2003). Mainstream citizenship educators advocate teaching a strong civic knowledge base of the legal-politico democratic structure and citizens' rights and duties (Parker, 2003). Progressives, on the other hand, recognize the importance of a civic knowledge base, but contend that citizenship education must provide students with opportunities for practicing substantial participation in public life (Parker, 2003). At play, in both camps, is a different vision of the active citizen. Progressives cast doubt on the notion that civic knowledge leads to active involvement in public affairs.

These different perspectives have important implications for school curriculum. While there is an explicit commitment to educate active, engaged citizens, classroom-based research in Canada (see, e.g., Evans, 2006; Llewellyn, Cook, Westheimer, Molina, & Suurtamm, 2007; Llewellyn, Cook, & Molina, 2010; Molina-Girón, 2012) and elsewhere (see, e.g., Kahne & Sporte, 2008; Pace, 2008; Rubin & Hayes, 2010) reveals that, for the most part, citizenship education favors a mainstream approach that stresses teaching young people the knowledge and skills required to become informed and responsible citizens. Less emphasis is placed on developing knowledge and skills for reflective action in the public sphere. In addition, a closer examination to the construction of active citizenship in official citizenship education curricula shows that, across Canadian provinces, "active citizenship is consistently coupled with cautious words" that stress ethical, responsible, and dutiful citizen behavior in the public sphere (Kennelly & Llewellyn, 2011, p. 903). Words associated with influencing public decision making like "activism, activist, or protest" are hardly ever used to describe active citizenship (Kennelly & Llewellyn, 2011).

This empirical research examines the practice of citizenship education in three public high schools in Ottawa, Canada. More specifically, it is concerned with whether and how teachers prepare students to be active citizens. My goal is to elucidate the multiple meanings that educating for active citizenship has and the roles that students as active citizens can play in civic and political life. Central to this inquiry is the investigation of the three teachers' conceptions of active citizenship and the ways in which their conceptions impact their day-to-day citizenship instruction.

CITIZENSHIP THEORIES[2] AND THEIR INFLUENCE IN EDUCATING FOR ACTIVE CITIZENSHIP: A THEORETICAL FRAMEWORK

There are three prevalent theoretical approaches to citizenship: the liberal, the communitarian, and the civic republicanist. Each set of theories puts forth different understandings of what citizenship comprises and the roles and duties of citizens. These distinct understandings of citizenship influence citizenship education in distinct ways, since they delineate different priorities, goals, and expectations in educating active, democratic citizens. Many of the underlying premises behind predominant citizenship theories strongly influence instructors, course developers, and policy makers in their knowledge and understanding of what it means to be an active citizen and what approaches best advance their visions.

Boyte (2004) connects the liberal citizenship theory with a predominately individualist, rights-based approach to citizenship education. The communitarian tradition, in his view, provides support for citizenship programs that stress social and moral responsibility, while civic republicanism emphasizes a vision of citizenship education concerned with democratic political participation. Following is a brief explanation of the assumptions about citizenship, the citizen, and public participation underlying each theoretical approach.

The liberal theoretical approach. Liberals regard citizenship primarily as legal status. The citizen is seen mainly as a rights bearer whose status entitles him/her to certain state benefits. The citizen is autonomous, independent, and free to pursue his or her own personal interests (Jansoki & Gran, 2002; Miller, 2000; Shafir, 1998). How citizens exercise their rights is irrelevant, as long as they do not preclude someone else's rights. Citizenship is located within the state – more specifically, in the institutions, procedures, and regulations of citizenship representation (Isin & Turner, 2002). A more liberal theoretical approach to citizenship frames it as a direct, unmediated relationship between the citizen and the state and between the citizen and the polity (Boyte, 2004). Therefore, the relationship between the state and the citizen can be best understood as one of client provider wherein the citizens are the clients: the recipients of services and other benefits provided by the state (Boyte, 1994).

Legal understandings of citizenship center active citizenship participation at the individual level and frame it in terms of rights and civic responsibility. Active participation in the public sphere can be characterized as "contractual" (Jansoki & Gran, 2002, p. 19), meaning that for the rights and liberties granted to citizens, there are also civic duties to be fulfilled. In the liberal conception of citizenship, contends Miller, "a citizen is not conceived as being an active participant in politics," or in substantial matters of democratic decision making (2000, p. 46). Rather, what emerges are free agents whose participation in the public sphere is driven mainly by self-interest and personal preference and much less by concern for the common good or the quest for democratic ideals (Boyte, 2004; Miller, 2000).

The communitarian theoretical approach. Communitarians view citizenship primarily as an activity, a practice in the pursuit of the common good (Jansoki & Gran, 2002; Miller, 2000; Shafir, 1998). They oppose the individualism championed by liberal citizenship by putting strong emphasis on the community. As such, citizenship is situated in the public sphere and citizens are seen as active individuals committed to the welfare of others and of their communities (Jansoki & Gran, 2002; Miller, 2000; Shafir, 1998). Active involvement in civic affairs creates a sense of community, which in turn reinforces the idea of a committed citizenry whose own personal interests do not take primacy over those of the community (Jansoki & Gran, 2002; Miller, 2000). While there is full recognition of the importance of rights and the fulfillment of civic duties, such as voting and abiding by societal laws, the real meaning of being a citizen lies in a commitment to public life. For communitarians, citizenship supersedes individual status and formal structures and procedures; citizenship is rooted in the active involvement of citizens in civic and political communal affairs (Jansoki & Gran, 2002; Miller, 2000; Shafir, 1998).

The communitarian theoretical approach emphasizes the active nature of being a citizen by stressing social and moral responsibility in the community (Boyte, 2004). While many interpretations of community exist, Miller (2000) offers two interpretations that are critical to understanding active citizenship in the public sphere: one is community as a "moral ideal" and the other is the "political community." In the former, community is a place, most often a neighborhood, within which citizens are encouraged to be active and make valuable contributions – this is the spirit embraced by proponents of community service who stress volunteerism and acts of charity. The political community is a space where citizens engage to discuss and make decisions on substantial matters of public life (Miller, 2000). Informed by moral conceptions of community, the communitarian approach encourages a vision of the citizen as a collaborator, a "helper" (Walker, 2002), someone who does good deeds as a means of contributing to the well-being of others and their community. Community is constructed as a harmonious place where there is consensus, commonality, and solidarity among its members. Overlooked, however, are the unavoidable conflicts and competing interests that characterize social relations in a community.

The civic republican theoretical approach. In this tradition, citizenship is, above all, a practice, an activity in the political realm of the public sphere (Boyte, 2004; Miller, 2000). The citizen is conceived, using Barber's (2003) words, as a "political actor," actively involved in public decision making. As with the liberal theoretical approach, citizenship is situated in the public sphere, in the community, but unlike the liberal theoretical approach it is also situated in civil society. The citizen is not only active but politically active – a notion central to the civic republicanist citizenship theory.

The civic republicanist tradition stands in sharp contrast to a liberal conception of participation as something based on self-interest and as merely discharging one's responsibilities, and it is also in sharp contrast to a notion of citizenship being driven primarily by social concerns as the communitarian theoretical approach defines it. The civic republicanist theory views citizenship as a political practice and activity and conceives of community as political community directly linked to the values of participation, plurality, and justice (Boyte, 2004; Miller, 2000). In addition, community is envisioned as something that offers a sense of solidarity and mutuality to citizens amidst conflict, opposing interests, and sometimes even entrenched antagonism. Civic republicanism is concerned primarily with democratic political participation. In this context, citizenship is political participation and politics, as Boyte contends, "is the way people become citizens: accountable and contributors to the country" (2004, p. 79).

METHODOLOGY[3]

This article focuses on data from three Grade 10 civics classrooms taught in two urban high schools, data drawn from a larger project (Molina-Girón, 2012). Spruce and Willow High Schools belong to the Ottawa School Board (OSB)[4] and are located in residential neighborhoods near the downtown core. Data collection took place between January and June, 2008, in three Grade 10 civics classrooms. All teachers held a university degree in social sciences and had ample experience teaching the civics course. Class sizes ranged from 9 to 22 students.

Data collection methods included non-participant observations of class instruction, interviews with teachers and students, and citizenship-related document analysis. Observations in each classroom ranged from 10 to 15 sessions of 75 minutes each to account for a total of 58 hours of observations. Formal (along with informal) interviews were conducted with each civics teacher and 30 students taking the course. Interviews with teachers lasted from 45 minutes to an hour. Individual and focus group student interviews lasted between 15 and 40 minutes. All interviews followed a semi-structured format and were tape-recorded and later transcribed verbatim. Citizenship-related documents analyzed included the Ontario civics curriculum, ministry and school board guidelines, instructional materials (e.g., handouts and videos), and examples of students' classroom work.

Data analysis was iterative and it followed two phases: within-case and cross-case analyses (Stake, 2006). The cross-case analysis was approached as "the study of diversity," or the investigation of patterns of commonalities and differences present across cases in order to build theory about educating for active citizenship (Ragin, 2000, p. 22). What resulted from this exploration is that the cases "differ by kind or type" specifically in terms of the classroom practices teachers employ to promote active civic engagement (Ragin, 2000, p. 74).

TEACHING STUDENTS HOW TO BE ACTIVE CITIZENS: THE RESEARCH FINDINGS

How do teachers through their instruction promote active citizenship? What roles are students taught to perform as active citizens? Despite having common curricular guidelines, are there significant differences in educating for active citizenship across classrooms? To answer these questions, I examined the classroom citizenship pedagogy, with special attention to how methodological approaches construct particular understandings about what active citizenship is and what active citizens do. More specifically, I looked at the drivers and expectations of students' involvement in the public realm as well as the messages about what kind of actions they can perform to be active citizens that were conveyed throughout instruction.

All three teachers identified active citizenship as a critical goal and outcome of their instruction. Accordingly, all of them designed learning activities that aimed at promoting student engagement in public life. However, a closer examination of both the types of learning activities and the goals and expectations of those activities reveal that there is a wide range of visions of what active citizenship is and what students should do as active members of society. The cross-case analysis indicates that there are three distinct understandings of active citizenship: duty-based, make-a-difference, and politically oriented active citizenship. In the next section, a case has been associated with a particular approach to active citizenship. However, no case fits perfectly into just one category, and there are moments when there is more than one type at play. In addition, the students are not merely passive recipients of instruction, but they interpret, shape, and create new and different meanings of what it means to be an active citizen, as the cases show. I begin with a brief description of the teacher's self-reported conceptions of active citizenship and goals for teaching. Then I present examples of class instruction that aimed at promoting active citizenship to illustrate how this is done. Next, I describe the type of active citizenship that is advanced through class instruction.

Duty-Based Active Citizenship: Ms. Sarah Montgomery's Civics Class

For Ms. Montgomery, educating active citizens was a top goal of her instruction. She asserted, "I want my students to learn how to become active citizens. And that is what I am trying to get the students to become in this Civics course." To promote active citizenship, she explained, "the first thing is understanding how our system in Canada works, [the] government ... the ... political system, [and the] three different levels of government." For Ms. Montgomery, civic knowledge of "how the system works" is fundamental to enable active citizenship. In her view, this knowledge is critical, so the students "would know how things work so that they would know where to go to make complaints or to make suggestions." She further elaborated:

> If [the students] have a particular concern ... which is under the jurisdiction of the federal [provincial or municipal] government, they would know that they would contact their MP [Member of Parliament ... or], their MPP [Member of Provincial Parliament], [or] their city councillor, so they would able to be active citizens within their community.

For Ms. Montgomery, active citizenship implies a strong connection to the government, and, thus, citizens must know the government structure and organization to be able to effectively participate in their society. Accordingly, three quarters of instructional time was dedicated to civic knowledge acquisition, an emphasis that was echoed by the students I interviewed. All nine students reported learning about the structure and function of the government and its institutions compared to only two students who mentioned learning how to be active citizens involved in their community. Suzanne explained, "a lot of it [class content] is facts," as opposed to discussions of societal issues. Nathan reported learning about government officials, "what they do and who they are," while Daren learned "about the different parties ... the rule of law ... the way government does things, the different [types] of laws, The House of Commons ... , and elections."

Promoting Active Citizenship through Class Instruction

Although Ms. Montgomery's class instruction primarily stressed civic knowledge acquisition, her instruction had an active citizenship component whereby students undertook a civic action project to benefit the community. *The Make-a-Difference* project consisted on designing and implementing an action in response to an issue or problem that the students cared about, either individually or in small groups. After completion, they presented to the class the results of the project and wrote a five-paragraph essay. Other strategies that promote active civic engagement, such as class discussions, role playing, and research projects, were not observed. In fact, the teacher asserted that in class, "the students write ... and ... say opinions, but no, there has never been any debate."

In preparation to their civic action projects, Ms. Montgomery explained to the class that the main goal was "to make a difference in your community." Through this activity, she said, "you are making a difference as an active citizen." To guide the process, the teacher asked the students to complete an action plan with three steps: (a) brainstorming to identify an issue of concern, (b) explaining the action(s) they will take to make a difference, and (c) detailing the tasks, deadlines, and resources required. The preparation phase previous to the implementation of the project was rather minimal. Besides clarifying the goals and requirements, students were left on their own deciding what civic project to undertake. However, the preparation phase is critical to the outcomes of community involvement. It is in this phase when students can explore issues that they can act on as well as reflect on the intended results of their efforts (Billig, Root, & Jesse, 2005; Newmann, 1975; Wade, 2008).

A total of 10 civic action projects were undertaken, all of them implemented in the local community. Based on the scope and aims of the student projects (here and in the other class at Spruce High School), I was able to identify two kinds of projects: service-oriented and issue-based projects. Service-oriented projects align with the communitarian conception of active citizenship as they aimed to improve the community, help people in need, or contribute to a good cause. The goal of these projects was to do something positive and good, but not necessarily to try to create change or address an identified problem or social condition. In contrast, issue-based projects closely correspond to the civic republican approach. Students who undertook these projects tackled an existing problem and worked with private or public institutions to affect change.

Eight of the 10 civic projects students conducted were service-oriented projects. They included six cleaning campaigns in public parks or school grounds, one clothes donation to a women's organization, and one essay writing to raise awareness about global warming. Of the two issue-based projects, one consisted of petitioning to the City of Ottawa Traffic Control office to increase the crossing time in a traffic light close to school between 3:00 PM and 3:20 PM on weekdays. For the other project, a trio organized a corporate food drive. They requested donations from three food stores and collected 11 boxes of non-perishable food, which they donated to the Ottawa Food Bank. Both are issue-based projects because the students identified a problem and carried an action to address an identified situation.

Interestingly, half of the students who decided on doing cleaning campaigns had explored other options for their projects that involved providing a direct service. Suzanne, Adrian, and Thuc thought about reading to the blind and a food drive as potential projects, but as Adrian said, "that was the end of it because it was really few [choices] to choose from that she [Ms. Montgomery] suggested" to the class. Suzanne explained that they decided on a cleaning campaign, "mainly ... because we have very tight schedules right now. We could have done something bigger, [but] we found a decent way to be an active citizen."

Although all students developed a project that contributed to society in one way or another, there are significant differences in the projects that students undertook. Overall, issue-based projects (here and in the other class) required research, careful planning and execution, and working with public or private organizations to their completion. In addition, the type of project that students undertook shaped the type of knowledge they were exposed to and the type of public participation. Students who did issue-based projects became aware of public and social issues and developed an increased sense of civic efficacy in comparison to the students who did service-oriented projects.

Poverty was a social issue that the students were exposed to, but in issue-based and service-oriented projects a different kind of civic learning occurred. The students who did the corporate food drive explained that while doing research on the Ottawa Food Bank website, they "discovered that there is a hunger issue in Ottawa"; an issue that they were "pretty unaware of." They learned that an estimated "40,000 people per month rely on the Ottawa Food Bank" out of which "40% are children." The students highlighted that working collaboratively with the food bank operation manager helped to "put into perspective the importance of this project" especially since over the last few years, there has been a steady "decline in donations and an increase of food bank users." In contrast, the clothes donors learned about the services that the institution provides, such as "food, shelter, clothes, and counseling services to women who have been abused or for some reason cannot provide for themselves." In their view, their clothes donation will "help these women [to] get one step further to be on their own," as well as "to minimize [the] number of women who attend the center." However, while their efforts genuinely aimed at helping poor women, these students did not talk about women's poverty and violence against women – the very issue they were acting upon – as issues that demand intervention beyond satisfying the victims' basic needs.

With regards to civic efficacy, overall, all students regarded the Make-a-Difference project as a positive experience that helped them understand that they can make valuable contributions to society. However, an increased sense of civic efficacy – the sense of seeing oneself capable of effectively participating in public life (Kahne & Westheimer, 2008) – is reported principally by the students who did issue-based projects. Jessica, who petitioned to increase the crossing time at a traffic light near school, saw herself and her counterparts as capable of bringing about change in their community. She said:

> I never really thought that just us high school students could actually ... make a change in the community. ... We can reach the City of Ottawa and make big changes, and we are only 15 years old.

The Make-a-Difference project was instrumental to the development of important skills, such as teamwork, problem solving, developing action plans, and identifying ways of being a contributing member. However, students who carried out issue-based projects reported learning additional skills including contacting city officials, writing convincing letters and evidence-based petitions, and working collaboratively with government and private organizations. Consequently, students who engaged in issue-based projects had a more meaningful and real opportunity to learn first-hand what it takes – the processes and constraints – to being involved in promoting change, which in turn contributed to strengthening students' sense of internal civic competence (Kahne & Westheimer, 2008).

Besides the civic project, throughout instruction, Ms. Montgomery favored certain forms of active involvement and deterred students from other forms of participation that could be considered more political. Ms. Montgomery showed the video *The Cochabamba Water War*, which addressed disparities in water abundance and access to drinking water among countries.[5] The video narrates the organization of Cochabamba citizens in Bolivia after their municipal government privatized the water supply system. Under the new administration, the price for water doubled and tripled, turning drinking water into an expensive commodity. Cochabamba citizens formed a civil organization to protest and change the new system. The video explores the role that citizens have in acting on public issues, especially in situations where access to vital services is in jeopardy. The video ends with 10 ways to conserve water, such as taking short showers and using rain water to water gardens and wash cars. After watching the video, the teacher told the students that in order to make a difference "you do not have to get involved" and that following the "ten ways to conserve water" is sufficient to make a difference. It seems that for Ms. Montgomery to be an active citizen, it is enough that students contribute to laudable causes and behave responsibly (e.g., by conserving water). Other forms of involvement that might help students to become conscious of local and global inequities and ignite a desire to promote change were not encouraged by the teacher.

Duty-Based Active Citizenship

This type of active citizenship falls within the liberal citizenship theoretical approach, which frames citizenship primarily as legal status – the combination of rights and duties that legal members of the nation-state have (Jansoki & Gran, 2002; Miller, 2000). By large, this is the most minimalist version of active citizenship as it stresses above all civic responsibility.

Teachers who adopt this conception of active citizenship teach their students about the citizen as an individual with state-granted rights and responsibilities. This frames citizenship as a direct relationship between the individual and the state as well as the individual and his or her fellow citizens. Congruent with the liberal approach to citizenship, active participation is located within the system through the array of government institutions, avenues, and processes provided for such ends (Isin & Turner, 2002). Another characteristic of this type of active citizenship is that it stresses a "contractual" (Jansoki & Gran, 2002) relationship that exists between citizens and the state, which mediates citizens' active public participation. To illustrate, Ms. Montgomery highlighted how students need to know the jurisdictions of different levels of government to know who to complain to if your garbage is not picked up on schedule, something that is part of the contract between citizens and their municipality, not their provincial or federal government. Central to this conception of active citizenship is teaching the workings of democracy, meaning how the government works, and developing in students an appreciation for core democratic principles.

A duty-based active citizenship promotes an image of the citizen as an informed observer who knows how the system works, and participates accordingly. When this conception dominates instruction, active participation in the public sphere is encouraged by exercising rights and fulfilling responsibilities. Consequently, students are socialized into a view of politics where they are politically passive, but active as voters, taxpayers, constituent, responsible citizens, and perhaps as volunteers in the community (Barber, 2003; Boyte, 2004; Walker, 2002; Westheimer & Kahne, 2004). Thus, good citizens recycle, join cleaning campaigns, contribute to laudable causes, and assess and vote for representatives in charge of public decision making. These are seen as ideal avenues to be active citizens. For Ms. Montgomery, for example, completing the civic projects was the most important objective, not the actual contributions students made as active citizens to better their communities – although these issue-based projects were more meaningful than service-oriented projects in engaging students with social problems.

A duty-based conception of active citizenship seems to endorse the view that citizens ought to give back to society by acting responsibly and fulfilling their responsibilities (Westheimer & Kahne, 2004). In response to critical issues like water scarcity, Ms. Montgomery discouraged students from politically active forms of engagement in favor of acting responsibly by using water rationally. Duty-based active citizenship resonates with understandings of the good citizen, to use Suzanne's words – a Grade 10 student – as someone who "knows about the country and how it is run, and is aware even if they are not always active, but he is always aware of what is going on."

Make-a-Difference Active Citizenship: Ms. Judith Keller's Civic Class

For Ms. Keller, there are two kinds of citizens: "a minimally good citizen" and "a good citizen." Minimally good citizens are "informed. They understand how their government works ... the political system; the parties ... who is running in their riding ... [and] their rights and responsibilities with regards to the law." In contrast, a good citizen

> [w]ould be one who is a *little bit more active*. Maybe writes a letter from time to time on something that upsets them, or does some kind of work in the community to improve things and not just letting other people do everything.

Civic knowledge acquisition and active citizenship are two components central to the goals and expectations Ms. Keller has set for the course. She explained:

> My goals for the civics class are to give them an overview of ... how the government works and their connection to the government. But, my main goal is to show them how they can do something, or kind of empower them ... to greater civic responsibility .... At the minimum, they are going to vote, and at the maximum, they are going to do more actions ... based on their beliefs.

Student interviews reveal that Ms. Keller achieved her goals. The majority of students interviewed reported learning that citizenship is about the relationship between the government and those who are governed as well as citizens' active involvement in the community. Edward's response is a good example: "what I have learned the most is about the government, how it works, what it does for us, and how to get involved, participate [and] become an active citizen."

Promoting Active Citizenship through Class Instruction

Class discussions and the Make-a-Difference project were the two pedagogical approaches geared toward developing active citizenship. Every Friday, the students discussed news articles of their choice. I observed five class discussions on the topics related to the creation of a water park, cell phones allergies, Facebook, the legalization of marihuana, and the adoption of a Nunavut child by non-Aboriginal people. While many of the news articles the students selected relate to things that were of interest to them, the articles differed in terms of their civic content and significance in discussing public issues. With few exceptions (i.e., the legalization of marihuana and the adoption of a Nunavut child), the news articles that students chose tended to focus on soft news, which report about less critical events, and much less on hard news.[6] In addition, I observed that Ms. Keller led discussions on relatively safe, controversial topics like the pros and cons of legalizing marihuana, but did not discuss controversial issues that address structural inequity and injustice. To illustrate, the class discussion on the article about an Inuit teenage mother who gave her baby up for adoption centered on the reasons couples or individuals have to adopt. Critical issues such as the fact that Aboriginal communities have the highest levels of teen pregnancy in Canada or the reasons why teen mothers decide to give their children up for adoption were not discussed.

To promote active citizenship, Ms. Keller also implemented the Make-a-Difference civic action project. The requirements were the same as in Ms. Montgomery's class; however, Ms. Keller did various activities to prepare her students to undertake their projects. Besides explaining the project goals and completing the three-step action plan, she read inspirational stories of citizens who contribute with their time and money to laudable causes (i.e., shelters). She also helped students to identify issues that they could address through their projects. Working in groups, Ms. Keller asked the students to name three issues that they were concerned about. Then, she invited them to propose at least one action for each issue that could be taken to improve the situation. Finally, she asked them to assess the feasibility of the suggested actions. For the students who had difficulty identifying an issue for their civic action projects, Ms. Keller suggested searching the websites of aid agencies, such as CARE and World Vision.

Four civic action projects were undertaken in this class: two service-oriented and two issue-based projects. In the two service-oriented projects, students fundraised for the Canadian Cancer Society and World Vision. The two issue-based projects focused on the environment. Vanessa took issue with a government building that kept the lights on throughout the night. She decided to write letters to the Minister of National Defense, her Member of Parliament, and to a local newspaper to request turning off the lights at the headquarters of the National Defense building. She also designed three posters that she put around the school that advised on three ways to save energy. One poster read, "if everyone in Ontario uses energy-efficient light bulbs instead of regular bulbs, we can save 600,000 watts." Albert and Edward participated in the Green Bin contest sponsored by the City of Ottawa, which consisted of designing a poster to support the city's new recycling program. I considered this an issue-based project based on the students' goals of promoting the city's waste management program. "Our action," they explained, "was to create this poster to inform people about the Green Bin .... We are trying to ask you to compost things ... to decrease the time to make another land field." Similar to the previous class, students who did issue-based projects report becoming aware of public and social issues and developing an increased sense of civic efficacy.

The students who did issue-based projects showed an increased concern for the environment. Vanessa began her presentation affirming, "global warming is a real issue ... We need to do something about the environment." For her, "raising public awareness about the environment in general and electricity in particular" as well as passing "better legislation [to save ...] energy" are two important steps in curbing global warming. Similarly, in their presentation, Albert and Edward expressed concern with the fact that humans "are speeding up the greenhouse effect." They spoke of their poster character as a superhero. Indeed, they affirmed, the Green Bin "is a super hero" because "it is getting rid of the garbage and composting it to make a greener world."

In contrast, both service-oriented projects focused on raising funds to tackle health issues nationally and internationally. The students were sensitive toward human suffering. For instance, the fundraisers for the Canadian Cancer Society asserted, "we chose to do a bake sale to help someone and save someone's life." However, none of these students seemed to have acquired a deeper knowledge of the very issues that they were acting on. For example, in their presentation, Rasil and Keifer limited themselves to say that "in some places like Kenya, they do not have basic medical needs ... like antibiotics for diseases."

With regards to civic efficacy, similar to the other class, the civic project was instrumental in helping students realize that they could make a positive contribution to society. Students, who helped others by fundraising, expressed a great sense of personal fulfillment. One of the cancer fundraisers remarked, "helping others makes you feel good and happy while [it] aids the people who get it." The students who did issue-based projects also found the projects to be personally rewarding. However, these students also expressed a sense of civic competence. Vanessa, who is critical of government inaction to protect the environment, stressed the need to take action to reduce global warming. "I feel like" she asserted, "if someone does not do something then the whole world is going to heat up and we are going to have malaria in Canada." Edward concluded that by doing this project he learned that:

> We are all able and ... we can all make a difference. [What] I want to achieve [with this project] is to inform people, to make them understand that this is an issue ... that ... it is very important and [that] it concerns all of us. And, if we all try, we can change the future.

Make-a-Difference Active Citizenship

The Make-a-Difference active citizenship aligns with the communitarian citizenship tradition. It emerges from care and concern for the well-being of others and the community as a whole; thus, it stresses social and moral responsibility (Boyte, 2004; Crick, 2007). Endorsing the moral ideal of community (Miller, 2000), this approach locates citizen action in the public sphere, in the community, and most often within the boundaries of local neighborhoods (Boyte, 2004; Crick, 2007). It stresses putting one's talents to the service of the common good and joining efforts with others in and out of the school in order to make valuable contributions (Crick, 2007; Kahne & Westheimer, 1996; Westheimer & Kahne, 2004). For example, Ms. Keller makes a distinction between minimally good citizens who vote and do "what is expected of them" and good citizens who are "empowered to a greater civic responsibility" in the community.

The make-a-difference approach to active citizenship emphasizes citizenship as a practice, but it does so in a depoliticized way. When this vision dominates instruction, citizenship educations couples civic knowledge of how the government works and civic action by encouraging students to undertake actions that can have a positive impact in the community. This approach encourages a vision of the citizen as a collaborator, a "helper" (Walker, 2002); someone who shows solidarity and is capable of putting others before his or her own interests (Crick, 2007; Kahne & Westheimer, 1996; Miller, 2000). This vision is very distinct from the individualism espoused on the previous approach. While in the duty-based approach active citizenship is seen as successfully completing a civic action project, for Ms. Keller even if the students do not complete the project, "at least they see that, yeah, it is possible to do something."

This approach embraces the vision of an active citizen that makes students believe that no matter who they are they can make a significant difference to fellow citizens and to society. As found in this research and elsewhere (Billig et al., 2005; Kahne & Westheimer, 1996; Wade, 2008; Walker, 2002), engagement in projects to better the community develops in students a sense of personal fulfillment, increased empathy and commitment to helping others, and a personal capacity to undertake actions that positively impact the community. However, students are not taught that through individual and public actions, they can have a say in issues affecting their lives. In this vision of active citizenship, as Jessica, a Grade 10 student, asserts, a good citizen is someone who "cares about the community and just would do things without expecting anything in return."

Politically Oriented Active Citizenship: Mr. Anthony Bennett's Civic Class

For Mr. Bennett, "civics is largely about politics." He espouses a Deweyian view of democracy as a work in progress and an ideal for living together.

Democracy, he asserted, "is something that is not easy ... that is very difficult" and to which "there is no easy solution." Therefore, an important goal of his instruction is to socialize students into politics and political processes. As he cogently observes, students are constantly exposed to a wide and conflicting range of political information. They "hear these names: Bush, Clinton, Harper, or Dion, and they formulate opinions on these people on very small amounts of information." Therefore, a central goal of his instruction is for students to develop

> [a] clear understanding of the political ideologies that are involved, so they have a broader ... grid in which to place characters [politicians] ... and events like the war, terrorism and other issues. I hope ... they [understand ...] that there are opposing views.

For Mr. Bennett, engaging with real issues at the local and international level is essential in educating active citizens. Thus, conflict, conflict resolution, and the common good are themes central to his citizenship pedagogy. With regard to conflict, he categorically states, "I believe it is my job to address it. ... So, my goal is to try and achieve some kind of understanding of the conflict." The vision of politics that Mr. Bennett has not only sees conflict as an inevitable part of democratic living, but also as something that cannot be neutral or left to be resolved through consensus and constitutional law (Crick & Porter, 1978). As he further asserts, "in order to understand the different conflicts ... you need to understand issues around the world." As such, for the most part, to provide instruction, he uses an issue-based approach, which he calls "political globalism."

For Mr. Bennett, educating an engaged citizen is something that "is very hard" to achieve. He further explains, "you cannot force somebody to participate. You can only show them that there is a need." In addition, he recognizes that there are different levels of civic engagement; thus, not all students are at the same stage and through the course they will reach different levels of citizenship engagement:

> Some [students] will never ... engage in civil, societal issues. Some of them will engage in societal issues in this course, and others have already engaged. Others will engage maybe in their twenties or thirties. It is different for everybody.

Promoting Active Citizenship through Class Instruction

Mr. Bennett's vision of civics as politics seemed to influence how he sees students engaging in public life. His instructional approaches aimed at practicing direct forms of citizenship participation, reflecting on one's personal political stances and practicing collective decision making. He engaged students in protest and letter writing. "I took students to a protest [against] university tuition fees increase," he affirmed. In addition, he involved the students in writing letters to government officials to express concern about an issue. The students "would be quite excited when they got a letter back from some officer. Hopefully, it shows them that they do have an input; that in a democracy, they [government officials] do respond to the people."

Mr. Bennett implemented learning activities that encouraged students to think politically. A good example is found in the way he planned and taught the unit on political parties. Mr. Bennett gave the students two handouts, *The Political Spectrum: Where Do You Stand?* and the *Political Statements Worksheet*, which had various political statements on issues related to post-secondary education, immigration, state-sponsored programs for disadvantaged groups, and minimum wage regulations. The students were asked to take a position whether they were in agreement or not with the statements. Then, the teacher asked them to identify the political ideology (right, center, or left-wing) and the political party (Conservative, Liberal, or the New Democratic Party [NDP]) that was more likely to support each statement. To illustrate, the statement "rising tuition costs are making post-secondary education inaccessible to many students. It's time to abolish tuition fees and have the government fund all levels of education" would have been identified with the words left-wing and NDP. In contrast, the statement "welfare programs are too rich in this country. People lose their initiative and their drive if it is too easy to go on welfare" would have been identified as right-wing and Conservative.

Role playing and simulations were the main teaching strategies Mr. Bennett used to practice democratic decision making. In a sweatshop role-playing exercise, the students explored labor relations of exploitation. Divided into four groups, the students came together to negotiate a 10% salary cut to workers at a shoe factory located in Honduras, a developing country. Each student represented a different stakeholder: the shoe company CEO, the factory owner, the assembly line workers, the First World consumers, and a labor rights NGO. According to the company's CEO, salary cuts were necessary "in order to stay profitable against heavy competition." Each representative received a handout outlining the positions they would take in the negotiation.

Before the simulation took place, Mr. Bennett discussed what a sweatshop is. Most students knew famous companies that use sweatshops to produce their products, like Nike, Adidas, and Guess. Students defined a sweatshop as "a place where you get paid funny." Mr. Bennett further explained that sweatshops rely on cheap labor from people in poor countries – a strategy that allows companies to ensure and expand their profit potential. "In sweat-shops," he told the students, "people work 12-hour shifts for a minimum salary and have no benefits." Students conceded that they buy these brands "because we are bombarded with advertisements." As a form of reflection, the teacher told the students that the professional golf player "Tiger Woods makes more money from Nike than all the people working for Nike in Indonesia." Then the teacher talked about the avenues workers have to negotiate salary disputes, such as forming a union and going on strike. By going on strike, "the company [can] lose millions of dollars," he told the students.

Of four groups, three could not come to an agreement and the workers decided to go on strike. In the group that came to an agreement, the workers accepted a 3% salary cut, with the promise that the salary cut would be reversed once the company's profits improved. In the discussion following the activity, a student reflected on the discrepancy between workers' salary and the company's profit. Cemal said, these "companies make millions of dollars every year … . Workers work eight hours a day for four dollars and they are still complaining." Jamila recognized how difficult is to boycott or giving up buying these brands. "I know what they do," she said, "but I will still buy their brands." To close the activity, the teacher remarked: "I hope you have a better understanding of what the situation is all about" and how we as "blind consumers are implicated in the exploitation of people around the world."

Politically Oriented Active Citizenship

This type of active citizenship adopts the civic republicanist conception of active citizenship as a practice in the *political* realm (Barber, 2003; Boyte, 2004). Teachers who endorse a politically oriented active citizenship combine civic knowledge and a broader engagement with politics and social and political issues. Their instruction highlights an understanding of effective participation in the public sphere that is driven primarily by the identification of societal issues that demand citizen and government attention as compared to the duty-based active citizenship that stresses fulfilling one's civic responsibilities and the make-a-difference active citizen-ship that champions charitable acts. As such, teachers who teach with this vision discuss with their students difficult and often controversial issues (e.g., government welfare programs and labor exploitation) in order to provide a language and context to understand politics and to develop political competence (Crick & Porter, 1978; Westheimer & Kahne, 2004). In contrast, in classrooms where the duty-based approach to active citizenship dominated, students were not engaged in class discussions and in classrooms where the make-a-difference was favored; students discussed safe, controversial issues to promote civic skill development.

The site for active citizenship participation is the political community, which is seen as a space – rather than a place, as conceived in the two previous approaches – where citizens debate, discuss, and propose actions on matters of public concern (Miller, 2000). If the realm for citizenship action is political, it follows that the citizen is conceived as a "political actor" (Barber, 2003), a "co-creator" (Boyte, 2004). Mr. Bennett, for example, taught students political forms of active citizenship, such as protesting and letter writing as mechanisms to affect societal change. In a politically oriented active citizenship, students are taught that the citizen is politically active and his or her participation can affect public decision making.

Teachers with a politically oriented conception of active citizenship take seriously the notion that citizenship is a reflective practice for enlightened engagement in the public sphere (Newmann, 1975; Parker, 2003). This type of active citizenship, for the most part, socializes students into a conception of politics as "give-and-take, messy, everyday public work through which citizens set about dealing with the problems of their daily existence" (Boyte, 1994, p. 79). As Adana, Grade 10 student, explained, good citizens are those who "stand up and speak out instead of just … hiding, because, then, it is not a democracy, really, if we, all, do not take part in it."

SAME CURRICULUM, THREE DIFFERENT UNDERSTANDINGS OF BEING AN ACTIVE CITIZEN

This research investigates an important goal of school-based citizenship education: educating active citizens consciously engaged in shaping the future of their societies. Overall, the research results reveal that there is a strong relationship between teachers' understandings of what active citizenship is and how students are taught to participate in the public realm. Despite having common curricular guidelines and expressing a commitment to educate active citizens, in practice, teachers' conceptions of active citizenship have profound implications as they construct and delineate the capacities deemed desirable and necessary for active citizenship and the actual roles that students as active citizens are expected to play in public life. The research findings reveal three distinct understandings of active citizenship that can be advanced through school-based citizenship education: duty-based, make-a-difference, and politically oriented active citizenship.

Teaching students different conceptions of active citizenship has important consequences. A key finding is that two of the three conceptions promote a vision of active citizenship as "an *alternative* to politics" (Boyte, 1991, as cited in Kahne & Westheimer, 1996, p. 597, emphasis in original). While the duty-based approach envisions an active citizen as an informed observer, the make-a-difference approach stresses the image of a helper. Although with different emphases a key priority for both approaches is developing the capacity for being law-abiding citizens and for acting responsibly by fulfilling one's civic responsibilities (e.g., voting and paying taxes), the make-a-difference approach, however, goes a step farther as it aims to foster core moral virtues, such as solidarity, generosity, and concern for others. To a large extent, being an active citizen in the public sphere is underlined by a call to the good person who willingly contributes and volunteers in altruistic initiatives to help those who are less fortunate (Crick, 2007; Kahne & Westheimer, 1996; Walker, 2002).

In contrast, the politically oriented conception of active citizenship situates active citizenship in the realm of politics. It promotes a view of the citizen as a "political actor" actively engaged in shaping the future of his or her society. What is unique to this approach is that the vision of an active citizen moves beyond fulfilling one's civic responsibilities and doing acts of kindness – although these are recognized as important qualities of good citizenship – to engaging in the public sphere; dealing with economic, political, and social issues; and problems and dilemmas of the day (Crick & Porter, 1978; Parker, 2003). Citizenship education that endorses this approach helps students make sense of their political world. Students are taught to grapple with conflicting interests, power differentials, and are encouraged to participate in activities of a political nature, like protesting as a mechanism for societal change.

This research also sheds light on the centrality of the educational practices employed to promote civic engagement. According to the findings, there is a high level of congruence between teachers' goals and expectations for public engagement and students' understandings of what active citizenship is and the roles they see themselves playing in public life. However, there were instances when this was not the case. Students who undertook issue-based projects that sought to address real issues reported civic learning that aligned with a more politically oriented vision of active citizenship, although the civic projects aimed at fostering moral and social responsibility.

Providing students with learning experiences that allow them to engage with real issues can be significant in helping students to begin to think and act politically.

The different understandings of active citizenship stress not only the development of different capacities for active citizenship. They also direct students toward very different paths for participation in the public sphere. The duty-based and make-a-difference conceptions of active citizenship teach students to accept a set of democratic principles (rights and responsibilities) and behave accordingly (Kennelly & Llewellyn, 2011; Miller, 2000; Parker, 2003). As such, the kind of public participation that is endorsed is contained within existing political structures. In other words, citizens are active within the system, not necessarily for public engagement, but for the smooth and unchallenged functioning of the state (Barber, 2003; Boyte, 2004; Parker, 2003). The duty-based and make-a-difference conceptions of active citizenship seem to embrace a civic minimalism that leads students to believe that any act in the public sphere is active participation as long as it is informed by an understanding of the rules of society. The actions of an active citizen can require a significant amount of effort or not. They can be practiced frequently or only once in a while, and they can range from voting to helping someone to cross the street. Absent in these conceptions of active citizenship is a vision of public participation geared toward influencing public decision making in order to promote social change (Barber, 2003; Parker, 2003; Walker, 2002; Westheimer & Kahne, 2004). If educating active citizens concerned with the future of their societies is a priority, then we need a kind of citizenship education that teaches young people about democratic values and ideals as well as the issues, contradictions, and dilemmas that our democracy faces. It is in this context that the idea of the active citizen as a political actor can emerge: as someone who not only is concerned with the future of his or her society, but that is willing to work with others to create a more just and democratic society.

NOTES

1. In 1998, England introduced the *Education for Citizenship and the Teaching of Democracy in Schools* (House of Commons, 2007), while in 1997, Australia launched the *Discovering Democracy* national program (Australian Government, n.d.). In United States, *The Civic Mission of Schools Report* was released in February 2003 (Carnegie Corporation of New York & CIRCLE, 2003).

2. There are other citizenship theories, such as the cosmopolitan, the ecological, and multicultural citizenship. However, further research is needed to determine how

these relatively new theories impact upon citizenship education. For a review of these citizenship theories, see Isin and Turner (2002) and Shafir (1998).

3. The names of all people, schools, and school boards are pseudonyms.

4. The OSB is the largest board serving the City of Ottawa. It has under its supervision a total of 73,243 students and 147 schools, out of which 116 are elementary and 26 are secondary schools (OSB, n.d.).

5. The unit entitled *The Impact of Globalization and the Privatization of Water* has been suggested for civics and other school subjects as this unit meets the OMET curricular standards. To teach this unit, a complete teaching kit has been developed (Ontario Secondary School Teachers' Federation [OSSTF] & Canadian International Development Agency, 2007). Materials can be accessed from the OSSTF website.

6. In journalism, news stories are divided in two kinds: soft and hard news. Soft news provides background information mainly about events and incidents. In contrast, hard news includes major significant political, socioeconomic, and war-related news that require a government response (Patterson, 2000).

ACKNOWLEDGMENTS

The author would like to thanks Joel Westheimer, Sharon Cook, Daniel Schugurensky, and Derek Smith for their feedback in earlier versions of this work. Thanks are also extended to the anonymous reviewers and guest editors for their insightful comments and suggestions. This research was supported by the Social Science and Humanities Research Council.

REFERENCES

Australian Government (n.d.). *About civics and citizenship education.* Retrieved from http:// www.civicsandcitizenship.edu.au/cce/about_civics_and_citizenship_education,9625.html

Barber, B. (2003). *Strong democracy: Participatory politics for a new age* (2nd ed.). Berkeley, CA: University of California Press.

Billig, S., Root, S., & Jesse, D. (2005). *The impact of participation in service-learning on high school students' civic engagement.* CIRCLE Working Paper No. 33. The Center for Information and Research on Civic Learning and Engagement (CIRCLE). Retrieved from http://www.civicyouth.org/PopUps/WorkingPapers/WP33Billig.pdf

Boyte, H. C. (1994). Reinventing citizenship. *Kettering Review, 78,* 78–87.

Boyte, H. C. (2004). *Everyday politics: Reconnecting citizens and public life.* Philadelphia, PA: University of Pennsylvania Press.

Carnegie Corporation of New York & CIRCLE. (2003). *The civic mission of schools.* New York: Carnegie Corporation.

Crick, B. (2007). Citizenship: The political and the democratic. *British Journal of Educational Studies, 55*(3), 235–248.

Crick, B., & Porter, A. (Eds.). (1978). *Political education and political literacy*. London: Longman.

Evans, M. (2006). Educating for citizenship: What teachers say and what teachers do. *Canadian Journal of Education, 29*(2), 410–435.

House of Commons (2007). *Citizenship education: Second report of session 2006–07*. Retrieved from http://www.publications.parliament.uk/pa/cm200607/cmselect/cmeduski/147/147.pdf

Isin, E., & Turner, B. (2002). Citizenship studies: An introduction. In E. F. Isin & B. S. Turner (Eds.), *Handbook of citizenship studies* (pp. 1–10). London: SAGE.

Jansoki, T., & Gran, B. (2002). Political citizenship: Foundations of rights. In E. F. Isin & B. S. Turner (Eds.), *Handbook of citizenship studies* (pp. 13–52). London: SAGE.

Kahne, J., & Sporte, S. (2008). Developing citizens: The impact of civic learning opportunities on students' commitment to civic participation. *American Educational Research Journal, 51*(3), 738–766.

Kahne, J., & Westheimer, J. (1996). In the service of what? The politics of service learning. *Phi Delta Kappan, 77*(9), 592–599.

Kahne, J., & Westheimer, J. (2008). The limits of efficacy: Educating citizens for a democratic society. In B. C. Rubin & J. M. Giarelli (Eds.), *Civic education for diverse citizens in global times: Rethinking theory and practice* (pp. 175–199). New York: LEA.

Kennelly, J., & Llewellyn, K. (2011). Educating for active compliance: Discursive constructions in citizenship education. *Citizenship Studies, 15*(6–7), 897–914.

Llewellyn, K., Cook, S., & Molina, L. A. (2010). Civic learning: Moving from the apolitical to the socially just. *Journal of Curriculum Studies, 42*(6), 791–812.

Llewellyn, K., Cook, S., Westheimer, J., Molina, L. A., & Suurtamm, K. (2007). *The state and potential of civic learning in Canada: Chartering the course for youth democratic and political participation*. Ottawa, Canada: Canadian Policy Research Networks.

Miller, D. (2000). *Citizenship and national identity*. Cambridge, United Kingdom: Polity Press.

Molina-Girón, L. A. (2012). *Educating good citizens: A case study of citizenship education in four multicultural high school classrooms in Ontario*. Unpublished doctoral dissertation. University of Ottawa, Ontario, Canada.

Newmann, F. M. (1975). *Education for citizenship action: Challenge for secondary curriculum*. Berkeley, CA: MrCutchan Publishing Corporation.

Ontario Ministry of Education and Training. (2005). *The Ontario curriculum grades 9 and 10: Canadian and world studies (Revised)*. Retrieved from http://www.edu.gov.on.ca/eng/curriculum/secondary/canworld910curr.pdf

Ontario Secondary School Teachers' Federation & Canadian International Development Agency (2007). Tapped out: The world water crisis. Retrieved from http://www.osstf.on.ca/tapped-out-resource

Ottawa School Board. (n.d.). *Public education: Doing it W.E.L.L.: Director's annual report to the community 2010–2011*. Retrieved from http://www.ocdsb.ca/ab-ocdsb/annual_Reports/Documents/16289%20OCDSB%20Annual%20Report%202010-2011_Ev_V7a%20FINAL-s.pdf

Pace, J. (2008). Teaching for citizenship in 12th grade government classes. In J. Bixby & J. Pace (Eds.), *Educating democratic citizens in troubled times: Qualitative studies of current efforts* (pp. 25–57). New York: Sunny Press.

Parker, W. (2003). *Teaching democracy: Unity and diversity in public life*. New York: Teachers College.

Patterson, T. E. (2000). *Doing well and doing good: How soft news and critical journalism are shrinking the news audience and weakening democracy – And what news outlets can do about it*. Retrieved from http://www.hks.harvard.edu/presspol/publications/reports/soft_news_and_critical_journalism_2000.pdf

Ragin, C. C. (2000). *Fuzzy-set social science*. Chicago, IL: University of Chicago Press.

Rubin, B., & Hayes, F. (2010). "No backpacks" versus "drugs and murder": The promise and complexity of youth civic action research. *Harvard Educational Review, 80*(3), 352–378.

Shafir, G. (1998). Introduction: The evolving tradition of citizenship. In G. Shafir (Ed.), *The citizenship debates: A reader* (pp. 1–28). Minneapolis, MN: University of Minnesota Press.

Stake, R. (2006). *Multiple case study analysis*. New York: The Guilford Press.

Wade, R. (2008). Service-learning. In L. S. Levstik & C. Tyson (Eds.), *Handbook of research in social studies education* (pp. 109–123). New York: Routledge.

Walker, T. (2002). Service as pathway to political participation: What research tells us. *Applied Developmental Science, 6*(4), 183–188.

Westheimer, J., & Kahne, J. (2004). What kind of citizen? The politics of educating for democracy. *American Educational Research Journal, 41*(2), 237–269.

ENGAGING YOUNG PEOPLE? THE EXPERIENCES, CHALLENGES, AND SUCCESSES OF CANADIAN YOUTH ADVISORY COUNCILS

Christopher D. O'Connor

ABSTRACT

Purpose – *In recent years, various communities across Canada have recognized the need to include young people's input in community/urban decision-making processes. As a signatory to the United Nations Convention on the Rights of the Child (CRC), Canadian governments and policy makers are obligated to take young people's views into consideration when decisions about them are made. The aim of this chapter is to examine how some communities have attempted to involve young people in such decision making by creating youth advisory councils.*

Design/methodology/approach – *This chapter draws on an open-ended small-scale survey conducted with youth council members and adults familiar with the operation of youth councils.*

Findings – *The findings suggest that many youth councils were mostly initiated by adults for youth. However, the successes of these youth councils were many. Participants reported that youth councils provided*

Youth Engagement: The Civic-Political Lives of Children and Youth
Sociological Studies of Children and Youth, Volume 16, 73–96
Copyright © 2013 by Emerald Group Publishing Limited
All rights of reproduction in any form reserved
ISSN: 1537-4661/doi:10.1108/S1537-4661(2013)0000016008

young people with a voice on an array of issues ranging in scope from local to national/international. Despite these successes, the ability of young people to have a voice in decisions that affected them was hindered by the many challenges that youth councils faced (e.g., lack of adult support).

Originality/value – *This chapter provides strategies to help overcome barriers to genuine youth participation in the decision-making processes of communities/cities. It also critically engages with the concept of participation as it relates to youth councils as an avenue for enhancing young people's civic and political lives. Finally, it adds to the literature by examining the Canadian context which has often been overlooked in research on youth councils.*

Keywords: Youth; youth councils; citizenship; participation; Canada; policy making

INTRODUCTION

Canada's as well as other countries' urban landscapes have undergone many changes in recent decades due in part to increasing globalization and technological innovation and also because of an increasing influx of people into cities from a variety of different backgrounds (Hiller, 2005). As Canada enters this new era, questions are being raised about the nature of Canadian identity and citizenship. Central to these discussions have been the experiences of young people and the way that they create and respond to the culture around them. This chapter explores how Canadian communities have attempted to facilitate youth participation and engagement in community decision-making processes by creating youth advisory councils. In doing so, this chapter also adds to the literature on civic and political participation by examining young people's participation in youth councils as both a rights issue and an urban/community issue.

CITIZENSHIP, RIGHTS, AND YOUNG PEOPLE

Probably the most common understanding of citizenship is one that attributes place of birth/residence to a particular nationality/country. While this conception acknowledges the limits that are often placed on who can be considered a citizen, it fails to address the complexity of what it means to be part of a citizenry. Nowhere is the need for a more complex understanding of citizenship more apparent than when we examine young people as citizens. Young people may be afforded rights by being born in a country, but they are by no means afforded the full rights of a citizen (Wall, 2012). Instead, young people are most often thought of as "citizens-in-the-making" (Gordon, 2010). This conception of citizenship relates closely with the transition to adulthood where young people eventually *become* citizens/ adults. Here being a citizen is a destination one arrives at when they reach a certain age, presumably with the requisite skills/training to be a fully engaged citizen (Bessant, 2004; Lodge, 2005). For young people, age is one of the greatest sources of inequality when it comes to exercising full citizenship rights (Gordon, 2010).

With the adoption of the United Nations Convention on the Rights of the Child (CRC), there has been increasing attention paid to how young people exercise their rights while being considered something less than full citizens. Traditionally, social research has tended to focus on young people as either the future generation in need of protection or as troublemakers who threaten the status quo (Checkoway et al., 2003; Cohen, 2005; Stasiulis, 2002). A similar trend is also seen in how the media portray young people to the public (Gordon, 2010). However, since the adoption of CRC, the academic literature at least has attempted to move beyond these innocent – troublemaker narratives by paying attention to what it means to be a child/ youth citizen as well as young people's right to participate in decisions that affect them (Reynaert, Bouverne-de-Bie, & Vandevelde, 2009; Veerman & Levine, 2000).

YOUTH PARTICIPATION IN CIVIC AND POLITICAL LIFE

The principles contained in the CRC include such rights as freedom from discrimination, the right to life, the right to survive, and the right to develop. Of particular interest for this chapter is Article 12 which states "States Parties shall assure to the child who is capable of forming his or her own views the right to express those views freely in all matters affecting the child, the views of the child being given due weight in accordance with the age and maturity of the child" (United Nations, 1991, p. 6). As communities have attempted to implement the intent of the CRC, the term "participation" has often been used to help clarify ways young people engage in civic and political life (Reynaert et al., 2009).

Participation, of course, means different things to different people. However, for the most part, the term as used in reference to young people's civic and political lives has come to refer to providing genuine avenues for young people to influence the decisions that affect them and to have a dialogue with, and to contribute to, their communities (Lodge, 2005; Middleton, 2006; Morrow, 1999). Participation initiatives incorporate a diverse range of methods including youth councils, avenues for artistic expression, youth surveys, and young people lobbying on specific issues in their communities (Blanchet-Cohen, 2006; Middleton, 2006). Overall, the term participation is used to examine the multiple ways and varying levels in which children and young people do/could contribute to their communities.

The language of participation often describes young people as competent citizens who are able to create positive changes in their communities (Checkoway et al., 2003; Lodge, 2005; Stasiulis, 2002). It has been found that when young people participate, they can help to create more sustainable communities (Bridgman, 2004; Kjorholt, 2002), provide valuable input into how municipalities are managed (Guerra, 2002), and contribute to the making of a healthy democracy (Gordon & Taft, 2011). There has been recognition in the literature on youth participation that while children and young people may have different experiences than adults, they are no less capable of contributing to public dialogue. For example, young people have been found to be just as capable as adults in voicing their ideas when they participate in public policy decision making (Speak, 2000). Similarly, Sutherland (2001) argues that young people can often see problems and their solutions more clearly than adults because they spend more time involved in community activities.

The overarching idea is that getting children and young people to actively participate in community affairs holds much potential to benefit society. For example, by engaging young people in community activity, positive relationships can be created between adults and youth which can help to overcome some of the mistrust that often exists between these two groups (Chawla, 2001). It also increases the likelihood that young people will go on to participate in community initiatives as adults (Speak, 2000), or put another way it holds the potential to increase social capital (Putnam, 2000). Further, as young people are able to express their concerns (e.g., lack of recreational facilities, police harassment) to local policy makers, it promotes an atmosphere of inclusion while at the same time engages and empowers young people (Bah & Johnston, 2001; Chawla, 2001). By extension, the consequences of not providing avenues for children and young people to participate are argued to be many. Some potential consequences of not including youth in decisions that affect them include low levels of participation in civic activity (Adsett, 2003; Elections Canada, 2004; O'Toole, Lister, Marsh, Jones, & McDonagh, 2003; Wyness, Harrison, & Buchanan, 2004), health problems (Centre of Excellence for Youth Engagement, 2003; Cook, 2008), as well as youth frustration, alienation, and disenfranchisement (Adsett, 2003; Blanchet-Cohen, 2006; Caputo, 2000; Chawla, 2002).

Having said this, participation is by no means an uncomplicated concept. While there might be much agreement in the academic literature that a key ingredient of successful participation should be *genuine* youth involvement, this is often not how it plays out in practice. Instead, youth participation in public policy making often takes the form of tokenism rather than genuine participation. Genuine participation then involves legitimate opportunities for young people to influence decisions that affect them, while tokenism simply offers the *appearance* of influence. Essentially the incorporation of youth voices into public policy making is sought out but not listened to or incorporated into policies that are developed (Gurstein, Lovato, & Ross, 2003; Perrons & Skyers, 2003; Wyness et al., 2004). Often, adults end up planning for young people rather than working with young people as equal partners (Bridgman, 2004, Wyness, 2009).

The exclusion/marginalization of young people from decision-making processes occurs in part because young people inhabit an ambiguous space somewhere between being children and being adults (Jenks, 1996; Simpson, 1997). As previously noted, children and young people are considered citizens-in-the-making rather than full citizens (Gordon, 2010). This is a problematic space for young people to occupy given that who is considered to be a "young person" is socially constructed and thus, it is not always readily apparent to city governments and policy makers what roles young people should occupy, how much responsibility they should be given, or to what degree their input should be considered in public policy making (Gurstein et al., 2003; Such & Walker, 2005; Zeldin, Petrokubi, & MacNeil, 2008). As a result, adults tend to retain much control over urban processes given young people's ambiguous status.

YOUTH COUNCILS AS A FORM OF PARTICIPATION

Recently, the importance of including youth in decisions that affect them has been brought to the forefront of many community agendas in Canada and elsewhere. In part, this has been prompted by the adoption of the CRC and also by the suggestion that civic and political participation is in serious decline (Putnam, 2000). While this perception has been critiqued for ignoring new/different ways youth have participated in civic and political life in recent years (e.g., participating in online boycotts and petitions rather than joining a bowling club) (Gordon & Taft, 2011; Hustinx, Meijs, Handy, & Cnaan, 2012), the perception of decline still prevails among government and policy makers who have set out to remedy the situation. It is also likely that participation initiatives at the community level have become popular because the principles of the CRC are easier to implement at the local level than they are at a national level (Veerman & Levine, 2000). Adding to this literature, this chapter examines how young people participate in civic and political affairs in Canada through youth councils.

A youth council is probably best described as a formal organization that is consulted by governments (mostly municipal) and community organiza-tions on issues of concern to youth. In turn, youth councils allow young people an opportunity to express their concerns to governments and community organizations as well as allowing them to have their voices heard on topics that are important to them (Bah & Johnston, 2001; Caputo, 2000; Matthews, 2001). As a signatory to the CRC, Canadian governments and policy makers are obligated to take young people's views into consideration when decisions about them are made and young people have a right to provide input regarding decisions that affect them. Youth councils provide just one example of how young people's input can be utilized to inform public policy making and how some of the principles of the CRC have been put into practice in Canada.

Unfortunately, the rights outlined in the CRC have not been realized for most children and youth. Canada's implementation of the CRC has been primarily focused on making changes to youth crime legislation and family law (Stasiulis, 2002) while often ignoring the need to include young people's input in public policy decision making. Interestingly, a notable exception to this trend has been the community level, or local level, recognition of the need to include youth input in community decision-making processes. Although in its infancy, active youth citizenship has been promoted by initiatives run for and by youth in various communities across Canada (Blanchet-Cohen, 2006; Caputo, 2000).

While youth councils form part of this movement to encourage young people to actively participate in civic and political affairs, we know little about how these councils operate in Canada and what their impacts have been on participation efforts. When youth councils have been examined elsewhere, mostly in the United Kingdom, concerns have been raised about how effective they have been at providing young people with avenues to make genuine political change. It has been found that adults tend to control much of the processes and are reluctant to share decision making with young people for fear that they might open themselves up to scrutiny. Adults also tend to control the resources allocated to these councils. In addition, youth councils have been critiqued for their inability to recruit diverse segments of the youth population which has raised concerns about whose voices these councils actually represent (Matthews, 2001; Middleton, 2006; Wyness et al., 2004).

Overall, these findings raise questions about how genuine youth participation can be achieved when it is dependent on the good will of adults. There are also larger questions that need to be addressed in terms of whether youth councils do indeed truly help to create active citizens who can make genuine change in their communities or do they simply work to responsibilize youth and temper expectations? Also, what types of citizenship do youth councils promote and what impacts can they have on young people's civic and political lives? In the sections that follow, I begin to address these questions by exploring young people's experiences and the successes and challenges they have encountered participating in youth councils in Canada.

METHODS

This chapter draws on an open-ended small-scale survey conducted with adults and young people involved in youth councils. Questions inquired about the lessons learned in setting up and maintaining existing youth councils in Canada and were divided into two themes. The first theme explored the structure of the participant's youth council. This entailed asking questions about the youth council's size, funding, meetings, governing structure, and members. The second theme explored the activities the youth council was involved in including the successes, challenges, and lessons learned from the participant's involvement with youth councils. Questionnaires were administered between November 2002 and April 2003. Participants were assured confidentiality and were only identified by questionnaire number and as either an adult (e.g., A1) or a youth council member (e.g., Y14).

Participants could either fill out the questionnaire on their own or participate in a telephone survey. Self-administered questionnaires were emailed to participants who then filled out the questionnaires at their convenience. Once questionnaires were returned, follow-up questions were emailed if clarification was needed or if a participant's answers required further investigation. Participants opting to participate in a telephone survey were emailed the questionnaire in advance and a convenient time was arranged for the survey.

The main challenge in conducting this exploratory research project was identifying existing youth councils in Canada. A variety of techniques were utilized to identify possible participants. First, the Federation of Canadian Municipalities (FCM) and the Canadian Commission for UNESCO (United Nations Educational, Scientific, and Cultural Organization) helped identify possible participants and existing youth councils throughout Canada. Second, an Internet search of youth councils was conducted in order to identify possible contacts. Finally, once contact was made with a participant, s/he was asked to help identify other youth council contacts in his/her region. The goal of the research was not to provide an exhaustive list of all youth councils in Canada but to try to identify at least one within each province and territory.

The final sample included completed questionnaires from 32 different participants/youth councils across Canada. Many of the youth councils were located in either the province of Ontario (n = 13) or Quebec (n = 8). Completed questionnaires were also obtained from British Columbia (n = 3), Alberta (n = 3), the Yukon (n = 1), Saskatchewan (n = 2), Prince Edward Island (n = 1), and Newfoundland and Labrador (n = 1). Of these youth councils, two were national youth councils with headquarters in Ontario and five were provincial/territorial youth councils. The remaining youth councils (n = 25) were described by participants as local/municipal/regional councils. Unfortunately, I was unable to contact youth councils in the Northwest Territories, Nunavut, Manitoba, New Brunswick, and Nova Scotia to participate in this study.

The participants included 21 adults and 11 young people. The young people were all current members of active youth councils, while the adult participants included municipal and provincial government officials and representatives from community organizations. The majority (n = 18) of adult participants were working with active youth councils in their respective communities. Questionnaires were also administered to two adults who had previous experience working with youth councils (the youth councils were no longer active) and one adult who was developing a youth council in their community. Twenty-four of the questionnaires were self-administered which included six questionnaires administered in French and translated into English for analysis. Another eight questionnaires were completed over the phone.

Before discussing the findings of this research project, I want to briefly address one major limitation of this research – the sample of youth councils that was utilized. Despite considerable effort, it was difficult to reach participants from youth councils in provinces/territories with smaller populations. Also, the majority of youth councils were identified through their websites and the Internet search. Therefore, youth councils without websites or links to the Internet were less likely to be included in this research project. Many youth councils were likely excluded due to my inability to identify and contact them. Given this, it is impossible to know exactly how representative this sample is of youth councils in Canada; however, I am confident that the sample represents the diversity of youth councils that existed within the various regions of the country.

YOUTH COUNCIL STRUCTURE

Youth councils appear to be a relatively recent phenomenon within Canada with most having been created in the past 10 years through initiatives by mayors, city councilors, and/or city staff who wanted input from youth on issues of concern to youth. For example, some youth councils evolved out of city committees or task forces, while other youth councils were created in fulfillment of a mayor's election promise or from an initiative of a city's youth center staff. Some young people had initiated the process of creating a youth council in their community, but it ultimately took adult support for their plans to come to fruition.

It should also be noted that in Quebec and Newfoundland and Labrador, the creation of youth councils was expedited by provincial government policy. For example, in Quebec, the government's 1998–2001 Action Plan required that each regional development council in the province set up a youth council. Similarly, the creation of 20 economic development zones in Newfoundland and Labrador prompted the creation of a provincial youth council and the need for youth representation in each of these zones.

Youth councils typically received funding and "in-kind" services (e.g., meeting space, photocopying) from multiple sources including governments, the private sector, and community organizations. However, the majority of youth councils received at least part of their funding from their local municipalities. Funding amounts varied widely and ranged from in-kind services to pizza/coffee/doughnuts for meetings, to thousands of dollars for special events. The funding allocation often depended on the role the youth council was playing. For example, if the youth council was planning a youth conference or a large youth entertainment event, significant funds were required to get the event going. On the other hand, if the youth council mainly advised on youth issues, the costs were very low. Usually, the only significant costs were for a youth coordinator and/or support staff who were hired to work with and assist the youth council. However, these people usually split their time between the youth council and other city departments or activities.

Youth councils ranged in size from as little as six members to having hundreds of members. While the size of these youth councils varied considerably each year, they overall tended to be very small with the majority having less than 20 members. Often, the size of a youth council was determined by its resources and/or purpose. For example, some youth councils had few resources and needed to limit membership, while other youth councils were funded for large diverse memberships where various youth views were garnered from across a municipality/city/area.

The specific governing structures of youth councils also tended to vary considerably, but there were some common themes that are worth noting. First, the majority of youth councils had some form of governing executive. For example, most youth councils had a chairperson, vice-chairperson, and various directors who were either elected by the young people on the youth council or appointed by adults (e.g., mayors, youth coordinators). Directors oversaw such portfolios as city council relations, communications, finances, memberships, and community projects. Ad hoc committees were also formed to deal with emerging issues and special events that the young people on the council deemed to be important. Often these committees were utilized to get younger members oriented toward the councils' operations so that they could replace older outgoing members. Finally, the majority of youth councils were governed by some form of mission statement. Generally, these mission statements were broad in scope and included such goals as empowering young people, providing youth with a voice, and creating positive images of youth.

Most youth council members met on a regular basis, most frequently once a month. In addition to the regularly scheduled meetings, the executive and working committees (or subcommittees) often met outside of established times. The majority of youth councils also had a formal reporting structure in place. Given the close ties to municipalities, many youth councils reported to youth coordinators or city staff on the activities of the council. Youth councils were often in a unique position within municipal governments because their input could be provided on a wide range of issues. Thus, youth councils tended to also report directly to various departments (e.g., youth services, recreation) within city governments as well as to city councils and mayors. For example, youth councils were often asked to provide input to city governments on how money should be spent on youth services in municipal budgets.

YOUNG PEOPLE PARTICIPATING IN YOUTH COUNCILS

The young people who participated in youth councils encompassed such age ranges as 12–19, 11–17, 12–25, and 15–30. However, despite setting age limits, many youth councils had flexible age restrictions. For example, if the age limit for a youth council was set at 15–18 and a 14-year-old wanted to join, s/he would likely be allowed to participate. Also, age guidelines tended to be established by what worked best for the group or by what common issues a particular age group thought they shared. For example, some youth councils felt that age 29 was too old to identify with youth issues because many people of this age were working and/or had families. However, other youth councils felt that it was important to include older youth in order to take advantage of their experience and knowledge and to help mentor younger council members. The majority of youth councils also had some form of screening process where young people were either interviewed or participated in some other form of application process (e.g., the completion of a nomination form, writing an essay) before being accepted to the council.

Participants were asked to identify the best ways to encourage youth to initially join and then sustain their participation in youth councils. One key suggestion was to provide youth with incentives to participate. Young people were busy with school, work, and recreation and thus providing an incentive encouraged them to volunteer their time to youth councils. As one young person stated:

> When youth volunteer and they don't see fast change ... they tend to ... want to quit, but with an incentive be it monetary (meaning they aren't losing money by being involved), travel opportunities, or even an exciting opportunity where they get to address the Prime Minister or something, then it keeps them excited and keeps them involved (Y8).

Free food, fun activities, volunteer credit hours, and transportation to and from meetings were all mentioned as good ways to get youth to participate, but keeping them participating often took more. For example, having strong youth leaders and positive adult encouragement helped newer members adjust more easily to the demands placed on them by the youth council. It was also helpful if youth councils provided interactive activities mixed with talking/discussions and were flexible with meeting schedules and the issues that they addressed.

Most importantly, it was important to provide young people with an opportunity to make a difference and to implement their ideas:

> The key to getting young people to participate is to empower them to make a difference. There is nothing more powerful than witnessing one's ideas come to life (Y1).

> Show them that giving voice to their ideas can have a dramatic (and positive!) effect on the government's decisions (A2).

> Let them be the process and have ownership in what they do (A18).

As the above quotes suggest, it was essential to empower youth to take action on topics that they felt passionate about.

When participants were asked to identify what types of young people were represented on their youth councils, the majority stated that their youth councils had diverse memberships that were representative of their communities in terms of gender, race/ethnicity, and socioeconomic status and that they contained representatives from marginalized groups of youth. Interestingly, and somewhat contradictory, many participants also stated that their youth councils did not specifically attempt to recruit marginalized youth and that it was very difficult to contact marginalized youth in order to recruit them to participate in youth councils. This inconsistency might be partly explained by the wide net cast for who was considered marginalized which included young people generally, youth living in poverty, street kids, pregnant teens, homosexual youth, skaters, abused youth, single mothers, youth living in foster care, Aboriginal youth, differently abled youth, those who have had contact with the justice system, and environmentalists. Regardless of this ambiguity, as we will see from the topics youth councils addressed, marginalized youth issues were often included in youth councils' agendas.

SUCCESSES OF YOUTH COUNCILS

When participants were asked to identify topics that their youth councils focused on and the successes they had achieved, it was apparent that youth were involved in a wide variety of issues through their youth councils. The nature of topics addressed by youth councils affected young people at the community, provincial, national, and international levels. Table 1 illustrates the diverse activities that were engaged in by youth councils.

The majority of participants stated that youth councils provided an avenue for young people to have their voices heard on issues that were of concern to them. An interesting example of this was where one youth council conducted an evaluation of government services and city establishments. These establishments were evaluated for "youth-friendliness." The project was undertaken because many young people felt that they were treated differently than adults when using city establishments. For example, youth often had time limits set for them in restaurants or were followed in stores. Many participants also stated that young people were able to promote youth activities and available services to youth within their area through their youth councils and that youth councils helped to create a positive image of youth in their communities, molded a new generation of

Table 1. Projects Worked on by Youth Councils.

Local Events/Activities		
Youth drop in centers	Youth conferences/forums	Youth achievement awards
Youth festivals	Talent showcases	Youth week celebrations
Youth newspapers	Youth program planning	Youth event nights
Promoted city services	Promoted youth activities	Heritage days
Santa Claus parades	Coffee houses	Dances
Nutrition programs	Road cleanups	Fundraisers
Food/toy drives	Art festivals	Grant giving
Youth surveys	Skateboard parks	City service evaluations
Talking circles	Graffiti projects	Youth magazines

Local Issues		
Promoted volunteerism	School violence/bullying	Keeping school pools open
City budget input	Sports initiatives	Employment programs
Training programs	Suicide prevention	Public transportation
Antiviolence campaigns	Antidrug campaigns	

Provincial/National/International Issues		
HIV/AIDS awareness	Poverty	Racism conferences
Young offender legislation	Smoking reduction strategies	Prostitution awareness
Child health awareness	Environmental awareness	Nuclear phaseout campaign
Homelessness	Minimum wage policy	National unity
Landmines abolition	Input on graduated (driver) licensing	World Summit on Sustainable Development

leaders, and promoted a sense of civic pride among members. Overall, the majority of participants felt that their youth councils had empowered young people to make positive changes in society.

CHALLENGES YOUTH COUNCILS ENCOUNTER

The above successes were not achieved without difficulty. Various issues arose during the operation of youth councils that threatened their success and sustainability. The most frequent challenge cited by participants was a lack of youth commitment or participation. For example, many participants stated their youth councils had a high turnover rate, especially from "keeners" or "over-achievers" who often only participated in youth councils to improve their résumé or to help themselves get into post-secondary school. These young people did not take a serious interest in the council and usually quit within months of joining because it was not something they felt passionate about. Participants also expressed concerns over the lack of knowledge by young people about the existence of youth councils in their area. Further, given the transitory nature of the age groups involved in youth councils, it was often difficult to maintain continuity between members from year to year. For example, many members graduated and moved to other cities which often left youth councils with a new group of young people each year.

Another challenge frequently mentioned by participants was dealing with a lack of adult support. This included a lack of adult respect, adults not having confidence in youth, and adults not listening or allowing young people to participate:

> People [adults] look at youth and think that if they give us something that we are going to make mistakes, or they think that youth are too young to accomplish anything, and they have this inherent belief that we are going to do wrong or bad things, which isn't true, ageism would be the biggest challenge (Y8).

Participants felt that adults often had a "we know better" approach when dealing with youth which often made it very challenging for youth to have their voices heard on issues. For example, it was often difficult to get adults to recognize the difference between genuine youth participation and token youth involvement (e.g., giving youth "busy work"). Genuine participation allowed youth voices to be heard, considered, and incorporated into decision making, while token involvement often involved envelope stuffing or picking up garbage at youth events.

Also, dealing with bureaucracy and politics was especially challenging for youth council members. For example, young people wanted to see action on issues relatively quickly, but dealing with what was perceived as adult government departments and other organizations was often a lengthy process. The remaining challenges expressed by participants mainly involved aspects of the operation of youth councils. Obtaining secure funding, transportation of young people to and from meetings (because of its associated costs, especially for some youth councils with more dispersed memberships), recruiting marginalized youth to participate, finding consensus on meeting times, and balancing member's busy schedules were all mentioned as challenges.

KEYS TO A SUCCESSFUL YOUTH COUNCIL

Participants were asked to identify the key lessons they had learned from operating their youth councils, to provide advice to young people thinking about starting their own youth councils, and to state what they would do differently if they could start their youth councils over. Out of these three questions evolved the "keys to a successful youth council."

The most common response from participants was that a successful youth council required adult support. Adult support included a commitment from the municipality, city council, or affiliated organization that the views of young people would be taken seriously:

> Show that you value their [the young people's] opinion and let them make decisions even if you disagree ... this is about them not you (A5).

For example, one way city councilors and mayors could/did show their support was by meeting with youth council members and/or attending their meetings. This was identified as a critical element because it added legitimacy to young people's work, helped show young people their views were being taken seriously, and motivated young people to continue pressing on with their issues. It was also noted by most participants that an important way to gain adult support was to have "youth-friendly" adults help bridge the gap between reluctant adults and youth council members. For example, it was suggested that adult support should be provided at the "sidelines" or that adults should play an advisory role. That is, adults should avoid telling young people how they must proceed and instead young people should be left to learn from their own experiences including their mistakes.

Many participants also stated that staff working with youth councils should have experience working with young people so that youth are not exploited for someone else's agenda. For example, it was not helpful to have politicians involved with youth councils, who were only concerned about youth issues when photo opportunities arose. Also, staff members should work for the young people and treat them as they would treat adults. It was important to have staff that could work with youth and deal with the bureaucracy of the organization or municipality so that youth council members could work on their issues. Often, staff members working with youth councils split their time among various committees and projects which often resulted in youth councils being treated as their last priority. Further, participants noted that there must be a balance struck between the needs of adults and young people. For example, participants stated that youth must recognize that there is a process to follow that is worth waiting for in the long run, but in turn adults must recognize that concrete results need to be accomplished if young people are to continue to provide input on issues. If young people saw that their views were being taken seriously and that their ideas were being acted upon, this helped motivate them to continue doing their work.

Another frequent suggestion from participants was that in order for youth councils to be successful, they needed to ensure that they produced results and took action on projects while at the same time providing a voice for youth. Generally, this meant that young people needed to be provided with the power to produce change:

It is youth who are in the best position to know about youth issues (Y30).

Many participants stated that it was important for young people to have as much input as possible into the operation of youth councils. For example, one youth council had many operational problems because its structure was set by the city and the youth council had no power to change that structure or its own constitution. One problem that arose was that when young people left the council, there was no mechanism to replace them until the following year. This left the youth council with fewer members than they needed to accomplish their goals which in turn frustrated the remaining members.

It was also noted by participants that it was helpful to have young people be able to decide for themselves the issues that they wanted to address. This was often difficult for adults because youth often advanced issues that exceeded their comfort levels. In order to produce results and provide a voice for youth, it was suggested that set goals needed to be attainable within a short time period. For example, it was noted that it was best not to have projects extend over several years but instead make projects attainable in the short term so that successes could be realized. An interesting way some youth councils accomplished this was by incorporating a grant-giving function into their youth councils. These youth councils were allotted a sum of money (e.g., from the municipality) and they decided on what projects to fund.

Several participants also stated that it was important to have free, interactive, and fun activities. If meetings were entirely about policy and agenda items, youth often got bored and lost interest. There needed to be a combination of fun and business to keep young people interested and returning to participate in youth council meetings. A good example of a fun and interactive activity was where one youth council grew a garden, cooked the food, and served it at a youth shelter. Also, providing free activities, food, and transportation encouraged young people (who often had little money) to attend meetings. Finally, one of the most important suggestions to come out of this research was that young people needed training in how to conduct meetings and on legal issues surrounding youth councils. Young people were inexperienced at running meetings and reporting to city councils or city departments. They needed to be provided with an opportunity to learn about the process. Young people were unable to provide genuine input, for example on the municipal budget, if they did not have a good understanding of how the budget process worked. An important lesson learned by participants was that if young people were to provide useful input on a topic, it was likely that they needed training on how the process worked.

DISCUSSION

It was evident from the attempts by many municipalities to establish youth councils in their communities that Canada is slowly making progress in meeting some of its CRC obligations. Of course, youth councils are only one part of this larger effort, but it is important to examine the actual impacts these councils have had on youth participation. Essentially, are these councils enhancing young people's civic and political lives and helping to prompt a more youth-friendly society or are they simply training young people to be good/obedient, and one day adult, citizens?

Examining the structures and successes of youth councils as well as who participated, it was clear that youth participation in youth councils mostly hinged on, or was somehow tied to, relationships with adults. For example, the structures of youth councils were closely aligned with adult institutions (e.g., municipal governments) which often controlled the funding of these councils. Both young people and adults in this study agreed that it was very difficult for youth to develop youth councils and accomplish their goals without adult support. In particular, "youth-friendly" adults, which many of the participants in this study could be considered, were mentioned as being essential to bridging the gap between youth and adult worlds.

Given this heavy adult influence, it is easy to critique youth councils for treating young people as "citizens-in-the-making" (Gordon, 2010) rather than as agents of social change. For example, youth councils exist and are designed in part to work within existing governing structures as a way of advancing young people's positions. By encouraging this type of citizenship, youth councils open themselves up to the critique that they simply "manage" or "responsibilize" young people rather than "empower" and "provide a voice" (Westheimer & Kahne, 2004). In addition, it could also be argued that rather than acting as a "bridge" to the adult world, youth-friendly adults might actually be acting more like a "tether," tying young people to the adult world instead of acting as a reciprocal "pathway/bridge." While this is a valid critique of youth councils, it only tells part of the story.

The more interesting part of this story is that participants in this study suggested that young people often did not participate in youth councils unless they were seeing some form of tangible result from their participation. Essentially, young people refused to be "managed" without being provided some power to make genuine change. If their voices were not being heard and acted upon, young people were unlikely to participate in, or engage fully with, the youth council. Thus, while youth councils on the one hand might work toward training young people to be "good" citizens, young people also appeared to be active participants in shaping what this citizenship looked like. Thus, youth councils appear to promote an active, albeit structured, and cooperative form of citizenship. For example, the successes of Canadian youth councils were numerous, but they were also tempered by adult intervention. That is, young people participating in youth councils did not have complete free reign to do what they pleased, but they also did not have adults completely control the agenda.

The creation and utilization of youth councils are good first steps toward creating a more active youth citizenry; however, more can be done to facilitate youth participation and engagement in decision-making processes. Given the successes youth councils have accomplished and the benefits of including youth in decisions that affect them, I suggest, similarly to Middleton (2006), that adults relinquish more control of societal institutions to young people. In addition to expanded roles for youth councils, young people can be consulted through a variety of ways including youth surveys, forums, and conferences. This would help quell criticisms that youth councils and other forms of participation are simply managing young people instead of working toward a society genuinely shaped by young people. In addition, and as other researchers have noted (Bessant, 2004; Stafford, Laybourn, Hill, & Walker, 2003; Wyness, 2009), a more diverse set of consultation methods and engagement techniques is needed in order to help capture the diversity of youth voices that exist and in particular the voices of marginalized youth. As this study has shown, there is much work to do in recruiting marginalized youth to participate in youth councils. If diverse recruitment is not attempted, it is then difficult to claim that consultation is representative of "youth."

One key way to facilitate youth participation is for municipal govern-ments to take more seriously the obligations outlined in the CRC by ensuring that legislation affecting young people is not passed without first formally consulting young people. Making reference to the CRC in legislation affecting young people would show both youth and adults that a genuine attempt is being made to adhere to the principles outlined in the CRC. Further, provincial/territorial governments can facilitate youth consultation (as we saw in the cases of Quebec and Newfoundland and Labrador) by requiring that young people be consulted on issues at the local level. This approach would not only benefit youth–adult relations but also municipalities themselves given that it has been found that incorporating young people's perspectives into public policy helps create cities that are more sustainable and inclusive of the diverse range of people living there (Blanchet-Cohen, 2006; Bridgman, 2004; Gurstein et al., 2003; Speak, 2000).

Now, it is clear from the findings of this study that consultation does not necessarily equal genuine participation and actual incorporation of youth voices into public policy decision making. However, as other authors have suggested (Barber, 2007; Carlson, 2006; Christens & Dolan, 2011), it is important for communities to have a structure in place that institutionalizes the requirement to consult young people so that opportunities can be created for their participation. Or put another way, if consultation is thought of as a routine and important requirement of passing legislation, more opportunities should arise for genuine youth participation. This, of course, does not ensure buy in by either youth or adults, but it does ensure that once there is buy in from both parties, there is at least a process in place that can help to facilitate participation. Similarly, Gordon (2010) found that youth activists were more successful at getting their voices heard when they utilized their connections to, and worked with, adult organizations.

Youth participation, as many have already noted (Bessant, 2004; Middleton, 2006; Wyness, 2009), is by no means an easy process and as the findings from this study have shown in regards to participation in youth councils, many challenges still remain. For example, one key issue that arises with youth councils and youth participation more generally is how to determine what topics require youth input and which ones just simply might be nice to have but are not completely necessary. Given the wide variety of topics young people have engaged with through their youth councils, the topics that affect and are of interest to young people seem to be unlimited. This suggests that determining topics to focus on might be best left to the specific local level involved. While this might be an issue to resolve, it also seems that the more pressing concern is not what to focus on but how to create genuine change/consultation once a focus is discerned. This seems to be the key ingredient in moving participation toward the empowering side rather than the managing side of youth participation. It also appears that if participation is genuine, it increases young people's likelihood of participating in civic and political affairs in the future; however, negative experiences can have many deleterious results (e.g., skepticism, disengagement) (Graham & Fitzgerald, 2010; Stafford et al., 2003).

The difficulties young people encountered in getting their voices heard on issues that affect them raise some larger questions about Canadian citizenship. First, what does (or should) full Canadian citizenship look like? Is it earned or given to people? Should rights be determined by some arbitrary age or should they be determined by something more concrete? That is, should the ability to perform an act (e.g., obtaining a driver's license, voting) be the criteria for determining whether something is a right rather than arbitrarily determining rights based on age (Skott-Myhre & Tarulli, 2006)? Although this chapter has only begun to address these questions, the evidence suggests that young people are considered something less than full citizens given that adults influence many aspects of youth participation in decision-making processes. It also appears that young people must earn full citizenship based on adult-approved criteria if they are to fully participate in decisions that affect them (Harris, 2001). At the same time, youth resistance to adult-imposed strategies holds promise for a more collaborative youth-influenced approach to participation at least when it comes to youth councils.

CONCLUSION

Overall, it appears that youth councils hold the potential to enhance young people's civic and political lives. When given the opportunity, youth councils can be utilized by young people to provide input on a variety of topics and to help shape public policy from a youth perspective.

Interestingly, many of the issues that young people chose to work on were complicated (e.g., racism, homelessness) and the issues were not easily resolved, but the interest to work on difficult topics was apparent. This suggests that societal issues might be better understood and dealt with if they were actually considered societal issues rather than being considered adult issues needing to be resolved *for* young people instead of *with* young people. This also suggests that young people are not immune from so-called adult issues and that young people have important things to say about the culture that they inhabit.

More importantly, youth participation in youth councils should be seen as a complex mix of avenues for empowerment that provide opportunities to change the status quo and at the same time avenues to work within it. There is evidence that youth councils can help create genuine social change by incorporating youth voices and experiences into adult decision-making processes, but as it stands politically and civically, these are still adults' decisions to make. Young people can gain access to these decision-making apparatuses and influence them through youth councils, but they do not ultimately control them. In addition, it has been found that adults sometimes actively work against youth which poses another limitation on participation (Gordon, 2010). While youth councils can be considered a somewhat measured/reserved form of active youth citizenship, it might also be considered a form of cooperative/collaborative citizenship given that the impact young people can have on decisions that affect them is closely tied to how well youth and adults can collaborate on dealing with community issues. Collaboration/cooperation will be the ultimate arbiter of what youth can accomplish through their youth councils and whether youth participation is empowering or simply a way to train young people to be good citizens of the state.

ACKNOWLEDGMENTS

This research could not have been completed without the help of some very dedicated and hardworking individuals. I would like to thank Tullio Caputo for his insightful comments on previous drafts of this paper. I would also like to thank Genevieve Talbot of the Canadian Commission for UNESCO and Janet Neves of the Federation of Canadian Municipalities for their support and help with this research project. Their dedication to youth issues is impressive and inspiring. I would also like to thank the editors and anonymous reviewers whose comments made for a much stronger paper.

REFERENCES

Adsett, M. (2003). Change in political era and demographic weight as explanations of youth 'disenfranchisement' in federal elections in Canada, 1965–2000. *Journal of Youth Studies, 6*(3), 247–264.

Bah, K., & Johnston, A. (2001). *Toronto youth profile.* Toronto: The City of Toronto.

Barber, T. (2007). Young people and civic participation: A conceptual review. *Youth & Policy, 96*, 19–39.

Bessant, J. (2004). Mixed messages: Youth participation and democratic practice. *Australian Journal of Political Science, 39*(2), 387–404.

Blanchet-Cohen, N. (2006). Young people's participation in Canadian municipalities: Claiming meaningful space. *Canadian Review of Social Policy, 57*, 71–84.

Bridgman, R. (2004). Criteria for best practices in building child-friendly cities: Involving young people in urban planning and design. *Canadian Journal of Urban Research, 13*(2), 337–346.

Caputo, T. (2000). *Hearing the voices of youth: Youth participation in selected Canadian municipalities.* Ottawa: Health Canada.

Carlson, C. (2006). The Hampton experience as a new model for youth civic engagement. *Journal of Community Practice, 14*(1/2), 89–106.

Centre of Excellence for Youth Engagement. (2003). Youth engagement and health outcomes: Is there a link? Retrieved from http://www.tgmag.ca/centres/index_e.html.

Chawla, L. (2001). Growing up in cities. *UNESCO Sources, 133*, 4.

Chawla, L. (2002). Toward better cities for children and youth. In L. Chawla (Ed.), *Growing up in an urbanising world* (pp. 219–242). United Kingdom: UNESCO.

Checkoway, B., Richards-Schuster, K., Abdullah, S., Aragon, M., Facio, E., Figueroa, L., ... White, A. (2003). Young people as competent citizens. *Community Development Journal, 38*(4), 298–309.

Christens, B. D., & Dolan, T. (2011). Interweaving youth development, community development, and social change through youth organizing. *Youth & Society, 43*(2), 528–548.

Cohen, E. (2005). Neither seen nor heard: Children's citizenship in contemporary democracies. *Citizenship Studies, 9*(2), 221–240.

Cook, P. (2008). Understanding the effects of adolescent participation in health programmes. *The International Journal of Children's Rights, 16*, 121–139.

Elections Canada. (2004). Youth electoral participation: Survey and analysis of Canadian trends (October 2003). Retrieved from http://www.elections.ca/content.asp?section=med&document=survey&dir=eveyou/forum&lang=e&textonly=false.

Gordon, H. R. (2010). *We fight to win: Inequality and the politics of youth activism.* New Brunswick, NJ: Rutgers University Press.

Gordon, H. R., & Taft, J. K. (2011). Rethinking youth political socialization: Teenage activists talk back. *Youth & Society, 43*(4), 1499–1527.

Graham, A., & Fitzgerald, R. (2010). Progressing children's participation: Exploring the potential of a dialogical turn. *Childhood, 17*(3), 343–359.

Guerra, E. (2002). Citizenship knows no age: Children's participation in the governance and municipal budget of Barra Mansa, Brazil. *Environment and Urbanization, 14*(2), 71–84.

Gurstein, P., Lovato, C., & Ross, S. (2003). Youth participation in planning: Strategies for social action. *Canadian Journal of Urban Research, 12*(2), 249–274.

Harris, A. (2001). Dodging and weaving: Young women countering the stories of youth citizenship. *Critical Psychology, 1*(4), 183–199.

Hiller, H. (2005). The dynamics of Canadian urbanization. In H. Hiller (Ed.), *Urban Canada: Sociological perspectives* (pp. 28–47). Don Mills, Canada: Oxford University Press.

Hustinx, L., Meijs, L., Handy, F., & Cnaan, R. (2012). Monitorial citizens or civic omnivores? Repertoires of civic participation among university students. *Youth & Society, 44*(1), 95–117.

Jenks, C. (1996). *Childhood*. London: Routledge.

Kjorholt, A. T. (2002). Small is powerful: Discourses on 'children and participation' in Norway. *Childhood, 9*(1), 63–82.

Lodge, C. (2005). From hearing voices to engaging in dialogue: Problematising student participation in school improvement. *Journal of Educational Change, 6*, 125–146.

Matthews, H. (2001). Citizenship, youth councils and young people's participation. *Journal of Youth Studies, 4*(3), 299–318.

Middleton, E. (2006). Youth participation in the UK: Bureaucratic disaster or triumph of child rights? *Children, Youth and Environments, 16*(2), 180–190.

Morrow, V. (1999). 'We are people too': Children's and young people's perspectives on children's rights and decision-making in England. *The International Journal of Children's Rights, 7*, 149–170.

O'Toole, T., Lister, M., Marsh, D., Jones, S., & McDonagh, A. (2003). Tuning out or left out? Participation and non-participation among young people. *Contemporary Politics, 9*(1), 45–61.

Perrons, D., & Skyers, S. (2003). Empowerment through participation? Conceptual explorations and a case study. *International Journal of Urban and Regional Research, 27*(2), 265–285.

Putnam, R. (2000). *Bowling alone: The collapse and revival of American community*. New York: Simon & Schuster.

Reynaert, D., Bouverne-de-Bie, M., & Vandevelde, S. (2009). A review of children's rights literature since the adoption of the United Nations Convention on the Rights of the Child. *Childhood, 16*(4), 518–534.

Simpson, B. (1997). Towards the participation of children and young people in urban planning and design. *Urban Studies, 34*(5/6), 905–925.

Skott-Myhre, H., & Tarulli, D. (2006). The immanent rights of the multitude: An ontological framework for conceptualizing the issue of child and youth rights. Paper presented at the conference *Investment and Citizenship: Towards a Transdisciplinary Dialogue on Child and Youth Rights*, St. Catharines, Canada.

Speak, S. (2000). Children in urban regeneration: Foundations for sustainable participation. *Community Development Journal, 35*(1), 31–40.

Stafford, A., Laybourn, A., Hill, M., & Walker, M. (2003). 'Having a say': Children and young people talk about consultation. *Children & Society, 17*, 361–373.

Stasiulis, D. (2002). The active child citizen: Lessons from Canadian policy and the children's movement. *Citizenship Studies, 6*(4), 507–538.

Such, E., & Walker, R. (2005). Young citizens or policy objects? Children in the 'rights and responsibilities' debate. *Journal of Social Policy, 34*(1), 39–57.

Sutherland, M. (2001). Melbourne: Having a say in Frankston. *UNESCO Sources, 133*, 5–6.

United Nations. (1991). *Convention on the rights of the child*. Hull, Canada: Canadian Heritage.

Veerman, P., & Levine, H. (2000). Implementing children's rights on a local level: Narrowing the gap between Geneva and the grassroots. *The International Journal of Children's Rights, 8*, 373–384.

Wall, J. (2012). Can democracy represent children? Toward a politics of difference. *Childhood, 19*(1), 86–100.

Westheimer, J., & Kahne, J. (2004). What kind of citizen? The politics of educating for democracy. *American Educational Research Journal, 41*(2), 237–269.

Wyness, M. (2009). Children representing children: Participation and the problem of diversity in UK youth councils. *Childhood, 16*(4), 535–552.

Wyness, M., Harrison, L., & Buchanan, I. (2004). Childhood, politics and ambiguity: Towards an agenda for children's political inclusion. *Sociology, 38*(1), 81–99.

Zeldin, S., Petrokubi, J., & MacNeil, C. (2008). Youth-adult partnerships in decision making: Disseminating and implementing an innovative idea into established organizations and communities. *American Journal of Community Psychology, 41*, 262–277.

BRIDGING WORLDS IN THE SOCIAL STUDIES CLASSROOM: TEACHERS' PRACTICES AND LATINO IMMIGRANT YOUTHS' CIVIC AND POLITICAL DEVELOPMENT

Rebecca M. Callahan and Kathryn M. Obenchain

ABSTRACT

Purpose – *Prior research suggests that high school experiences shape young adult political behaviors, particularly among immigrant youth. The U.S. social studies classroom, focused on democratic citizenship education, proves an interesting socializing institution.*

Methods – *Through qualitative inquiry, we interviewed Latino immigrant young adults and their former teachers regarding their high school social studies experiences and evolving political and civic engagement.*

Findings – *Armed with experience bridging the worlds of the school and home, immigrant students respond and relate to the content and pedagogy of the social studies classroom in such a way that they (1) participate in*

Youth Engagement: The Civic-Political Lives of Children and Youth
Sociological Studies of Children and Youth, Volume 16, 97–123
Copyright © 2013 by Emerald Group Publishing Limited
All rights of reproduction in any form reserved
ISSN: 1537-4661/doi:10.1108/S1537-4661(2013)0000016009

civic discourse and (2) nurture a disposition toward leadership through teachers' civic expectations of them and instructional emphasis on critical thinking skills.

Social implications – *The ability to engage in civic discourse and a disposition toward leadership are both necessary to foster America's democratic ideals, and to take on leadership roles during adulthood. With focused effort on the unique perspective of immigrant youth, high school social studies teachers can nurture in these students the ability to become leaders in young adulthood, broadening the potential leadership pool.*

Originality – *This study highlights how the social studies curriculum may be particularly salient to Latino immigrant youth as they transition from adolescence to young adulthood and develop their political and civic identities.*

Keywords: Immigrant; civic development; high school; adolescence; social studies; pedagogy

INTRODUCTION

First- and second-generation immigrant youth are one of the fastest growing segments of the US population. Children of immigrant parents (first- and second-generation youth) now comprise one in four students in U.S. schools (Capps, Murray, Ost, Passel, & Herwantoro, 2005), and Latinos make up the largest proportion of this growing population (Fry, 2008). Despite this demographic shift, we know relatively little about the factors that shape Latino immigrant youths' civic (e.g., community volunteering) and political (e.g., voting) engagement as they enter into adult society. U.S. high schools in general, and social studies coursework in particular, may provide a social and educational nexus for immigrant students balancing two worlds.

Prior research indicates that both high school social studies courses and achievement shape young adult political participation for all adolescents (Atherton, 2000; Chaffee, 2000; Nie, Junn, & Stehlik-Barry, 1996; Niemi & Junn, 1998). The fact that Latino immigrant young adults tend to engage politically and civically at lower rates than their non-Latino, non-immigrant peers (Jones-Correa, 1998; Verba, Scholzman, & Brady, 1995) makes social studies experiences much more important to explore. As prior research suggests a strong relationship between social studies course taking and political behaviors among immigrant youth in particular (Callahan, Muller, & Schiller, 2008), we set out to explore how the social studies classroom may influence the civic perspectives of Latino immigrant young adults. It is our hope that these analyses will shed light on how Latino immigrant youth interact with the social studies classroom in the process of their political and civic development. Specifically, we explore how Latino immigrant young adults and their former social studies teachers perceive the youths' high school social studies experiences to have influenced their civic and political development in young adulthood. As the Latino population continues to grow at an unprecedented rate (Passel & Cohn, 2008; U.S. Census Bureau, 2006), ensuring enlightened political engagement (Parker, 2003) among its youth can only strengthen the future of our democracy. The civic and political futures of school districts with large and/or growing Latino immigrant populations may depend on the ability of their social studies programs to reach these citizens.

SCHOOLS, IMMIGRANT STUDENTS, SOCIAL STUDIES, AND POLITICAL ENGAGEMENT

An historical function of U.S. public schools has been to prepare youth, and immigrant youth in particular, to participate in the democratic process, to vote, and to actively engage in their communities (Cremin, 1951; Goodlad, 1984; Tyack, 1974). In essence, school has served as a political and cultural socializing agent. In particular, social studies coursework offers more than just political preparation; it also provides a context within which immigrant youth observe, relate to, and identify with their teachers and peers. That experience offers the opportunity to both socialize and counter socialize students (Engle & Ochoa, 1988) into the dominant culture through the content, skills, and dispositions learned and modeled. Sherrod (2003) found that political knowledge during adolescence predicts voting during young adulthood, knowledge gained, at least in part, from social studies coursework. For immigrant students in particular, research suggests that the accumulation of social studies credits plays a key role in the likelihood of voting and registering to vote (Callahan et al., 2008). Behind the credits and the grades, however, lies the development of civic and political initiative. This study explores how immigrant youth respond and relate to experiences in high school social studies classes in ways that may shape later civic and political development.

Adolescence: A Critical Juncture on the Pathway
to Adult Civic Engagement

In U.S. society, adolescence represents a time when both an individual's sense of self and the social world widen (Lesko, 2001). During childhood, an individual's world and identity are primarily defined and determined by his or her family and home (Corsaro, 1997; James, Jenks, & Prout, 1998); in middle and high school, focus begins to shift outward. During adolescence, youth begin to develop a sense of self as peers and connections made in the school and outside the home increase in importance (Borman & Schneider, 1998). This outward expansion includes relationships with friends, teachers, and mentors (Cauce, 1986; Ryan, 2001) as the social connections of the school increase in relevance. Schools have the potential to shape youths' political and civic growth through connections (Putnam, 2000), as well as social studies pedagogy and content.

Adolescence is particularly important in the foundation of political identity and engagement as research demonstrates an association between youths' high school experiences and political behaviors in young adulthood (Atkins & Hart, 2003; Frisco, Muller, & Dodson, 2004; Glanville, 1999). Adolescence is a time to gain independence, form new relationships, take on new social roles, and begin to make choices about group membership. Adolescence lends itself to the emergence of new identities, social and otherwise. The present study explores youths' development of civic and political identities, determining where and how one fits into the larger community.

Immigrant Youth: Balancing School and Home

From an early age, all immigrant youth learn to negotiate and balance two worlds, that of the home and school. By definition outsiders to the dominant culture, immigrant students daily practice negotiating perspectives different from their own; this inherent emphasis on empathy may make them open to the social studies curriculum which emphasizes awareness of societal needs (Sherrod, Flanagan, & Youniss, 2002). In particular, immigrant youths' experience learning to balance these worlds (Cooper, Cooper, Azmitia, Chavira, & Gullatt, 2002) may prime them to connect to central tenets of social studies which stress not only a recognition of alternate perspectives but also the ability to defend the logic behind often disparate points of view.

As children of immigrant parents, these students' lives – social and academic – are defined by their roles as mediators between their home culture and expectations, and those of their new community, which may at times collide. Kao and Tienda (1995) illustrate how immigrant youth incorporate their parents' expectations for them to buffer school contexts that are often marked by racial and economic disparities in achievement. Similarly, both Gibson (1987) and Zhou and Bankston (1998) illustrate how Punjabi and Vietnamese immigrant youth, respectively, draw from the supportive structures inherent in their home cultures to craft successful identities for themselves within the adopted school contexts. This ability to recognize and utilize key aspects of the home culture and balance these with the world of school may allow immigrant students to incorporate key elements of the social studies classroom to their benefit.

Critical Thinking Skills and the Development of Civic Discourse

While early research suggested that social studies coursework might not matter in furthering political engagement (Langton & Jennings, 1968), later research suggests otherwise, linking curriculum to the development of political knowledge and subsequent political activity (Atherton, 2000; Chaffee, 2000; Niemi & Junn, 1998). While curriculum itself is crucial, several studies also highlight the importance of teachers' pedagogical practices in the development of civic and political engagement among youth. For example, Kahne, Chi, and Middaugh (2006) argue that the social studies curriculum alone does not promote civic engagement, but rather teachers' pedagogical practices also shape the degree of student political engagement later in life. In particular, the authors find that simulations and role modeling contribute to students' expectations of and for civic participation (Kahne et al., 2006). These kinds of practices create opportunities for students to construct, rather than reproduce, knowledge. Students incorporate prior experiences and learning with new information to construct – through processes of analysis, synthesis, and evaluation – new knowledge that may be applied to other settings in and out of school, including civic life. These practices also create the opportunity to practice civic or political skills, such as construction of an argument, deliberation, and negotiation. Understanding how immigrant adolescents respond to these practices requires that we take youth agency into account. Ultimately, youth are responsible for developing their own agency and initiative (Larson, 2000); how immigrant youth respond and relate to their experiences in high school social studies classes merits further exploration.

Balancing Perspectives: Engagement and Voice in the Curriculum

In their review of the literature investigating social studies pedagogical practices, ten Dam and Volman (2004) argue that teachers can create environments where multiple perspectives are recognized and defended, but that ultimately teachers must encourage students to develop these skills within themselves. Providing evidence to support this perspective, Marri (2005) found that high school social studies teachers operating from a multicultural democratic education perspective actively engage their students in critical thinking skills development. According to Marri, as well as Parker (1996), multicultural democratic education adheres to three defining characteristics: democracy is viewed as a shared path; citizens belong to both small and large publics; and diversity is an asset. These teachers require students to engage with the information at hand, effectively communicate their position to others, negotiate alternate perspectives, and view the existence of diverse perspectives as positive.

Multicultural democratic education is particularly appropriate for this study in its conceptualization of democracy as participatory, the membership of citizens in various small (e.g., family, school) and large (e.g., nation) publics, as well as the view that a diversity of opinions strengthens democracy. The existence of such an open, safe environment in which students can actively engage in debate and discussion has been shown to contribute to schools' ability to foster civic engagement (Torney-Purta, 2002). The rich social studies pedagogy described above requires that students are not simply passive recipients of instruction, but rather that they are engaged actors, directing their own civic growth and development. Social studies instruction that requires students to engage in their communities allows youth to own and shape their civic futures (Youniss, McLellan, & Yates, 1997). Adolescents, particularly racial and ethnic minorities, and/or immigrant youth, who might otherwise be marginalized, may be particularly primed to integrate community-focused ideals of civic instruction (Ginwright, Noguera, & Cammarota, 2006). The goal of producing enlightened and engaged citizens lies at the heart of the social studies curriculum (Parker, 2003). It could be argued that social studies has the potential to maximize immigrant adolescents' balancing experiences, facilitating their ability to incorporate the multiple perspectives necessary to move beyond one's own needs to recognize those of the group (Sherrod et al., 2002). These balancing experiences may enhance immigrant youths' ability to respond to and interact with social studies teachers and materials. In particular, they may approach the social studies curriculum in such a way as to internalize argumentation and persuasive skills which may be conducive to future political and civic engagement and leadership.

PURPOSE OF THE STUDY

The unique space where immigrant adolescents interact with the social studies classroom presents an intriguing area of inquiry. All immigrant youth travel into and through adolescence learning to negotiate and balance two worlds; as outsiders to the dominant culture, they negotiate and participate in perspectives different from those of their parents on a daily basis. This position may leave them particularly open to social studies experiences that not only articulate the dominant culture but also encourage its examination, interrogation, and critique.

METHODS

The qualitative inquiry was designed to explore the forces potentially associated with civic and political development among Latino immigrant youth, in particular the high school social studies context. In spite of the wealth of knowledge provided by the previously discussed theories, as well as findings from prior research, gaps remain in our understanding of the forces that drive the political development of immigrant youth, especially Latinos who tend to participate at lower rates than their non-Latino, non-immigrant counterparts (Bass & Casper, 2001; Cassel, 2002; Ramakrishnan & Espenshade, 2001; Torney-Purta, Barber, & Wilkenfeld, 2007). Grounded theory methods afford a way to explore issues of this nature without the initial imposition of an analytical framework. By carefully choosing participants, engaging in data analysis during data collection, and using these processes to inform and shape further data collection (Charmaz, 2006), we were able to create a plan to explore how Latino immigrant youth and their high school social studies teachers perceived their social studies experiences to have shaped these youths' future political and civic development.

Participants

We drew from two distinct groups of participants for this study. First, we sought out National Board Certified (NBC) high school social studies teachers who teach in high Latino immigrant impact communities. Second, we identified Latino immigrant young adults, most of whom had taken high school social studies coursework with these teachers. Given the relatively low rates of both political participation *and* social studies course taking among Latino immigrant youth, we purposefully designed the present study to explore the potential impact that focused civic development could have – within immigrant communities, but also with respect to the society as a whole.

High School Social Studies Teachers
Our focus on board-certified teachers adds a degree of consistency in content and pedagogy across our purposeful sample. While we recognize that variation in content and pedagogy are to be expected when investigating classroom experiences, national board certification provides a measure of peer recognition in the field, as well as a rigorous application and certification process for teachers. Prior research indicates significantly higher levels of achievement among the students of NBC teachers compared to students of non-nationally certified teachers (Goldhaber & Anthony, 2007; Vandevoort & Berliner, 2004). In addition, national certification offers a tangible measure of pedagogical and curricular expertise across our sample.

We drew our sample from four high Latino, high immigrant communities: southern California; southern Florida; Chicago, and Texas. Using the national board certification database, twenty-six high school social studies teachers actively working with immigrant students in high Latino enrollment schools in each of the regions were randomly selected and contacted; nine teachers consented to participate. Although the NBC teachers were geographically diverse, the six men and three women had all taught at least 7 years and were white, with the exception of one non-immigrant Latina. All names are pseudonyms, and due to the rarity of nationally certified teachers in some areas, regions, rather than cities, are listed to protect participants' identities.

Latino Immigrant Young Adults
Through snowball sampling (Patton, 2002), we contacted Latino immigrant young adults who had studied with one of the NBC social studies teachers in our sample, and who would have been eligible to vote in the 2008 presidential election. We contacted these young adults based on the recommendations of the teacher participants. Recruitment targeted both foreign-born (first generation) and U.S.-born (second generation) immi-grant Latinos. Many, although not all, of the young adults were former

students of the teacher participants. In some instances, the teachers initiated contact with their former students and the young adults contacted the researchers; in others, the teachers provided the contact information and the researchers made the initial contact. Nineteen students were recommended and contacted; 11 Latino young adults, all in college at the time of data collection, agreed to participate in the study. Again, all names are pseudonyms.

Data Sources and Data Collection

Audio-taped, semi-structured interviews with the 20 participants served as the data sources for the study. Individual interviews lasted between one and two hours and were conducted by the first author and were conducted in the language preferred by the participants (English). While the majority of interviews were face to face, due to logistical constraints, the Florida interviews were conducted via telephone. All interviews were conducted first with the NBC teacher participants in a region, followed by the Latino young adult participants in the same region. To explore how Latino immigrant youth responded and related to social studies, interview topics for this study included issues of curriculum, pedagogical practices, in- and out-of-class activities, service learning opportunities, teacher–student relationships, and immigrant youth civic and political participation. While some scholars conflate civic engagement and political participation (Parker, 2003; Walzer, 1989), we chose to explore them separately in the interviews. For example, *"What kinds of political participation, if any, do you feel are engendered by classroom assignments?"* and *"What could your school do that it might not be doing now to promote civic behaviors?"* address related, but distinct behaviors. As Keeter, Andolina, and Jenkins (2002) explain, political participation is typically confined to electoral activities, including voting and working on political campaigns, while civic participation focuses on community issues, volunteering for nonprofits, participating in fund-raising activities for charitable organizations, and so on. These activities or behaviors may overlap. Further, political participation may be seen as a distinct category within a broader construct of civic life. The terms political and civic are used throughout this chapter consistent with this distinction.

Prior to each interview, the interviewer explained the study's focus on the factors that shape Latino immigrants' political and civic lives, followed by an introduction to and explanation of prior research indicating a positive relationship between social studies course taking and political participation for children of immigrant, but not U.S. born, parents (Callahan et al., 2008). The interview began with the interviewer asking the participant to expand on the social and academic processes in their high school social studies classrooms. Based on the content of this expansion, the interview proceeded with relevant probe questions. This procedure was followed for all participants.

Teachers
There were 9 one- to two-hour-long semi-structured interviews with the NBC social studies teacher participants. Generally, the teacher participants did not share their immigrant students' social and academic histories, yet they did display a marked sensitivity to their Latino immigrant students' positions negotiating two worlds. The teachers shared stories, opinions, and insights into what happens in the social studies classroom. Topics ranged from pedagogical practices and activities, the curriculum, inter- personal relationships and skill development, and anything that the NBC teachers believed might encourage immigrant students to become more engaged in civic life and the political process. Focused interview questions explored teachers' definitions of political participation and the mechanisms at play in the social studies curriculum in particular. In addition, teachers discussed their motivations, strategies, and perceptions regarding social studies instruction, as well as beliefs, expectations, and perceptions regarding their immigrant students' political preparation and future civic and political engagement. To a person, all of the teachers commented on the focus required of immigrant youth to bridge the world of school and home.

Young Adults
The 11 young adult participants were between 18 and 24 years old; the 2008 general election represented the first time that most would have been eligible to vote. Interviews included discussion of their current civic and political engagement as well as reflection on social and academic processes during high school that they believed may have shaped their current civic positioning. Participants shared their involvement in and reaction to the election, as well as any current political and leadership activities. In addition, the immigrant young adults discussed their high school social studies experiences, as well as current and prior community and political engagement, and any relationships they perceived between the two.

Data Analysis

Due to the interpretive nature of the study, data analysis occurred in an ongoing and iterative manner. Through a process of open, axial, and selective coding (Strauss & Corbin, 1997), the researchers looked for themes within regions and across teachers and young adults. We generated coding schemes independently and then collaborated to refine the codes and to generate the broader thematic findings. Specifically, we analyzed the interview data during two main phases of coding: (1) an initial phase involving naming segments of data followed by (2) a focused, selective phase that used the most salient or frequent initial codes to sort and organize large amounts of data. During the initial coding process, we used action words to label segments of data and to flag particular comments that proved central to our research objectives (Charmaz, 2006). Following the initial coding, data were summarily reviewed and annotated to determine the viability of the thematic coding.

FINDINGS

Below, we first provide composite portraits of both the teacher and young adult participants, followed by their perceptions of the social studies experiences they believed may have shaped the political and civic development of the Latino immigrant young adults.

High School Social Studies Teachers

The desire to foster enlightened political engagement (Parker, 2003) among the next generation resides at the core of high school social studies curriculum in the United States (Atherton, 2000), and our participants' interviews reflected a perspective consistent with this purpose. Although we did not ask teachers to name the specific texts and resources, the reported content covered and strategies implemented prove relatively consistent across our participants. This curricular consistency was likely due to our purposeful sampling of NBC teachers, as well as high school social studies course content that is reflective of the dominant culture. Overall, the NBC teacher participants provided a comprehensive overview of their perceptions of their role, the role of the curriculum, and what might be expected of students in terms of civic and political engagement.

Latino Immigrant Young Adults

The levels of civic and political integration and dedication to the community among the Latino immigrant young adult participants proved noteworthy. Each of the Latino young adults demonstrated various kinds and levels of civic participation on their college campus, many taking active leadership roles and integrating themselves into the surrounding community. Nearly all participated in some form of political participation in their community during the 2008 presidential election: organizing voter registration drives, holding debates, volunteering on campaigns, spearheading fundraisers, and even developing Facebook forums related to the elections. Many held leadership positions in their civic lives: for example, mentored other undergraduates, middle and high school students; led community service projects; volunteered in campus and city health care clinics providing health education services. Their employment also leaned toward civic-minded pursuits: for example, advocate in the office for student disabilities; intern on a senate campaign; health sexuality peer educator. We found the Latino young adults' disposition toward leadership in their communities of interest, especially due to its consistency across the participants.

CONSTRUCTED THEMES BRIDGING TWO WORLDS: CIVIC DISCOURSE AND A DISPOSITION TOWARD LEADERSHIP

As data analysis progressed, we constructed two interacting broad themes that are the foundation of our findings. We argue first and foremost that immigrant youths' bridging experiences shape their incorporation of two key foci of high school social studies: how teachers perceive immigrant youth to be predisposed to understand and connect with the tenets of the social studies curriculum, and how these perceptions in turn might enable immigrant youth to develop both the ability to participate in civic discourse and a disposition toward leadership. Students' participation in civic discourse and future leadership potential are both strengthened by teachers' emphasis on the development of critical thinking skills.

Professionally focused on shaping the political engagement of youth, these teachers were acutely aware of how their immigrant students might identify with the curriculum and the content in a way that children of U.S.-born parents might not. Teachers viewed immigrant students' awareness of political systems outside the United States as a motivator to actively engage with and internalize current social studies content. As Mr. Jones, a U.S. history teacher, noted, in the adopted U.S. context, many immigrant youth:

> look to the social studies classes to learn more about the political system and ... the
> history of the country ... they see opportunity, they see freedom ... they are eager to
> participate. But in order to participate, they have got to become informed and
> knowledgeable about the system.

In the teachers' view, immigrant youths' very *being* as mediators between the two worlds necessitated and motivated their desire to engage with social studies.

Interestingly, it was the teachers, not their former students, who elaborated on the youths' positions bridging cultures. The Latino immigrant young adults themselves did not speak directly to their position bridging cultures. We hypothesize that this may be because as outsiders, the teachers recognized students' bridging experiences perhaps because these acts stood in contrast to the teachers' own experiences. However, the Latino young adults who grew up bridging did not speak to it directly in the interviews, perhaps because for them, it is a normal experience.

Ultimately, we argue that the teachers' perceptions of immigrant students' bridging experiences, and their subsequent civic expectations based on these perceptions, may have shaped how the students responded and related to the social studies emphases on developing civic discourse and a disposition toward leadership. The teachers' perceptions in this case may have emboldened the youths' civic identities. Prior research suggests that teachers' beliefs about and expectations for their students are highly correlated with students' actual performance (Jussim & Harber, 2005). Through our analysis, it became clear that the teachers saw the balancing required of immigrant youth as a benefit to students' interaction with the social studies curriculum, and this translated into their expectations for students' performance. In particular, the teachers believed that Latino immigrant students' experience balancing the perspectives of their parents and the school facilitated their integration of core civic concepts, and ultimately, their civic and political development in young adulthood. The levels of community involvement evidenced among our Latino immigrant young adult participants reflect the expectations their teachers reported holding for them during high school.

Even though the Latino young adults we interviewed may not have perceived their bridging experiences as worthy of comment, their sensitivity to multiple perspectives, a focus of social studies, was decidedly present. The

Latino young adults, with a lifetime spent learning to recognize when and how their home and dominant cultures collided, seemed to recognize that their experiences may have been particularly salient to the social studies classroom. Specifically, Isabel reported that the social studies classroom validated this awareness as, "a very important stepping stone for us ... with the two different cultures, we were already made sensitive since birth. ... But we just developed a bigger, a lot more sensitivity in that class." Her voice reflects how the social studies classroom validated her experiences bridging two worlds and helped her turn this into an awareness of other, alternate perspectives.

Consistent with the young adults' perspectives, throughout the course of the interviews, the teachers highlighted how immigrant students' unique perspectives often facilitated comprehension and internalization of the social studies lessons. To illustrate this, Mr. Rocca, a European history teacher, shared:

> I also stress to them that sometimes Americans get very complacent about their own democracy. They complain about having to go out and vote; standing in line; missing their favorite television programs and things like that. And I call to their attention that, in places around the world when people go out to vote, they quite literally take their life in their hands; it can be a life threatening experience. And I always get a lot of, you know, head nodding from a lot of the Latin American students about that. I have a young man this year, he's just great. His family has just come from Venezuela and ... he is very much in agreement with what I said. He actually spoke in class to the fact that what I said was very, very true; that ... people in countries like that very often suffer intimidation or actual physical violence.

The board-certified teachers in our sample reported emphasizing aspects of the social studies curriculum that they believed immigrant youth might connect with in particular. The teachers recognized that the immigrant youth in their classes do, in fact, bridge two cultures, and used the social studies curriculum as a vehicle to connect students' experiences to the course content.

In fact, teachers seemed to capitalize on their immigrant students' dual references and positions outside mainstream American society, drawing on students' lived experiences to prompt recognition of alternate perspectives, capitalizing on students' positions bridging two worlds. Consistent with Newmann, Marks, and Gamoran's (1996) discussion of the construction of knowledge in the social studies curriculum, as the Latino immigrant young adults were bridging two worlds in high school, they were constructing, rather than reproducing, the knowledge of the dominant culture as they brought in their life experiences to expand the conceptual understanding of the social studies content. In addition, their experiences and perspectives give voice to often unexplored perspectives on course content. Civil rights issues were a particularly popular topic, as teachers encouraged students to relate the topic to their own, lived experiences. Ms. McDougal, a U.S. history and world studies teacher, noted:

> Right now we're talking about Jim Crow, and the grandfather clauses, and the polling taxes, and the literacy tests ... what does it mean to not be able to understand the ballot? .... When I'm with my Mom's group, it's, *You're an American. You should learn to speak English. Our documents should not be published in any other language but English.* I say this to my kids; 'that is what my mother's generation thinks, the World War II generation'. (I ask) How do you respond to that? Why? Let's talk about that. What languages should it be available in? *Well, Spanish.* Is that the only one? *Well, we're the dominant minority.* So, you're going to lock out the other minorities? How about before you were the dominant minority? *Oh.* Well, what other languages are important? *Well, we're in a school with Polish speaking kids, well, we can have Polish.* Is that it? *Well, I don't think that we should have whatever languages they speak in the Middle East.* Well, why not? *Because they're all terrorists.* Ok. Here we go again.

This eagerness to engage immigrant students' lived experiences with the curriculum highlights teachers' recognition that these youth approach the social studies curriculum already having to negotiate two worlds, already having to think about how others experience the world. A central premise of the social studies curricula lies in the necessity to learn to recognize others' perspectives in order to persuade, engage, and lead (http://www.socialstudies.org/positions/powerful). The fact that these young adults bridge two cultures and their ability to adopt others' perspectives in order to do so frame our two specific findings. First, participation in civic discourse and, second, development of a disposition to lead are products of the intersection of the young adult immigrants' life experiences with their secondary social studies school experiences, as perceived by our participants.

Participating in Civic Discourse

If one key to civic and political engagement in young adulthood is the ability to recognize and utilize others' perspectives to understand and engage with one's community, a second is the ability to persuade. Using the course content as a springboard to develop and defend an argument, these teachers guided their students to take a position and defend it with evidence, to engage in this aspect of civic discourse, a hallmark of authentic intellectual work (Newmann et al., 1996). Rather than being passive recipients of the teacher's instruction, the students are required to find their civic voices. In this process, the students begin to shape their civic identities. The Latino young adults repeatedly remarked on their teachers' insistence that they be able to defend a position that might not be their own, an ability built upon the students' experience recognizing and relating to alternate perspectives. Both participant groups spoke of the importance of argumentation, defined as the ability to actively seek out, identify, and employ evidence to support one's position. Teachers reported developing a multilayered argumentation process using interactive instructional activities such as debates and role plays that required students to defend their perspectives.

Frequently, the content of the activity was almost secondary to the teachers' focus on developing empirical question-and-answer processes. Mr. Gordon, a world history teacher, went so far as to emphasize his focus on logical, persuasive arguments regardless of curricular content, stating, "My goal is to develop critical thinking, through the manipulation of evidence, through the manipulation of information ... It's really a skills-oriented class. In any given year I ask them, *What topics do you want to look at?* The content is almost irrelevant." Consistent with an issues-centered approach to teaching social studies (Evans, Newmann, & Saxe, 1996), this emphasis on argumentation, evaluation of evidence, and articulation of one's perspective dominated both teacher and young adults' reflections about the formative elements of high school social studies. Teacher participants reported engaging students in activities which forced them to question, and defend oftentimes competing positions. Likewise, the Latino young adults reported having to actively defend contentious positions – often positions that ran counter to their own beliefs – in the very public forum of the social studies classroom. The *question–interrogate–defend* pattern was repeated across courses and content.

Argumentation

Specifically, teachers and young adults found value across different classroom activities which required one to question assumptions, evaluate evidence drawn from historical and current primary sources of evidence. These activities encompassed reading and writing, as well as debate and role plays designed to motivate students to interrogate sources of information in order to critically evaluate them. Mr. Tomasi, a world history teacher, articulated the teachers' belief in the importance of identifying, and questioning the sources of any given information.

> Well, I think there are things that we do in our curriculum ... where you challenge, (you) don't accept the status quo just because someone's saying it, that's where you go back to

the source. *Who's* saying it? *Why* are they saying it? *What's* the end game? *What* are the objectives? Look at it that way. Try to be more objective ... dispassionate. (Find out) more of the story and don't get caught up in the emotions. Try to understand what's being said, for what purpose ... . I think the government class talks a lot about these issues.

In a separate interview, Ms. Jewel, a civics and government teacher, affirmed the civic importance of developing critical consumers of information.

> In my law class they have to find a current events article that has to do with law; they have to identify any bias in the article, in the headline, in the article. I'm trying to get them to read, be thinking readers. That gives us an opportunity to talk about the media and the media's influence on us as consumers of the media.

The use of classroom discussions and learning to defend one's position with evidence (Flynn, 2009; Newstreet, 2008) is particularly important for immigrant young adults as they make their way in a political system new to them and their parents, processing information from a media also largely new to their families. Several young adults reflected (with mock frustration) on their teachers' tactics, ultimately praising the outcome. For example, Fernando noted:

> (My government teacher) was really good at wanting you to say what you really feel about a subject. ... You sort of get angry because he is baiting you into these things, and you lay out your opinion and then he will ask you, *Why do you think that?* And that question sort of puts you on edge. It's like, '*wait a minute*'! And you have to go back and rethink everything to double check that, yeah, this is really what I think.

Similarly, when asked in the interview about how she learned to make and support the arguments that she wields as a young adult, Amanda recalls a high school teacher who insisted that, "If you have a *position* you better damned well be able to back it up or else I am not going to listen to you, and I'm not going to let anyone else listen to you (either)." Recounting this admonishment with pride, Amanda valued her ability to use evidence to persuade others to her way of thinking. In general, proficiency in constructing an informed and persuasive position is critical in the development of individual civic discourse, and civic and political debate within a community.

Similar to the skills necessary in oral argumentation, writing assignments were referenced as key in helping youth develop their opinions and support their arguments with relevant evidence. These substantive conversations, as part of classroom instruction, are key in preparing students to articulate, analyze, and evaluate their ideas (Scheurman & Newmann, 1998). The immigrant young adults referenced teachers' insistence that they defend a

point of view as a key point of their connection with social studies. For
instance, Ramiro reflected that:

> (My teacher) emphasized our writing and being able to write a thesis. He always asked
> us: *What is a thesis? What is our argument? What details are going to prove this argument?*
> And that instilled a change in how I think because it allowed me to justify what my
> arguments are, and if I can't justify my argument then what is the point of arguing it
> which really it helps a lot.

In fact, teacher-utilized questioning techniques and writing assignments
defending a thesis were often allayed into broader discussions – debates
centered on shared readings and writings, wherein participants questioned
and defended opposing viewpoints. Prior research highlights the effectiveness of questioning, discussion, and writing assignments among racially and
socioeconomically diverse students (Rubin, 2007), such as the Latino
immigrant youth interviewed here. These discussions allowed the students to
question assumptions they may have made while honing their ideas for
change into policies and plans. Mr. Jones explained:

> There is a writing assignment (the students) write their own U.S. Immigration Policy;
> they have to come up with ... five to ten ideas – basically starting anew. How would they
> address the immigration policy? The following day we put some of them up on the
> board ... let the class decide what they like and what they don't, and then we begin to
> break down what are the problems with this and again that might be a point that is
> probably the most frustrating because it generally comes down to; gee, those are great
> ideas but where do we generate the revenue, what do we cut in order to provide for that?
> And again, the students have a wide variety of issues and ideas ... you get everyone
> understanding all of the issues out there and then they make it a forum.

Ultimately, argumentation experiences are useful in learning that while
the student voice is important and to be respected, it will be best heard when
supported with relevant facts.

Debates
Another popular activity designed to shape students' ability to adopt and
defend opposing viewpoints was the classroom debate centered on relevant
current events. Teachers reported working to ensure that students could
not always select a position toward which they might naturally lean;
Ms. Martínez, a world and European history teacher, reported that she
debriefs with her students following a class debate, asking, "How did you go
about researching this when you didn't believe it? How did you actually
consider arguments?" Here, the debriefing process was as important as the
debate itself; the connections students made to a topic they might not have
agreed with informed the development of their perspective.

Recognizing the need to adopt a different perspective is important for all students, but may be especially salient for immigrant students who approach the high school social studies curriculum having already learned to balance their two worlds. Many of the Latino young adults reported how defending an alternate perspective through debate made them acutely aware of the strengths and weaknesses of their own point of view. One young woman, Fatima, noted:

> I think also one very big part of what made me specifically want to get my opinions out was she made us participate in debates. And it was very interesting because ... I argued for the legalization of prostitution and my views are not in accordance with that. But I wanted a challenge.

Immigrant youth may be predisposed to incorporate the concept of walking in another's shoes, that is, the multiple perspectives that are central in the social studies classroom and developed further through the use of debates and other forms of civic discourse.

Many of the teachers reported how their immigrant students adopted alternate perspectives in debate. For example, Ms. McDougal noted that debates provide "a wonderful growing experience and knowledge experience ... To have to conduct these debates, (students) have to defend their positions, let their colleagues listen to them, and then have the groups make informed decisions." Not only are the teachers modeling their expected norms of civic discourse, but they are also providing the students with the tools to become engaged citizens in their current and future communities. Consistent with Dewey's (1900/1990) view of the school as an embryonic society, as well as the goals of social studies education (i.e., citizenship education), our participants reported that the teachers provided the tools necessary to develop the knowledge, behaviors, and attitudes for participation in a democratic society. The public display inherent in debates emphasizes the importance of knowing the available evidence, as well as how to evaluate that evidence, articulate, and defend a position valuable practice in political discourse, preparing these immigrant youth for civic and political engagement.

Role Plays

Teachers also prompted students to reflect on current political issues such as civil liberties through role plays. Immigrant students' balancing experiences were perceived to help them relate to social studies concepts. For instance Ms. Martínez discussed her work developing empathy in her students:

> Imagine that you're a Jew living in Germany and you never know when they're going to revoke your citizenship ... you live in fear every day. Here you are contributing what you

can to society and you never know; they can take it away. And so we talk about that with the new immigrants coming in as well. And ... it connects it, not because they read it, but because they actually experienced those feelings even if it was only for two weeks. You know, they experienced those feelings. They felt that they knew what that was like ... I love that simulation. ... They become so invested in their roles.

Here, Ms. Martínez guided her students to connect issues in the Nazi-era role play with policy issues relevant to immigration today. Ms. Martínez and the other teachers encouraged debates and discourse concerning immigrants in today's society students to link the curricular content to lived experiences. This connection was especially relevant among immigrant youth who linked their parents' experiences to those of generations past.

Teachers also drew on immigrant students' lived experiences to develop agency and empathy in the study of history (Seixas, 1993). For example, world history teacher, Mr. Schroeder, describes his use of the following vignette to examine human willingness to cede individual freedoms to authorities.

Right before we go into the 1930's and fascism, (I teach) how easy it is to scare people. I do it in three parts. I tell the kids ... *Ok. We got this grant money ...* I walk them through a wish list of how they'd like to spend the grant money... I have a form all made up with the school letterhead and I have somebody record the results. (Then, the next day, I say) *Ok. Now, the principal wants us to know that ... we're not going to get all that we want because so much of it has to go to some of the problems of the school.* And they guess it right away, "Oh, graffiti."... And I say, *Yeah. Some of the graffiti was racist ... it's really severe right now and that brings us to another issue. We can't have everything that we want ...* It's leading them down a path, you promise them (one thing) ... and then you tell them, (they) can't have it...I usually ... do anti-Hispanic because we were a white school a long time ago and I usually have two or three white kids in my class and that's it. It's all Hispanic. And so it's so easy to get the Hispanics to turn against the white kids. And so I move them to the front of the room and I go through their binders and look for ... any kind of writing. And they just give it up. They so allow me to go through their backpack. And (they say), *Really, this doesn't mean anything.* And, (I reply) *It's going to have to go to the office."* And when anybody says, *Wait, this isn't fair ... Come on, we can work this out. ...* Which leads to a discussion, after (which I say) ... , *Look at all the rights that you just gave up because of fear.*

This exercise prompts the students to recognize that individual actors had the agency to make decisions about their rights in the past, while reflecting on the historical context in which the decisions were made. Exploration of the context through role play helps students develop historical empathy and allows students to question their own assumptions – in this case, their willingness to cede their freedoms when faced with a perceived threat.

Striking in participants' discussion of argumentation, debate, and role play activities was how teachers built upon the immigrant youths' bridging experiences to develop empathy as a facet of civic development. By definition, all immigrant youth negotiate and balance their worlds. Our social studies teacher participants repeatedly reported capitalizing on this experience to facilitate the integration of alternate perspectives. Teachers' integration of immigrant students' lived experiences has the potential to contribute to their future political and civic development.

A Disposition toward Leadership

In line with balancing and bridging experiences, our Latino immigrant young adult participants demonstrated a disposition toward leadership which they perceived to draw in part from their social studies experiences. While this disposition was explored earlier through a composite portrait of the youth, it is further detailed in this section using participants' voices. This disposition was especially apparent as the Latino young adults struggled to model the civic discourse developed in the classroom in their homes and their communities. Sam and Anthony both related the struggle to engage their parents in political conversations.

> **Sam**: Every once in awhile my mom will say something about a certain politician. I won't refute her opinions or her stances on a political sense, but ... I've taken a lot of classes that force you to think critically and ask these kinds of questions. So ... I ask my mom, '*What about this or what about that?*', seeing what she says and what she thinks and what she feels. I feel like a lot of her opinions ... come from what the news sources say. And like a lot of her friends that she talks with, they have the same news sources ... I just want ... (her to think) about these things in a different sense, more critically.

> **Anthony**: [Mom's] super active. My dad's ... take on politics is that he doesn't like it. He does not want anything to do with it. My dad tries to be a U.S. citizen and (he says) I'm a resident right now and nothing is bothering me. But my mom voted. And, I told her, did you vote in 92? And I'll ask questions about what Reagan did; did you like Reagan? Did you like Clinton?

The desire to maintain a respectful stance in their homes, while also prompting family members to think critically about information sources and potential biases, is not uncommon among immigrant youth navigating two worlds (Valdés, 1996). Expressed sensitivity to their parents' perspectives suggests an acute self-awareness among the immigrant young adult participants, as well as the disposition to be engaged and informed. This disposition also reflects Parker's (2003) enlightened political engagement, and it builds upon immigrant youths' bridging and balancing experiences.

Similarly, leadership among their peers emerged as a common theme among the Latino young adults. Their engagement in civic discourse during high school may have primed them to take on leadership positions in their communities as young adults. Sam was reflective about his potential for leadership, as well as how he might have the most impact. Noting his extensive involvement in high school and his recent transition to the university, he noted, "I'm one person and that made me think a lot about the way I can impact other people or the way that I can influence them. So I thought a lot about my leadership capabilities and the best way to reach people." Several young adults referenced formative social studies experiences with teachers who pushed them to articulate their arguments, to evaluate information, and to understand the perspectives of others. The youth saw these experiences with teachers as contributing to their disposition to lead, sometimes by example, sometimes in specific positions of power.

In discussing her role engaging other college students in the 2008 presidential debates, one young Latina made a connection between her long-standing interest in politics and her lived experiences negotiating two worlds. Amanda discussed encouraging her voting-age peers to keep up with politics, noting that, "I try to keep it light (with) references to stuff that everybody knows about … Palin … Tina Fey on SNL; (I) draw that into the conversation and then try to cut deeper from there." Amanda recognized her own draw to politics and her ability to engage her peers through the use of humor and pop culture. Only once she engaged her peers could she guide the discussion to a deeper level. Her leadership expanded beyond her personal likelihood of voting to the importance of encouraging her peers to vote, to become informed, and to be aware of the influence of politics on their lives.

Teachers' awareness of Latino immigrant young adults' bridging and balancing experiences, we argue, facilitates their ability to engage in a critical way in the social studies classroom. Teachers perceive immigrant youth as predisposed to participate in civic discourse and, as such, plant the seeds for future community leadership. However, neither of these social studies foci could be fully developed without the critical thinking skills at the heart of the social studies teachers' pedagogical practices. Our data emphasize the importance of engaging practices designed to develop critical thinking skills in order to realize the potential of the immigrant student perspective.

CONCLUSIONS

(Our social studies teacher) would challenge us to say, "Hey, I want you to take this cause and speak". … It was something that we got involved (in). And he … opened our eyes and told us who we were. He made it clear … You know most people won't even hear you

out; ... You've got to understand what you're ... fighting for, what's your position. What do
you think about that? So, us being 17 and 18 we react(ed) to that, **Anthony**

Like many of the Latino young adults we interviewed, Anthony saw his teachers' belief in him as primary and central to his expectations of himself in young adulthood. Anthony and his peers responded to their teacher's beliefs that they were predisposed to become leaders in their communities by becoming leaders in young adulthood. Mirroring earlier findings regarding youths' responses to teacher expectations (Jussim & Harber, 2005), Anthony and his peers' emergence in young adulthood as civic and political leaders may partially reflect their teachers' expectations that they had the skill set required to balance two worlds, a predisposition to be a leader. Across our teacher interviews, it was this belief that immigrant youth in particular are primed to lead in the civic sphere that drove their teachers' expectations for their futures. Mr. Gordon succinctly describes the teachers' perceptions of the relationship immigrant youth have with the social studies curriculum in particular:

> With our immigrant population at the school ... that by taking more social studies the feeling of isolation ... is dissipated ... so many of the topics that are dealt with (in social studies) ... plant the seed for a semblance of personal responsibility and also a confidence in the power of one, or in the power of a collective one.

Our Latino immigrant young adult and nationally certified social studies teacher participants alike all recognized the unique experience of immigrant youth and their families acclimating to a new society. Latino immigrant students' bridging experiences allowed them to incorporate two key foci of the social studies classroom: the ability to engage in civic discourse and the disposition to lead in their communities. Simultaneously, Latino immigrant youths' development of these core social studies foci was fostered by teachers' awareness of the youths' sensitivity to others' perspectives – a sensitivity necessitated by youths' lives spent bridging worlds. Latino immigrant students' experiences bridging worlds, coupled with teachers' focus on civic discourse, leadership, and core social studies concepts, may work together to present a perfect storm for future political engagement.

At the start of the last century, Dewey (1900/1990) argued that an effective democracy requires not only that the highest academic performers participate, but also that the entire citizenry acquire a basic level of social studies preparation in order to actively engage in the democratic process. As a rapidly growing segment of the voting-age population (Passel & Cohn, 2008), Latino immigrant youth arguably hold the future of our democratic tradition. Together, the social studies classroom and curriculum have the potential to capitalize on Latino immigrant youths' experiences to enhance and fortify our nation's democratic tradition.

Ultimately, through our synthesis of students' and teachers' perspectives, we suggest that it is immigrant youths' bridging experiences that facilitate their incorporation of the social studies teachings that allow individuals to explore and adopt alternate perspectives, engage in civic discourse, and adopt leadership positions in their communities. As an institutional force, the social studies classroom has the potential to actively engage Latino immigrant youths' experiences to foster civic and political engagement.

ACKNOWLEDGMENTS

This research was supported by a grant from the Russell Sage Foundation (RSF Project no. 88-06-12, Chandra Muller, PI, and Rebecca M. Callahan, Co-PI) and a supplemental Presidential Award. In addition, this research was supported by grant 5 R24 HD042849 *Population Research Center*, awarded to the Population Research Center at The University of Texas at Austin by the Eunice Kennedy Shriver National Institute of Health and Child Development. The authors extend their gratitude for initial data collection and exploratory analyses to Dr. Allen Lynn for his work while a Graduate Research Assistant (GRA) on the project.

REFERENCES

Atherton, H. (2000). We the people ... Project citizen. In S. Mann & J. J. Patrick (Eds.), *Education for civic engagement in democracy: Service learning and other promising practices* (pp. 93–102). Bloomington, IN: ERIC Clearinghouse for Social Studies/Social Science Education.

Atkins, R., & Hart, D. (2003). Neighborhoods, adults, and the development of civic identity in urban youth.. *Applied Developmental Science, 7*(3), 156–164.

Bass, L. E., & Casper, L. M. (2001). Differences in registering and voting between native-born and naturalized Americans. *Population Research and Policy Review, 20*(6), 483–511.

Borman, K., & Schneider, B. (1998). *The adolescent years: Social influences and educational challenges* (Vol. Part I). Chicago, IL: National Society for the Study of Education.

Callahan, R. M., Muller, C., & Schiller, K. S. (2008). Preparing for citizenship: Immigrant high school students' curriculum and socialization. *Theory and Research in Social Education, 36*(2), 6–31.

Capps, R., Murray, J., Ost, J., Passel, J. S., & Herwantoro, S. (2005). *The new demography of America's schools: Immigration and the No Child Left Behind Act*. Washington, DC: The Urban Institute.

Cassel, C. A. (2002). Hispanic turnout: Estimates from validated voting data. *Political Research Quarterly, 55*(2), 391–408.

Cauce, A. M. (1986). Social networks and social competence: Exploring the effects of early adolescent friendships. *American Journal of Community Psychology, 14*(6), 607–628.

Chaffee, S. (2000). Education for citizenship: Promising effects of the Kids' Voting Curriculum. In S. Mann & J. J. Patrick (Eds.), *Education for civic engagement in democracy: Service learning and other promising practices* (pp. 87–92). Bloomington, IN: Eric Clearinghouse for Social Studies/Social Science Education.

Charmaz, K. (2006). *Constructing grounded theory: A practical guide through qualitative analysis.* Thousand Oaks, CA: Sage Publications.

Cooper, C. R., Cooper, R. G., Azmitia, M., Chavira, G., & Gullatt, Y. (2002). Bridging multiple worlds: How African American and Latino youth in academic outreach programs navigate math pathways to college. *Applied Developmental Science, 6*(2), 73–87.

Corsaro, W. A. (1997). *The sociology of childhood.* London: Pine Forge Press.

Cremin, L. A. (1951). *The American common school: An historic conception.* New York: Teachers College Press.

Dewey, J. (1900/1990). *The school and society and the child and the curriculum.* Chicago, IL: University of Chicago Press.

Engle, S. H., & Ochoa, A. (1988). *Education for democratic citizenship: Decision making in the social studies.* New York: Teachers' College Press.

Evans, R. W., Newmann, F. M., & Saxe, D. W. (1996). Defining issues-centered education. In R. W. Evans & D. W. Saxe (Eds.), *Handbook on teaching social issues: NCSS bulletin 93* (pp. 2–5). Washington, DC: National Council for the Social Studies.

Flynn, N. K. (2009). Toward democratic discourse: Scaffolding student-led discussions in the social studies. *Teachers College Record, 111*(8), 2021–2054.

Frisco, M. L., Muller, C., & Dodson, K. (2004). Participation in voluntary youth-serving associations and early adult voting behavior. *Social Science Quarterly, 85*(3), 660–676.

Fry, R. (2008). *Latino settlement in the new century.* Washington, DC: Pew Hispanic Center.

Gibson, M. A. (1987). The school performance of immigrant minorities: A comparative view. *Anthropology and Education Quarterly, 18*(4), 262–275.

Ginwright, S., Noguera, P. A., & Cammarota, J. (Eds.). (2006). *Beyond resistance! Youth activism and community change: New democratic possibilities for practice and policy for America's youth.* New York, NY: Routledge, Taylor & Francis Group.

Glanville, J. L. (1999). Political socialization or selection? Adolescent extracurricular participation and political activity in early adulthood. *Social Science Quarterly, 80*(2), 279–290.

Goldhaber, D., & Anthony, E. (2007). Can teacher quality be effectively assessed? National Board Certification as a signal of effective teaching. *Review of Economics and Statistics, 89*(1), 134–150.

Goodlad, J. I. (1984). *A place called school.* New York, NY: McGraw Hill.

James, A., Jenks, C., & Prout, A. (1998). *Theorizing childhood.* Williston, VT: Teachers College Press.

Jones-Correa, M. (1998). *Between two nations: The political predicament of Latinos in New York City.* Ithaca, NY: Cornell University Press.

Jussim, L., & Harber, K. D. (2005). Teacher expectations and self-fulfilling prophecies: Knowns and unknowns, resolved and unresolved controversies. *Personality and Social Psychology Review, 9*(2), 131–155.

Kahne, J., Chi, B., & Middaugh, E. (2006). Building social capital for civic and political engagement: The potential of high-school civics courses. *Canadian Journal of Education*, *29*(2), 387–409.

Kao, G., & Tienda, M. (1995). Optimism and achievement: The educational performance of immigrant youth. *Social Science Quarterly*, *76*(1), 1–19.

Keeter, S., Andolina, M., & Jenkins, K. (2002). *The civic and political health of the nation: A generational portrait*. New Brunswick, NJ: CIRCLE and The Pew Charitable Trusts.

Langton, K., & Jennings, M. K. (1968). Political socialization and the high school civic curriculum in the united states. *American Political Science Review*, *62*(3), 862–867.

Larson, R. W. (2000). Toward a psychology of positive youth development. *American Psychologist*, *55*, 1.

Lesko, N. (2001). *Act your age! A cultural construction of adolescence. Falmer*NY: Routledge.

Marri, A. (2005). Building a framework for classroom-based multicultural democratic education: Learning from three skilled teachers. *Teachers College Record*, *107*(5), 1036–1059.

Newmann, F. M., Marks, H. M., & Gamoran, A. (1996). Authentic pedagogy and student performance. *American Journal of Education*, *104*(4), 280–312.

Newstreet, C. (2008). Paul revere rides through high school government class: Teacher research and the power of discussion to motivate thinking. *The Social Studies*, *99*(1), 9–12.

Nie, N. H., Junn, J., & Stehlik-Barry, K. (1996). *Education and democratic citizenship in America*. Chicago, IL: University of Chicago Press.

Niemi, R. G., & Junn, J. (1998). *Civic education: What makes students learn*. New Haven, CT: Yale University Press.

Parker, W. C. (1996). 'Advanced' ideas about democracy: Toward a pluralist conception of citizenship education. *Teachers College Record*, *98*(1), 104–125.

Parker, W. C. (2003). *Teaching democracy unity and diversity in public life*. New York: Teachers College Press.

Passel, J. S., & Cohn, D. V. (2008). *U.S. Population projections: 2005–2050*. Washington, DC: Pew Research Center.

Patton, M. Q. (2002). *Qualitative research and evaluation methods*. Thousand Oaks, CA: Sage Publications.

Putnam, R. D. (2000). *Bowling alone: The collapse and revival of American community*. New York: Simon & Schuster.

Ramakrishnan, S. K., & Espenshade, T. J. (2001). Immigrant incorporation and political participation in the united states. *International Migration Review*, *35*(3), 870–909.

Rubin, B. C. (2007). There's still not justice': Youth civic identity development amid distinct school and community contexts.. *Teachers College Record*, *109*(2), 449–481.

Ryan, A. (2001). Personality and social development: The peer group as a context for the development of young adolescent motivation and achievement. *Child Development*, *72*(4), 1135–1150.

Scheurman, G., & Newmann, F. M. (1998). Authentic intellectual work in social studies: Putting performance before pedagogy. *Social Education*, *62*(1), 23–25.

Seixas, P. (1993). Historical understanding among adolescents in a multicultural setting. *Curriculum Inquiry*, *23*(3), 301–327.

Sherrod, L. R. (2003). Promoting the development of citizenship in diverse youth. *PS: Political Science and Politics*, *36*(2), 287–292.

Sherrod, L. R., Flanagan, C., & Youniss, J. (2002). Dimensions of citizenship and opportunities for youth development: The what, why, when, where and who of citizenship development. *Applied Developmental Science, 6*(4), 264–272.

Strauss, A. C., & Corbin, J. (1997). *Grounded theory in practice.* Thousand Oaks, CA: Sage Publications.

ten Dam, G., & Volman, M. (2004). Critical thinking as a citizenship competence: Teaching strategies. *Learning and Instruction, 14*(4), 359–379.

Torney-Purta, J. (2002). The school's role in developing civic engagement: A study of adolescents in twenty-eight countries. *Applied Developmental Science, 6*(4), 203–212.

Torney-Purta, J., Barber, C. H., & Wilkenfeld, B. (2007). Latino adolescents' civic development in the United States: Research results from the IEA civic education study. *Journal of Youth and Adolescence, 36*(2), 111–125.

Tyack, D. B. (1974). *The one best system: A history of American urban education.* Cambridge, MA: Harvard University Press.

U.S. Census Bureau. (2006). *Hispanics in the United States.* Washington, DC: Retrieved from http://www.census.gov/population/www/socdemo/hispanic/hispanic_pop_presentation.html.

Valdés, G. (1996). *Con respeto: Bridging the distances between culturally diverse families and schools – An ethnographic portrait.* New York, NY: Teachers College Press.

Vandevoort, L. G., & Berliner, D. C. (2004). National Board Certified teachers and their students' achievement. *Education Policy Analysis Archives, 12*(46), 1–117.

Verba, S., Scholzman, K., & Brady, H. (1995). *Voice and equality: Civic voluntarism in American politics. Cambridge, MA.* Harvard University Press.

Walzer, M. (1989). Citizenship. In T. Ball, J. Farr & R. L. Hanson (Eds.), *Political innovation and conceptual change* (pp. 211–219). Cambridge: Cambridge University Press.

Youniss, J., McLellan, J. A., & Yates, M. (1997). What we know about engendering civic identity. *American Behavioral Scientist, 40*(5), 620–631.

Zhou, M., & Bankston, C. L. (1998). *Growing up American: How Vietnamese children adapt to life in the United States.* New York: Russell Sage Foundation.

"THEY HAVE THEIR HANDS ON THE PULSE OF THE CITY": TEACHERS' CONSTRUCTIONS OF STUDENTS' CIVIC KNOWLEDGE IN AN URBAN MIDDLE SCHOOL CLASSROOM

Shira Eve Epstein

ABSTRACT

Purpose – *This study focuses on seventh grade teachers' constructions of students' civic awareness as they planned for and enacted a civic engagement project with urban youth of color.*

Approach – *Drawing on critical and interpretive paradigms, I analyze the teachers' dialogues during colloquia on youth civic engagement and their pedagogy as observed in the classroom.*

Findings – *At the start of the project, the teachers hoped to involve students in critical thought and action on a local social problem. Yet, they doubted the depth of students' knowledge about injustices in their neighborhood. As the students shared their thoughts about budget cuts*

Youth Engagement: The Civic-Political Lives of Children and Youth
Sociological Studies of Children and Youth, Volume 16, 125–149
Copyright © 2013 by Emerald Group Publishing Limited
All rights of reproduction in any form reserved
ISSN: 1537-4661/doi:10.1108/S1537-4661(2013)0000016010

affecting a local park, the teachers expanded their constructs of the students' civic knowledge.

Value – *The paper argues that teachers' views of student knowledge are malleable and in the context of a learner-centered curriculum, they can position students as aware activists.*

Keywords: Youth civic engagement; civic knowledge; learner-centered curriculum; teacher thinking; counter-storytelling

INTRODUCTION

This study focuses on three teachers' constructions of students' civic knowledge as they planned for and enacted a civic engagement project in an urban middle school with low-income students of color. Such projects offer students opportunities to identify, research, deliberate, and take action around issues of social concern including gentrification, environmental degradation, and school inequity. The teachers wished for the project to tackle a local injustice that would promote high student motivation, yet they began the work concerned about the depth of their students' awareness of civic issues. Over time and in the context of a learner-centered curriculum, the students shared their thoughts about their community and illustrated their ability to engage with social problems. In learning of the students' ideas, the teachers expanded their views of the students, acknowledging their strengths. This article discusses the teachers' shift in thinking, suggesting how other educators can look for and value the civic insights of youth. The findings emerged as I addressed the following research questions: How do teachers construct students' knowledge of their community? How do curricular events shape teachers' views of students' civic knowledge?

When students' civic knowledge is aired and explored, students and teachers benefit. If students' civic knowledge is discounted, students are civically disenfranchised. Countering this tendency, if teachers honor and integrate students' civic experiences, students' sense of civic belonging and political agency can be augmented. As for teachers, when students' civic knowledge is shared, teachers learn valuable information about their students' lives that can be integrated into the curriculum. They can adopt students' concerns as their own and build on their change-making ideas and social insights. Furthermore, in casting the students as competent and agentic citizens, teachers can feel confident to enact robust civic projects. For these reasons, teachers should engage students as citizens who have knowledge to contribute and place students' concerns at the center of civic curricula, as opposed to constructing civic projects around predetermined topics or generic civic concepts such as the right to vote.

Such a framing of students as civic agents may not happen spontaneously; particular factors shape teachers' constructions of students' civic knowledge. In the case spotlighted in this paper, the teachers shifted their vision about the youth from a deficit perspective to a competency perspective in the context of learner-centered curriculum that created space for the students to communicate about a local civic problem: budget cuts facing a neighborhood park. This finding argues that teachers should enact learner-centered methods, in this case in a civically oriented curriculum, even when they doubt the knowledge that their students bring to it.

BACKGROUND

In their ideal form, youth civic engagement projects offer opportunities for youth to name and critique social problems, research them in a way that acknowledges their complexity, and take action to do something about them. The projects reflect Corsaro's (1997) view of young people as active participants in society and contributors to what may be understood as an adult world and the belief that this positioning fosters their sense of belonging and responsibility. Youth civic engagement projects also ideally develop youth's political skills and awareness. While civic engagement includes acts of community participation (e.g., volunteering, fundraising), it also includes forms of political engagement and political voice where citizens vote, protest, and canvass to express a point of view, often to influence the state (Levine, 2007). Participation in the political components of civic life involves a questioning of society's power structures. When students engage with politics by critiquing current policies, engaging with a diversity of opinions on public issues, and working with others to solve problems, they learn how to interface with political structures and also develop democratic patriotism (Westheimer, 2007).

Youth of color, such as those portrayed in this paper, may be inclined to engage in such politically oriented civic engagement so to critique and change their personal and communal circumstances. The members of low-income African American, Latino, immigrant, indigenous, and poor white communities often experience few individual rights, and so they work together to express collective political demands (Collins, 2010). Indeed, grassroots political organizing gives marginalized groups a form of resistance against social, economic, and environmental injustice. More specifically, students of color organized together can disrupt prevailing narratives about them as unable to succeed and easily abandoned by those who might support them (Hosang, 2006). They can organize and collectivize their experiences so as to advocate for more just political realities.

This paper looks at the way that teachers worked with students of color during a youth civic engagement project, at first doubting their ability to understand their political realities and critique social problems and later praising their civic knowledge as it emerged. This focus on teachers' views of students' civic knowledge is helpfully grounded in literature on how students' civic knowledge has been evaded and how it can be valued in the classroom.

Limiting Youth Civic Knowledge

Researchers have engaged in many efforts to understand students' civic knowledge, generally through the use of tests with a series of questions assessing the skills that the researchers deem important in civic life (Rubin, 2007). For example, one study focusing on the civic competencies of students with and without disabilities presents the results of a written test administered to students that assessed three competencies: ability to acquire and process data on political situations; ability to gauge the necessary level of involvement in political situations; and ability to utilize the political system to promote and protect public and private interests (Hamot, Shokoohi-Yekta, & Sasso, 2005). The authors acknowledged the limits of this test. Referencing a wide range of civic competencies, they write, "the reality exists that many of these competencies cannot be tested via a pencil and paper instrument," and they therefore only assessed "testable items" (p. 36). For example, Hamot et al. do not test for practices such as building solidarity with others or engaging in consensus-oriented decision making when determining a focus for civic action – two potentially quite important skills in civic engagement.

Such tests can yield some insights, yet they may inform a deficit view of students' civic knowledge. They assess decontextualized skills that do not amount to all that can be involved in civic participation. Studies with such close-ended designs "risk blinding us to the variety of forms of engagement that young people may be exploring" (Flacks, 2007, p. 79). Furthermore, these studies have contributed to evidence of a "civic achievement gap" between low-income students of color and middle-class or wealthy white students (Levinson, 2007), yet they leave it unclear how or why race, class, or educational attainment is related to civic learning (Rubin, 2007). Reflecting the way that the knowledge of low-income students of color is commonly skirted in classrooms, their civic skills and knowledge are similarly evaded in educational research.

Classroom teachers have also been seen to bypass students' civic insights. An international study, drawing on data from 200 civic-related teachers, shows that teachers in the United States were relatively unlikely to want to negotiate with students about what is taught in civic curriculum and were likely to favor standards-based teaching (Torney-Purta, Barber, & Richardson, 2005). Therefore, while teachers have reported a belief that students are involved in civic life (Feldman, 2007), they might be reticent to open the curriculum in a way that places students' concerns or experiences at the center. They are seemingly operating with an assumption that ideal youth citizenship is enacted when students can report back on standardized civic ideals, not necessarily on civic issues that impact them.

Standardized curricula often prioritize "official knowledge" as opposed to local knowledge of students situated in communities (Apple, 2000). Civic issues are more or less relevant for students depending on what social and economic conditions are impacting their lives. For some students, a pressing social issue may be gang violence, while for others it may be an oppressive school uniform policy, and for others the growing pressures they feel about school-based testing. Yet, these nuances are lost if teachers enact civic engagement projects on pre-determined topics, disregarding the students' experiences.

Finally, government programs and rhetoric can also reflect a deficit view of youth as citizens. For example, British mandates on civic education frame citizenship as involving a set of principles that need to be implanted in youth, side stepping what youth bring to the enterprise (Hart, 2009).

> Government policy and rhetoric on the need to control young people's behaviour and educate them in the values and practice of citizenship has meant that young people's relational experiences within their communities are often ignored, and also ones where they feel discriminated against and disempowered. (p. 648)

This framing of youth as needing to have a civic identity imposed on them, and the policy that extends from it, influences youth to have a diminished view of their own civic abilities. It also limits the likelihood that policy makers or teachers' will take action steps to foster young people's unique civic identities and ameliorate instances of youth discrimination that hinder their participation.

Honoring Youth Civic Knowledge

Despite trends to measure and seek to control students' civic identities in top-down manners, youth articulate and demonstrate sophisticated civic understandings. Drawing on interviews of youth from a range of socioeconomic and cultural positions of gender, class, race, and ethnicity, youth expressed how they experience citizenship in their lives and how they wish to participate (Hart, 2009). For example, they shared experiences of age-based discrimination – an important issue that they might address through a civic engagement project – and also their coveting of greater inclusion in an adult civic world. This confirms the finding that youth "place a high premium on constructive social participation" and are more aware of their responsibilities as citizens than politicians often assume (Lister, Smith, Middleton, & Cox, 2003, p. 251). More specifically, 16- and 17-year-old German youth engaging in politically active communities described shared political opinions, reported the practice of demonstrating with precision, and in general positioned themselves as part of a larger political movement (Pfaff, 2009). These studies illustrate the civic competencies of youth and, in using interview-based methodologies, present an alternative to tests that only measure civic skills the researchers deem important.

Research that spotlights the lived, contextual civic knowledge of youth has been particularly valuable in recasting the civic experiences of students of color. One key study of this type argues that urban youth of color are likely to experience a "disjuncture" between the civic ideal of justice and their own life stories, in comparison to their White affluent peers (Rubin, 2007). Again, instead of focusing on a pre-determined list of civic behaviors that the students may or may not embrace, this research draws on interviews and in-class discussions to describe how youth experience democracy. With knowledge of the "disjunctures," teachers can explicitly engage students around them and together explore how to navigate them.

Another study, employing a similar interview-based methodology, sought to understand the civic identities of secondary students from immigrant backgrounds and those from "dominant-culture" families (Myers & Zaman, 2009). They learned that the immigrant students favored "universal positions" that emphasized all people's shared rights while the dominant-culture students more often sought to balance their national and global interests. Yet, over half of the students took different positions on particular subcategories of these spectrums. These findings can help teachers recognize that students' civic identities are contextualized and nuanced and that students have civic ideas to share.

Presenting an alternative to enacting standardized civic projects, admirable teachers facilitate civic projects that affirm students' civic knowing. For example, teachers enact interactive class activities such as group work and in turn create environments in which students speak their minds and dialogue about social realities that shape their lives. In a study of Latino youth, those who attended schools that promoted an open climate for discussion and collaborative work reported greater positive views toward immigrants' rights than those who attended schools without this climate (Torney-Purta, Barber, & Wilkenfeld, 2007). All the Latino youth were assessed to have more positive views of immigrants' rights than their non-Latino peers, but their school environments had a relationship with the extent to which this was expressed. This suggests that when teachers welcome students' knowledge into the classroom, students embrace the opportunity to voice their opinions. Their perspectives can then become a source of knowledge from which teachers and students can learn.

Moving beyond discussion, youth work with adult mentors, who are at times school teachers, to take action on local problems that students identify, such as violence and poverty (e.g., Cammarota & Romero, 2009; Ginwright & Cammarota, 2007; Rubin, Hayes, & Benson, 2009; B. D. Schultz, 2008). These studies portray the power of mentors to enact curricula that are "decentralized and tailored to local school populations," as compared to those that teach standardized sets of political principles and practices (Gimpel & Lay, 2006, p. 13). The teachers seemed to be operating with an assumption that ideal youth citizenship entails youth speaking out on problems that matter to them. The studies also continue to illustrate the potential strength of student civic voice, and particularly, despite the proposed civic achievement gap between youth of color and their white peers (Levinson, 2007), the articles display the power of youth of color to advocate for change. For example, in one fifth-grade classroom in Chicago, students of color created and enacted an advocacy campaign for the building of a new school, reaching the press and politicians with their critical message, as their school suffered from great neglect and was in need of much repair (B. D. Schultz, 2008). Such projects enable students to take on and speak out about social injustices that impact their lives, ideally augmenting the possibility that they continue to do this in the future.

This paper builds on this work by illustrating how teachers' thinking generatively shifts during projects that center students' civic concerns. When teachers counter the trend to control or monitor students' civic identities through closed-ended tests and pre-determined civic curricula, students can be positioned as powerful civic actors, a positioning that is particularly notable for students of color. In turn, teachers can move past the assumption that students have little civic knowledge to offer, recognize their insights about their communities, and integrate them into their own evolving views of youth and social change.

PERSPECTIVES

The paper reflects multiple assumptions. First, I am oriented toward a view of curriculum as enacted. Within this perspective, teachers and students work together to create a lived curriculum that is responsive to students' needs and interests (Snyder, Bolin, & Zumwalt, 1992). This contrasts with situations in which teachers seek to implement a curriculum with fidelity in response to external pressures (i.e., teaching to the test or teaching a scripted curriculum with rigid sequencing). Enacting curriculum, as opposed to implementing it, allows teachers to embrace a learner-centered teaching philosophy, view students as the "starting point" in instruction and "co-participants" in the learning process, and prioritize "intense student engagement" (Paris & Combs, 2006, p. 576). These principles assume that students can direct the curriculum along with the teacher. It may be particularly important for students to gain such authority during civic projects, as these projects serve as a medium through which students learn to use power in society (B. D. Schultz & Oyler, 2006).

Second, while I position teachers and students as possible agents in curriculum enactment, I believe that teachers best ensure that students can use their empowerment in the classroom. In the norms of schooling, teachers are positioned with more power than students (Tyack & Cuban, 1995) and must often deliberately decide to share their authority if it is to happen. When addressing political issues, teachers are "the most essential element" in orienting students toward social justice (Lalas, 2007, p. 19). Given this, I direct my attention to teacher thinking during civic engagement projects. And, so to yield a nuanced picture of teachers, I avoid romanticizing or simplifying teachers' experiences and portray them with texture (Hargreaves, 1996).

Finally, I employ a critical analytic lens, spotlighting how some groups' knowledge is socially and historically de-legitimized, coupled with an interpretive perspective that views all experience as socially constructed (as seen in Rubin, 2007). Within the critical paradigm, critical race theory was helpful in looking at how teachers can oppose racial hegemony, and other forms of subordination, as they establish the relevance of their students' voices and challenge traditional views of people of color through counter-storytelling (Ladson Billings, 2000). The teacher participants in this study crafted such a counter-story about their students. Over time, they positioned the youth as informed and able to encourage change, countering a tendency to view students of color through a deficit lens. The interpretive perspective enabled me to view the teachers' views as malleable, given the assumption that knowledge and identity are built through interaction – they are not absolute (Lincoln & Guba, 2003). This is seen in spite of the way that stories can reflect entrenched hierarchies brought to the fore through critical theory.

SCHOOL SETTING AND TEACHERS

I learned about the Fields School,[1] the site for this study, upon attending a public event to celebrate sixth-grade students' studies on a local university's expansion into their urban neighborhood populated mainly by Black and Latino/a families with a low socioeconomic status. Through the event, the public K–7 school emerged for me as one that promoted civic projects that took students' local experiences into account. Specifically, the teachers and students had addressed the university expansion through a once-a-week project that was separate from content-area instruction. Impressed by the work, I inquired into the teachers' interest in enacting civic projects through the content areas, and was greeted with enthusiasm and questions about how it could be done.

In response to the teachers' interest, I invited them to attend a series of colloquia during which we would study pedagogical possibilities for civic engagement projects, and ultimately plan and reflect on an enacted project in their subject areas.[2] The most consistent attendees to the colloquia were the seventh-grade math/science teacher Mr. Sevino, the English/social studies teacher Ms. Holly, and a special education support teacher Ms. Oaks.

All the three teachers were people of color and had been teaching in the school for several years. Possibly for these reasons, the teachers commonly expressed concern for the social injustices characterizing the students' neighborhood. In one discussion about the lack of bookstores in the area, Ms. Oaks associated herself directly with the students: "Do they want our minds to grow or not? ... Do they want to open our minds, bring us more knowledge, more books that we can really get into?" Using words like "us" and "our" shows how Ms. Oaks positioned herself as a part of the students' world – despite the fact that she did not live in the neighborhood and never had. Ms. Holly similarly lived and was raised in a different area, but she spoke with knowledge and compassion about problems characterizing the school community including gentrification and low employment rates. Comparatively, Mr. Sevino was from the students' neighborhood and frequently shared his political concerns about it during the colloquia. For example, he raised conversations about the potentially unhealthy number of cell phone towers in the school's vicinity. Aware of high asthma rates, he also shared that when he takes runs in the area he can barely breathe and can go much farther in other environments.

Alongside the teachers' connections to and concerns about the students' community, they also distanced themselves from or critiqued the community's civic capabilities in some ways. For example, during our first official colloquia, Mr. Sevino explained that there are fewer problems in communities where the residents are better educated, noting that when an injustice occurs near the school, "People here won't question it." While he felt concern, and at times outrage, about the cell phone towers and other issues, he also looked down on the community for its perceived inability to fight back. It is this tension between honoring and critiquing local civic experience that is explored in this paper.

The teachers' content-area interests were also frontloaded during our opening colloquia. Ms. Holly and Ms. Oaks were interested in sharpening students' language skills and shared various ideas of speaking and writing assignments, related to the English and social studies content areas, that would address local civic issues. Mr. Sevino expressed more concern about finding room in the math and science curricula for conversations about relevant social issues, yet, as the colloquia began, he intended to find opportunities.

The teachers' goals for the project, reflected an ideal of youth engagement as involving knowledge and action. First, when I asked Ms. Oaks and Ms. Holly what they thought could happen during the project, they cited debates and research – examples of knowledge-building processes. Through research, the students could build the "awareness and information" that Mr. Sevino saw as important in civic engagement. Second, they cited action steps the students could take. Ms. Oaks talked about supporting them to voice their own opinions, and "not just repeat back what they have heard." Specifically, Mr. Sevino suggested that they could "reach community officials," and they envisioned the students speaking on community-based issues on the school loudspeaker. Ms. Holly was intrigued that students might take "real world, valid actions," noting that she was not used to doing that in her classroom. Overall, the teachers described an idealized form of citizenship that included both knowledge building and action, reflecting a vision of "enlightened political engagement" in which citizens take action in knowledgeable and principled ways (Parker, 2003, p. 33). The analysis presented in this paper explores how the teachers framed the students' abilities to pursue this ideal.

METHODS

Between December and June, 13 colloquia were held, each lasting approximately 45 minutes. Through the colloquia, we developed a community through which the teachers could "engage in existing practice" and also "begin to establish their own identity in its future" (Lave & Wenger, 1990, p. 115). At the beginning of our work, we explored samples of existing practice in civic education by learning about case studies of youth organizing around environmental injustices in Tar Creek, Oklahoma (Kesson & Oyler, 1999) and for a new school in Chicago, Illinois (B. D. Schultz, 2008). We also discussed and experienced pedagogical strategies used in civic engagement projects, including those that support research on local issues and deliberative discussions, and planned for the start of a project in their classes. Then, we held a colloquium when the project was being enacted to discuss how it was unfolding. The final colloquium was held at the end of the project and prompted the teachers' reflection on their experience.

Overall, during the colloquia, we constructed knowledge of how to facilitate meaningful youth civic participation. Indeed, the methodological decision to hold such colloquia reflects my belief that knowledge is emergent and displayed through interaction (Lincoln & Guba, 2003). I viewed the colloquia as prime locations for the teachers to build their visions and evaluations of civic education. All of the colloquia were audiotaped and transcribed.

I also visited the school to observe the project unfold in Ms. Holly and Ms. Oaks' English/social studies block. While the teachers and I looked for opportunities to extend this project into the math and science content areas, by late April, the math/science teacher felt that the curricula for these classes was too constrained to make room for the civic project. Conversely, Ms. Holly felt that the skills and approach of the project would fit nicely in her classes. In turn, she enacted a seven-week project, co-teaching with Ms. Oaks who worked most directly with students with learning disabilities and English language learners.

During five of the seven key weeks of the unit, I visited the class twice each week and observed a total of twelve lessons enacted during the combined English and social studies block. I recorded fieldnotes with a pen in my observation journal and extended them into lengthy, typed documents following each visit. During the lessons, I aimed to collect "unobtrusive data" (Hatch, 1995, p. 214) and generally observed without interfering with classroom events.

When entering the analysis process, I reviewed all transcripts from the colloquia and fieldnotes and engaged in open coding in which I filled the margins with notes about the data. Then I studied the codes, looking for common categories into which the data could be sorted. I ultimately created indexes of the data on categories including one entitled "teacher views on student civic knowledge and voice." I then divided each of the indexes into subsections, based on the coded findings. The index on teachers' views on students' civic knowledge and voice, the focus of this paper, included subsections on the teachers' doubts, interests, and praise for student knowledge and excerpts of illustrative data. Finally, I composed analytic memos about the overarching themes in each category, yielding the analysis presented below.

TEACHERS' MALLEABLE VIEWS OF STUDENTS' CIVIC KNOWLEDGE

Over the planning and project enactment period, the teachers were seen to (1) doubt the strength of students' civic awareness; (2) value learner-centered pedagogy that would promote student voice; and (3) praise students' emergent concerns and proposals for social change. As evident in these themes, the teachers' assumptions shifted and expanded throughout our work together. First, they claimed that the students had little civic knowledge to share, yet they also assumed that learner-centered methods should be used. Then, they came to propose that students' civic voices are powerful and that they do have insight to contribute.

Doubting the Strength of Students' Civic Awareness

Six weeks before the start of the project, the teachers argued that the students lacked social awareness. Concerning potential "disjunctures" between civic ideals and the students' experiences (Rubin, 2007), the teachers said the students "don't see it" and "don't recognize it." Mr. Sevino's concern led him to consistently question how he was going to craft a unit that interested the students. He remarked,

> How are we going to get those kids to be curious about something? ... The kids probably don't see a problem, a social issue going on here. They don't see it. So, we need to make them aware that there are issues that they should be concerned with. How are we going to do that?

This statement begins and ends with a question about how the work was going to ignite student concern, as he believed that the students did not have pressing concerns of their own.

Ms. Oaks and Ms. Holly agreed with this thesis. Ms. Oaks deemed that the students needed to be

> more in tune to what's happening in their own community ... If we go about taking a quick survey [about issues in their community], more than half are going to say, 'I didn't know.' And that's really unbelievable.

Here, Ms. Oaks inferred that the students were not "in tune" to events and trends in their community. Ms. Holly agreed that concerning social injustices and the need to "question the status quo," "They don't recognize it. They don't." These quotes illustrate the teachers' concerns that the students were unaware about social issues and were not involved in their amelioration. This aspect of the teachers' dialogue re-enforced a dominant narrative that frames poor youth of color in a deficit lens, mirroring the low expectations that they face in society (Nieto, 2004). More specifically, it reflected the finding that poor urban youth of color are lacking in civic knowledge (see Levinson, 2007).

At times, their dialogues contained more nuance, and the teachers spoke about issues of which they believed the students were more or less aware. Ms. Holly suggested that the students did have familiarity with "drugs, the gangs, the violence" because these problems are "closer to home" and issues that they "see everyday." Then, she continued, "Now, as far as the bigger issues, larger, like political and social issues," such as "the pollution coming from [the park] or the construction going on in the neighborhood" or "a comparison between desirable neighborhoods, or those that they might consider to be more desirable, and the problems in their neighborhoods ... I don't think they're aware of the issues." During this colloquium, she suggested that drugs, gangs, and violence are not large political and social issues, presumably because she saw them as ongoing and not linked to any timely campaign unfolding in the community. In comparison, in our colloquia, we studied how local community-based organizations were mobilizing around the particular issues of the maintenance of a nearby park and the construction of a bus depot, as civic bodies were imminently due to make decisions about them. Ms. Holly formed a hierarchy of more and less important civic issues and evaluated the students in reference to it. With the use of such hierarchies, educators or researchers make judgments about what students are able to contribute based on a pre-determined, limited list of civic skills or knowledge.

Given their assumption of the students' minimal civic awareness, the teachers were resolved to instigate its growth in the context of the project. Ms. Sevino commented, "We need to create some kind of awareness." More specifically, Ms. Holly remarked that the students know very little about the organizations that receive the money from their school charity project and told Ms. Oaks and Mr. Sevino that "we need to bring the information to them." While teachers can play an important role in introducing students to relevant information about their social contexts, this statement illustrates the way in which they generally positioned *themselves* as empowered, not the students, at the start of the colloquia. They felt that they could "bring" knowledge to the students, suggesting that you can "bank" social awareness in a top-down manner (Freire, 1970), or "create" awareness and assuming the students did not have important forms of awareness at the start. Mr. Sevino felt that the previous year's projects on the university expansion had "enlightened" the students and he wanted to continue on this trend. The teachers doubted the youth's abilities to contribute their own ideas on pressing civic issues and sought to enlighten them and fill the gap in their civic knowledge.

Valuing Learner-Centered Pedagogy

While the teachers claimed that the students lacked awareness or knowledge of social issues, they idealized learner-centered instructional strategies that would promote the students' voices. This was seen most sharply when they discussed how they would determine what social issue around which to organize. They did not want to tell the students which problem they should address; they wanted the problem to be named by the students. Ms. Holly articulated a vision. She said, "It should come from the bottom up," explaining that the idea should come from the students. Later, she presented her view of the students as potential civic agents by noting that there are "problems that kids could make the public aware of." She acknowledged that the students had civic concerns to draw on as well as civic abilities to raise awareness in their community.

The teachers suggested the use of multiple pedagogical strategies that could be used to learn about the students' concerns. First, Ms. Holly suggested that they "poll" the students: "We should poll. Let's get some ideas. What do they think are the bigger issues in their neighborhoods? What things do they look around and see are lacking?" She also suggested: "Maybe we could do some group work and have the kids pick the issue that they want to talk about. Like pollution, or maybe gangs." Ms. Holly explained that with data on the students' ideas, the teachers could "jot down their comments and make a little web of their major concerns." She was brainstorming ways for the teachers to prompt and then analyze the students' civic interests. This type of commentary suggested a shift from the previous type that reflected the assumption that the students' had few areas of concern or interest and it was the responsibility of the teachers to create awareness.

Then, Mr. Sevino presented the idea of giving students cameras and asking them to take pictures that document the social inequities in their community. He explained: "Photographs are a good starter for conversation. I think that is a good idea – have a walking tour, take some pictures." Mr. Sevino also suggested that during a community walk, they could ask the students to "write down what you notice, anything that pops into your head."

Finally, Ms. Holly offered that they hold an "open forum" during which students could orally share their concerns. Mr. Sevino advocated for it: "We should see what they have to say, give them a voice. Then, if we see that it's either too broad where they're going nowhere, then we could guide them to a particular spot." This suggestion gained the most interest among the teachers and they marked a date in their calendars during which they would hold it. The open forum would have provided a context for the students to engage in grassroots politics together – a powerful framing of community for people of color who may feel that in working together they can change their circumstances (Collins, 2010).

Counter to the finding that teachers do not want to negotiate with students about what is taught in civic-related courses (Torney-Purta et al., 2005), the Fields School teachers seemed quite committed to negotiating with them. At times, the teachers resisted positioning themselves as banking educators (Freire, 1970) and wanted to shape the curriculum with and around the students' ideas. To this end, they proposed the use of strategies that might have positioned the students as "starting points" in the curriculum – a key quality of learner-centered teaching (Paris & Combs, 2006). This is a particularly important move to make when working with students of color, as dominant knowledge generally ignores or distorts the experiences of marginalized groups. As students tell their stories, they can speak of their own ethnic and cultural backgrounds and add to the class texts available, as teachers struggle to find materials that represent all of their students' backgrounds (K. Schultz, 2009).

Furthermore, the teachers emerged as committed to instruction through which students express themselves in oral, print, and visual text. They imagined students speaking in an open forum, writing what they notice about their community, and taking pictures so to share their civic concerns. Such multimodal pedagogical strategies can offer students fruitful opportunities to participate (K. Schultz, 2009). For example, a student who is shy or thinks that his or her particular experience is not welcome in the classroom, possibly due to its race or class-based implications, might be more willing to air it through alternative, or arts-based modalities.

Overall, these activities could support students' empowerment as civic decision makers and actors, and the teachers' commitment to enacting them stood in potential contrast to their belief that the students were unaware of community issues. Indeed, it seems curious that the same teachers who agreed that the students "don't recognize" social problems suggested that the students' social insights should direct the curriculum. As the teachers talked about their plans, a counter-story about the students' civic knowledge began.

Centering Students' Emergent Concerns and Proposals

One week before the launching of the project, a clear civic concern was raised by students. In the face of large-scale state budget cuts, the services offered in a local public park were placed at risk. Two students brought a petition to the classroom that asked policy makers to ensure full funding for the park. Without this funding, the park's hours would be shortened and the outdoor pool would stay closed – two proposed limitations among others. The topic of the park had been discussed among the teachers, yet dismissed as something the students knew little about. However, once informed about the petition by the students, Ms. Holly and Ms. Oaks praised the students' identification of the problem and commented that they found a topic that "really excited the kids." They chose to pursue this topic raised by the students – a learner-centered teaching method.

The planned open forum was replaced with a forum in which they elicited students' opinions on the budget cuts. Ms. Holly told the students that they were going to run an "opinion machine," and asked them to walk around the class and find other classmates that felt the same way about the budget cuts as they did. After this activity, the teachers came to believe that the majority of the class was upset about the potential cuts and developed a project dedicated to restoring the budget. Over the following seven weeks, students researched the history of the park and present budget crisis, interviewed an official from the parks department, wrote letters to their local assemblyman protesting the cuts, and participated in a school assembly to inform other students about this issue, "the work they did, and its impact. As seen during the "opinion machine," the students aired their own values and concerns at varying points during the project – making them available sources of knowledge from which their peers and teachers could learn.

A lesson in which the teachers and students enacted a deliberative forum proved to particularly center the students' ideas. As the students were writing letters to the local assembly man, one student asked, "How are we going to tell him what we want?" Instead of only describing the problem of the deficit, this student wanted to present some ideas of how the park budget could be restored. In turn, Ms. Holly asked the students to brainstorm different solutions to the deficit. She wrote on the top of the board, "How can we reduce the budget cuts at [the park][3]?" and following each proposed solution, she prompted the students to consider its benefits and drawbacks (see *Teacher's guide to national issues forums (NIF) in the classroom*, 2005). Students' ideas were recorded on the board, in the form of a chart, and then transferred to a poster that hung in the class for the remainder of the project. By the end of the lesson, the students had proposed three solutions to the budget gap: (1) raise park service fees, (2) open a souvenir shop and visitors center in the park, and (3) hold a benefit concert or basketball game for the park. These ideas prove that the seventh graders were ready to think proactively about how to help the park stay fully functioning.

Their civic values and concerns were also illustrated in the benefits and drawbacks to these proposed action steps as noted by Ms. Holly on the chart. First, the students were interested in the social capital of the park. They thought that the souvenir shop would positively attract more tourists and the benefit concert, featuring perhaps a rap artist, would bring "fans" and "exposure" to the issue. Second, the students were concerned about the economic status of community members. They feared that if service fees were introduced, such as a charge to enter the park, the "fees may be too high for some visitors." Presenting an economic benefit for the community, they suggested that a souvenir shop would create jobs – a thought that was presented on the chart as "generate ongoing jobs for sales people." Third, they expressed worry about the financial and logistical feasibility of running a souvenir shop or a benefit event. Noted on the board was their concern about the "cost of sales goods" for the souvenir shop and "cost of support staff, security, food vendors, and sanitation" for the benefit events. These notes signified the students' insights about the needs of the community and the park.

This lesson is significant in two ways. First, it illustrates how the teachers honored the students' local and context-specific proposals by prompting them and recording versions of them on the board. Alternatively, the teachers might have ignored the students' ideas and told them, in a top-down manner, the solutions debated in the news or in the state government including the importance of raising taxes. The teachers supported an open discussion of a civic issue and in turn allowed students' knowledge of such issues to emerge (as seen in Torney-Purta et al., 2007).

Second, the lesson helped the teachers affirm and praise students' funds of knowledge (Moll, Amanti, Neff, & Gonzalez, 1992). In recapping the lesson to me later that afternoon, Ms. Holly remarked that the students came up with "really good ideas." Then, during the final colloquium, the following exchange occurred between Ms. Holly and Ms. Oaks as they described the deliberation:

> Ms. Holly: The ideas were things that I don't think I would have even ...
>
> Ms. Oaks: Come up with
>
> Ms. Holly: Come up with, because they have their hands on the pulse of the city. Oh, bring in a celebrity. You could do a rapper. You could do a basketball star. I was like, 'Wow,' I wouldn't have thought of that.
>
> Ms. Oaks: There was so much. They really had their passion.
>
> Ms. Holly: Even the souvenir shop idea. That was amazing ... That was a good idea, because other public venues have the souvenir shop. Why not [the park]? You know? Why not?
>
> Ms. Oaks: It was a small seed but it just kept blooming.

The teachers valued the knowledge the students expressed. In particular, Ms. Holly was intrigued by the students' suggestion that a rapper or basketball player could help bring positive attention to the park – a reaction that suggests she appreciated the students' knowledge and its role in the classroom. Indeed, hip-hop is a viable "vehicle for social change" and "platform from which to comment on the world" as the lyrics often speaks directly to the injustices in urban communities and is associated with black culture (Hallman, 2009, pp. 42–43). When the students suggested that rap could be used as a means to help the park and their idea was validated, the students and teachers entered a space where this cultural reference could be affirmed.

Later in the concluding colloquium, Ms. Oaks expressed the way she came to value the students' ideas. In fact, she identified her recognition of the students' knowledge as a significant part of her learning during this project. I asked the teachers what skills or values they plan to take with them into the future and Ms. Oaks responded: "What I'm taking out of this is a lot of knowledge of the kids. Don't underestimate them. They do have a voice and it's a powerful one. That's what I'm taking out of this."

THOUGHTS ON TEACHERS' CONSTRUCTIONS OF STUDENTS' CIVIC KNOWLEDGE

The three themes reviewed above illustrate the malleable nature of teachers' thinking about student knowledge. At the beginning of our work together, the Fields School teachers were concerned with gaps in student knowledge and (yet) committed to learner-centered methods, such as the use of a student poll and open forum, that implied that the students had knowledge to share. Then, the teachers chose to follow the students' lead in reference to their concern about the park and valued their proposals on filling the deficit. Alongside the use of learner-centered teaching methods, the teachers came to honor the students' civic mindedness that they had questioned at the start and embraced a counter-story about the students as activists. They began the project with a belief that the students knew little about social injustices, and expanded their views, ultimately suggesting that in some ways the students' knowledge trumped their own. The remainder of this paper reviews the significance of these findings.

Valuing Learner-Centered Methods

Potentially most importantly, the study suggests the value of learner-centered methods, as it was in the context of the teachers' use of such methods that they composed a counter-story about the students' social awareness. They used learner-centered methods both when they placed the students' interest in the park at the heart of the project and when they asked the students to draw on their own ideas in the deliberation on the deficit. As the students' knowledge about the park and possible solutions to the deficit was revealed, the teachers learned from it. When student insight emerges in this way, teachers can be inspired by what students have to offer and enact instruction based on the students' ideas. Also, when learner-centered strategies are used, students learn that their ideas matter. It was difficult for the teachers to draw the students away from the deliberation on solutions for the budget gap and had to remind them that it was lunchtime. Learner-centered methods motivate and deeply involve youth.

Such pedagogical moves might be particularly important for teachers who are working with students whose knowledge has been historically under-valued because of their race, class, age, gender, ethnicity, sexual orientation, or ability. In these communities, teachers should be vigilant to not reinforce a story about their students as unaware and utilize learner-centered methods to help them look for the valuable knowledge that they have to share. This can be the case with teachers with a range of racial identities, as in this case, teachers of color, who may be assumed to have an affirming view of students of color, learned to better value the students' knowledge in the context of a learner-centered civic project. When all teachers enact methods that ask students to share their ideas, they can learn about and can generatively draw on the motivations and experiences of their students.

Placing "Official Knowledge" on Hold

Second, this study is significant because it offers a rationale for placing "official" or predictable knowledge on hold as teachers center students' knowledge (Apple, 2000). This was illustrated in the lesson on solutions to the deficit, a lesson that seemed to especially enhance the teachers' counter-story about the students' civic knowledge. Critics may devalue this activity, as the solutions were not representative of those in the broader society. Parker (2003) argues that in deliberative forums, it is important to air a diversity of opinions that mirrors the opinions of all stakeholders. Based on this understanding, the Fields School students' proposals of raising service fees, opening a souvenir shop, and holding a charity event may seem inadequate, because they did not include solutions such as raising taxes or cutting funds from other state programs, aside from the parks. Government officials and interest groups readily debated these options, yet they were not raised by the students and potentially should have been by the teachers. To counter this critique, the teachers could be praised for the way they honored the students' voices and drew on ideas that came from the students. Had they entered the deliberative forum committed to airing three or four pre-established approaches – as is seen in standardized civic instruction and assessment – they may have had less of an opportunity to learn from and admire the students' ideas. Furthermore, the students would have been limited in their opportunity to share and develop their ideas about deficit. Or, if the students' ideas were bypassed completely, the students may have easily felt disinvested from the activity.

Given this potential debate over the strength of the "solutions" lesson, I believe that we can both praise and extend Ms. Holly and Ms. Oaks's pedagogy in this activity. When teachers listen for and honor students' unique civic ideas, as Ms. Holly and Ms. Oaks did, they acknowledge students as active and thoughtful citizens. In addition to validating students' ideas, teachers look for opportunities to discuss approaches to civic problems that are representative of those held by other stakeholders, yet not immediately apparent to the students. The teachers might have first welcomed the students' proposals on filling the budget gap, placing other ideas on hold, and then shared proposals such as raising taxes, crafting a web of ideas for the students to consider. Ultimately, as long as teachers *add to*, rather than seek to replace, students' ideas, the work remains learner-centered and expands the students' understanding of the issues at hand.

Prompting Shifts in Teacher's Thinking

Finally, and most generally, this study is significant in the way it can remind teachers and teacher educators how educators' thinking can and should shift over time. In particular, this study argues that they can grow increasingly adept at seeing and valuing student knowledge. Teachers may find themselves doubting their students' abilities and can reflect on this story of teachers and students in the Fields School to consider how to draw on students' civic, or otherwise, insights. Teacher educators can introduce cases such as this to prompt this reflection. Or, teacher educators may find it fruitful to craft assignments that ask teacher candidates to research students' civic knowledge, or interests in general. Such assignments where teacher candidates learn about individual students have been seen to help candidates question their original assumptions about students (Goodwin, 2002), as Ms. Holly and Ms. Oaks did.

Again, teachers of varied racial backgrounds can learn to better value students' knowledge. White teachers have been seen to frame racism as benign and struggle with developing cultural competence in comparison to teachers of color who recognize the real limitations that students of color face (Gere, Buehler, Dallavis, & Haviland, 2009). Therefore, teacher educators might focus on shifting white teachers' thinking in a way that helps them understand and affirm all their students' experiences. Yet, this project illustrates how teachers of color can also shift and expand their views of their students.

Before concluding, it is important to share two caveats in relation to these reflections. First, teachers do not necessarily build insight about their students, or develop a value-based view of them, in a way that essentializes them as all good. While the Fields School teachers' praise and interest in the students' insights seemed to grow as I continued working with them, I do not seek to argue that they eliminated all concern for their abilities. Indeed, through the enactment of project and letter writing process in particular, the teachers had multiple opportunities to feel concern for the students' skills and voiced them. If teachers are to move toward an increased appreciation of students' voices, I assume that their movement will be nuanced in which they acknowledge students' struggles, possibly at times doubt their abilities to achieve, yet continue to craft new, positive insights about them. What is essential is that movement happens, teachers question their initial assumptions, and deficit views that exclusively or routinely minimize students' abilities as civic actors and in other ways are questioned and shifted. It is this questioning and shifting that occurred for Ms. Holly and Ms. Oaks.

Furthermore, despite my praise for their learner-centered strategies, many obstacles can get in the way of their full use. It is possible for teachers to prompt students' voices, yet do so with an intention to fill gaps in their knowledge. Such a perspective might have led the teachers to enact an open forum, for example, in which they praise students' knowledge of the social problems that the teachers think are important and ignore contributions about others. Or, if teachers share additional civic approaches for the students to consider, their "adding on" might quickly become "imposing on" if the teachers' ideas become the only ones discussed as the project progresses. This could silence students who feel steered toward views that are different from their own. It would interrupt an opportunity for students to use a "language of community that potentially provides a functional statement of collective political demand" – a particularly productive move for communities of color (Collins, 2010, p. 16). Overall, teachers' enactments of what they believe are learner-centered strategies may not ensure that students' voices get fully heard. Also, it is difficult to reflect on the power of learner-centered methods without noting that Mr. Sevino did not perceive his content-area curricula as allowing him to use them in reference to civic engagement in the classroom. Teachers might feel comfortable brainstorming about open forums and community walks, but struggle to find space in the curriculum for this exploratory work or civic engagement in general. Rigid pacing calendars and top-down expectations particularly hinder learner-centered teaching.

These obstacles should be seen as real, yet not binding in an absolute sense, and so, I aim for this paper to support teachers to find opportunities, which might be small at first, to enact learner-centered curriculum uplifting students' civic ideas in the classroom, even when they are doubted. Students have real, lived civic concerns. Schools should offer them opportunities to voice them as they exist in the present and act on them (Biesta, 2007). While teachers in the Fields School first doubted student's civic knowledge, they ultimately experimented with the understanding that youth hold important civic insight and centered it in their instruction. As they enacted learner-centered methods, their thinking shifted and the students emerged as informed civic actors.

NOTES

1. The name of the school is a pseudonym as are all names of teachers and students, so to ensure the anonymity of the participants.
2. The original study of the teachers' experiences in the colloquia, the enacted civic curriculum, and the students' responses was conducted in association with The Kettering Foundation, Dayton, Ohio.
3. To protect the participants' anonymity, the official name of the park was eliminated and will be referred to as "the park."

REFERENCES

Apple, M. W. (2000). *Official knowledge: Democratic education in a conservative age.* New York: Routledge.

Biesta, G. (2007). Education and the democratic person: Towards a political conception of democratic education. *Teachers College Record, 109*(3), 740–769.

Cammarota, J., & Romero, A. F. (2009). A social justice epistemology and pedagogy for Latina/o students: Transforming public education with participatory action research. *New Directions for Youth Development, 123*, 53–65.

Collins, P. H. (2010). The new politics of community. *American Sociological Review, 75*(1), 7–30.

Corsaro, W. A. (1997). *The sociology of childhood.* Thousand Oaks, CA: Sage.

Feldman, D. (2007). Citizenship education: Current perspectives from teachers in three states. *Educational Research Quarterly, 30*(4), 3–15.

Flacks, M. (2007). "Label jars not people": How (not) to study youth civic engagement. In A. Best (Ed.), *Representing youth: Methodological issues in critical youth studies* (pp. 60–83). New York: New York University Press.

Freire, P. (1970). *Pedagogy of the oppressed.* New York: The Continuum International Publishing Group.

Gere, A. R., Buehler, J., Dallavis, C., & Haviland, V. S. (2009). A visibility project: Learning to see how preservice teachers take up culturally responsive pedagogy. *American Educational Research Journal, 46*(3), 816–852.

Gimpel, J. G., & Lay, J. C. (2006). Youth at-risk for non-participation. In P. Levine & J. Youniss (Eds.), *Youth civic engagement: An institutional turn* (pp. 10–15). Medford, MA: CIRCLE (The Center for Information and Research on Civic Learning and Engagement).

Ginwright, S., & Cammarota, J. (2007). Youth activism in the urban community: Learning critical civic praxis within community organizations. *International Journal of Qualitative Studies in Education, 20*(6), 693–710.

Goodwin, A. L. (2002). The case of one child: Making the shift from personal knowledge to professionally informed practice. *Teaching Education, 13*(2), 137–154.

Hallman, H. L. (2009). "Dear Tupac, you speak to me": Recruiting hip hop as curriculum at a school for pregnant and parenting teens. *Equity and Excellence in Education, 42*(1), 36–51.

Hamot, G. E., Shokoohi-Yekta, M., & Sasso, G. M. (2005). Civic competencies and students with disabilities. *Journal of Social Studies Research, 29*(2), 34–45.

Hargreaves, A. (1996). Revisiting voice. *Educational Researcher, 25*(1), 12–19.

Hart, S. (2009). The 'problem' with youth: Young people, citizenship, and the community. *Citizenship Studies, 13*(6), 641–657.

Hatch, J. A. (1995). Ethical conflicts in classroom research: Examples from a study of peer stigmatization in kindergarten. In J. A. Hatch (Ed.), *Qualitative research in early childhood settings* (pp. 213–222). Westport, CT: Praeger.

Hosang, D. (2006). Beyond policy: Ideology, race and the reimagining of youth. In S. Ginwright, P. Noguera & J. Cammarota (Eds.), *Beyond resistance! Youth activism and community change: New democratic possibilities for practice and policy for America's youth* (pp. 3–19). New York: Routledge.

Kesson, K., & Oyler, C. (1999). Integrated curriculum and service learning: Linking school-based knowledge and social action. *English Education, 31*(2), 135–149.

Ladson Billings, G. (2000). Racialized discourses and ethnic epistemologies. In N. K. Denzin & D. S. Lincoln (Eds.), *Handbook of qualitative research* (2nd ed., pp. 257–277). London: Sage.

Lalas, J. (2007). Teaching for social justice in multicultural urban schools: Conceptualization and classroom implication. *Multicultural Education, 14*(3), 17–21.

Lave, J., & Wenger, E. (1990). *Situated learning: Legitimate peripheral participation.* Cambridge: Cambridge University Press.

Levine, P. (2007). *The future of democracy: Developing the next generation of American citizens.* Medford: Tufts University Press.

Levinson, M. (2007). *The civic achievement gap.* Medford, MA: CIRCLE.

Lincoln, Y. S., & Guba, E. G. (2003). Paradigmatic controversies, contradictions, and emerging confluences. In N. K. Denzin & Y. S. Lincoln (Eds.), *The landscape of qualitative research* (pp. 253–291). Thousand Oaks, CA: Sage Publications.

Lister, R., Smith, N., Middleton, S., & Cox, L. (2003). Young people talk about citizenship: Empirical perspectives on theoretical and political debates. *Citizenship Studies, 7*(2), 235–253.

Moll, L. C., Amanti, C., Neff, D., & Gonzalez, N. (1992). Funds of knowledge for teaching: Using a qualitative approach to connect homes and classrooms. *Theory into Practice, 31*(2), 132–141.

Myers, J. P., & Zaman, H. A. (2009). Negotiating the global and national: Immigrant and dominant-culture adolescents' vocabularies of citizenship in a transnational world. *Teachers College Record, 111*(11), 2589–2625.

Nieto, S. (2004). *Affirming diversity: The sociopolitical context of multicultural education* (4th ed.). Boston, MA: Pearson.

Paris, C., & Combs, B. (2006). Lived meanings: What teachers mean when they say they are learner-centered. *Teachers and Teaching, 12*(5), 571–592.

Parker, W. C. (2003). *Teaching democracy: Unity and diversity in public life.* New York: Teachers College Press.

Pfaff, N. (2009). Youth culture as a context of political learning: How young people politicize amongst each other. *Young: Nordic Journal of Youth Research, 17*(2), 167–189.

Rubin, B. C. (2007). "There's still not justice": Youth civic identity development amid distinct school and community contexts. *Teachers College Record, 109*(2), 449–481.

Rubin, B. C., Hayes, B., & Benson, K. (2009). "It's the worst place to live": Urban youth and the challenge of school-based civic learning. *Theory into Practice, 48*(3), 213–221.

Schultz, B. D. (2008). *Spectacular things happen along the way: Lessons from an urban classroom.* New York: Teacher College Press.

Schultz, B. D., & Oyler, C. (2006). We make this road as we walk together: Sharing teacher authority in a social action curriculum project. *Curriculum Inquiry, 36*(4), 423–451.

Schultz, K. (2009). *Rethinking classroom participation: Listening to student voices.* New York: Teachers College Press.

Snyder, J., Bolin, F., & Zumwalt, K. (1992). Curriculum implementation. In P. W. Jackson (Ed.), *Handbook of research on curriculum* (pp. 402–435). New York: Macmillan.

Teacher's guide to national issues forums (NIF) in the classroom. (2005). Dayton, OH: Kettering Foundation.

Torney-Purta, J., Barber, C. H., & Richardson, W. K. (2005). *How teachers' preparation relates to students' civic knowledge and engagement in the United States: Analysis from the IEA Civic Education Study?* Medford, MA: CIRCLE.

Torney-Purta, J., Barber, C. H., & Wilkenfeld, B. (2007). Latino adolescents' civic development in the United States: Research results from the IEA Civic Education Study. *Journal of Youth & Adolescence, 36*, 111–125.

Tyack, D., & Cuban, L. (1995). *Tinkering toward utopia: A century of public school reform.* Cambridge: Harvard University Press.

Westheimer, J. (2007). Politics and patriotism in education. In J. Westheimer (Ed.), *Pledging allegiance: The politics of patriotism in America's schools* (pp. 171–188). New York: Teachers College Press.

PART III
CHILDREN AND YOUTH
CONSTRUCT ENGAGED
CITIZENSHIP

CIVIC ENGAGEMENT AND THE EMERGENCE OF RACE: AMERICAN YOUTH NEGOTIATE CITIZENSHIP

Shauna A. Morimoto

ABSTRACT

Purpose – *This paper aims to provide insight into high school students' understanding and experience of citizenship and civic engagement in the United States today.*

Methodological approach – *To supplement literature that reports the causes and correlates of youth civic engagement, this qualitative study explores the form and meaning of citizenship to young Americans. Drawing on observations and interviews with 116 high school students aged 14–19 years, this study explores how youth construct the meaning of citizenship and civic engagement.*

Findings – *I find that race and racial identity are emergent in young people's construction of citizenship. Youth articulate the status of citizen on the basis of "privilege" and feel fortunate to be American. Forms of civic engagement vary by race with white students positioning themselves as helpers and delineating lower income minorities as "others" while also*

Youth Engagement: The Civic-Political Lives of Children and Youth
Sociological Studies of Children and Youth, Volume 16, 153–175
ISSN: 1537-4661/doi:10.1108/S1537-4661(2013)0000016011

engaging in civic activity out of individual motivations and weak community connections. Minority youth express a desire to stay out of trouble, but also contest the boundaries of citizenship through forms of engagement that connect them to community.

Value of paper – *This paper contributes to understanding how race is emergent for young people's definitions of citizenship and civic actions. In addition to demonstrating how the categories of race and citizen are mutually constructed, it shows the value of looking beyond simple measurements of civic activity and exploring the meaning of youth civic work to gain insight into contemporary youth and democracy.*

Keywords: Citizenship; civic engagement; youth; race

INTRODUCTION

Research tells us that the civic prospects for low-income youth of color are grim. With regard to racial and ethnic minorities' formal participation in politics and civic life, Kahne and Middaugh (2008) find that "the very individuals who have the least influence on political processes – the voices schools need most to inform and support in order to promote democratic equality – often get fewer school-based opportunities to develop their civic capacities and commitments than other students" (Kahne & Middaugh, 2008, p. 9). Relative to white students, lower levels of participation among minority youth can be attributed to their unequal access to institutional opportunities for civic engagement as well as their likely cumulative socioeconomic and educational disadvantages (Flanagan & Levine, 2010; Levine, 2007).

While there are formal disparities in the rates of civic engagement among youth, these analyses treat civic engagement as a normative good for youth and citizenship as a static construct (Nenga, 2010). Drawing on interviews and observations with high school aged Americans in two Midwestern communities, I argue that young people today discursively construct citizenship as a privilege such that race and racial identity emerge as central to young people's engagement as citizens of the community. These racialized understandings of citizenship set into relief the ways racial minorities seek to expand the scope of the civic sphere.

The notion that citizenship is a raced construct is, of course, nothing new (Myrdal, 1944; Shklar, 1991; Smith, 1997; Roediger, 1991). However, such examinations of citizenship trace the ways the category of "citizen" became neutral through historical and legal processes of exclusion and boundary making (Glenn, 2002). In contrast, this study examines how young people, the "future of our democracy," reify the boundaries of racially based citizenship by tying racial identity to civic participation.

The adolescents I interviewed for this study believe that the United States is, without question, the best country in which to live. They indicate that being an American is a "privilege" that should not be taken for granted. While not invoking "white privilege" directly, white youth equated Americanism with both whiteness and privilege. Thus, in discussing citizenship, youth contrast their good fortune of being American with the plight of immigrant families – sometimes citing their own families' experiences. Accordingly, they perceive citizenship as a status position for those fortunate enough to be born in the United States, or lucky enough to be naturalized. Moreover, they implicitly invoke "whiteness" as an important marker of being an American by constructing boundaries around race. At the same time, however, by conceptualizing citizenship as a privilege, young people acknowledge global and racial inequity. Thus, contrary to colorblind racism (Bonilla-Silva & Foreman, 2000), this construction of citizenship allows youth to lament inequality while neither envisioning nor feeling empowered to pursue avenues for social justice or social change.

In the context of this racialized citizenship ideology, youth also tie their civic identity to being a "good" citizen through helping in the community and performing volunteer or service work. For white students, this often means engaging in nonpolitical service or altruistic helping because they feel better when they assist others, but also because service is a conscious policy strategy (Gordon & Taft, 2011; Nenga, 2010) that helps youth build their college resumes (Friedland & Morimoto, 2005). For youth of color, however, service is often linked to their racial identity as a means to foster the privilege of citizenship by investing in the community and expanding who participates in the public sphere. This gives their service work a purpose for the collective good and enhances their racial identity. Rather than measuring civic engagement as a static and normative "good," this study offers an understanding of the fluidity of youth citizenship and civic engagement. I argue that citizenship and civic engagement continually change in form and meaning through racialized understandings of civic participation.

The shifting meanings of youth civic engagement arise out of a fluid cultural terrain where young people's ties to both their identity and social institutions are in constant flux (Best, 2011). Postindustrial scholars argue that globalization, consumption, and communication continually alter both the public sphere and the identities of the young people who access it (Beck, 1992; Giddens, 1991). As a result, young people must continually negotiate ever-increasing forms and sources of information, obscuring their path to citizenship and the public (Morimoto & Friedland, 2011). Because boundaries are fluid, citizenship, therefore, is a negotiated status that relies on the construction of race and racial identity. Accordingly, the current generation both reproduces and confronts the civic lore associated with membership in the United States.

After a discussion of my data and methods, I review the literature on youth civic engagement and then examine how young people negotiate race and identity. Next, I offer qualitative data to demonstrate how youth view citizenship as a privilege, and how race emerges as critical to their understanding. This results in civic engagement where race is invoked with white students implicitly drawing the boundaries of citizenship and youth of color seeking to expand the privileged space of public action.

DATA AND METHODS

Most analysis of youth civic life is in the form of aggregate oriented methodological studies that consider causes, rates, and correlates of youth civic engagement. As Levine (2007) states, in the study of young people, "'civic engagement' is often operationalized as a list of variables" (p. 1). In an effort to reach beyond this formulation, I conducted qualitative research including interviews and observations with high school students to explore the meanings and understandings that young people attribute to their civic activity. My approach to this work is inductive, allowing me to consider the complex and emergent nature of what citizenship and civic activity means to young people.

Because my questions move beyond evaluation of civic engagement to encompass students' understanding of their citizenship status and civic activities, qualitative observation and interview methods are ideal for this work. The data analysis and design for this project are thus intended to consider both the action of individuals, and how they interpret, understand, and experience action (Giddens, 1984). As Burawoy (1998) notes, social science data are the theories social actors "carry in their heads" while they recreate and/or transform the institutions of their daily life. These "pre-constituted theories and concepts of participants" may only be obtained and understood "in relation to the context of their production" (Burawoy,

1991, p. 2). Thus, in understanding the construction of citizenship and civic engagement, I sought young people's understanding of these categories and spaces of social action.

Ethnographic observation, qualitative comparative methods, and in-depth interviews allowed me to explore and contextualize adolescents' connections to their communities and their experiences with civic activity. I relied on grounded theory techniques to develop my understanding as research proceeded (Strauss & Corbin, 1998). These methods permitted me to explore students' nuanced experiences of their civic activity while constructing a broader framework for understanding those experiences.

Research for this study was conducted in a Midwestern state in the towns of Springfield and Point Place.[1] Springfield is racially relatively homogenous, while Point Place is a bit more diverse. In Springfield, approximately 90% of the residents are white; 4% are African American; 4% are Asian; and the remainder Native American, Hispanic, or of other races. Point Place is 83% white, 1.5% African American, 3% Asian, 7% Hispanic, and the remainder Native American or other races. Springfield has a population of 208,000 and is relatively affluent, with a median annual household income of just over $50,000. Point Place is smaller, with a population of 108,000 and more working class, with a median household income of $38,800.

All of the respondents were high school students, between the ages of 14 and 19 years. In total, 116 students were interviewed. The racial composition of the sample included 15 African Americans, 5 Latino/Latinas, 5 Asian Americans, 1 Native American, and 1 Arab American. The remainder of the students interviewed were white. Sixty-five of the students were female. The majority ($n = 118$) of the respondents were contacted in high school settings and the remainder in a variety of other contexts including neighborhood centers, malls, and other hangouts. The young people interviewed for the study were generally engaged in their communities – most often through altruistic volunteerism, and also by involving in other forms of extracurricular participation, and, for some, through politics or activism.

With each participant, I conducted in-depth, semi-structured, and open-ended interviews, allowing students to discuss a range of topics related to their school, civic, and social lives. After establishing a rapport with interviewees, informants were asked about their activities, social lives, aspirations and expectations, home environment, and political beliefs. In addition, I asked specific questions about their ideas of citizenship and social responsibility and how these ideas related to their high school experience. Many of the youth interviewed for this study had numerous interests and would spend substantial time listing their activities, including sports, high school clubs, and volunteer work. To the extent that it informed their civic engagement, I asked follow-up questions about religion, social networks, and the community. In later interviews, I began asking students to complete a short form with some basic information about their activities, interests, their parents' occupations, their high school, and their religious affiliation. In addition to interviews, I observed high school aged students in various settings including at school, doing volunteer work or community activities, at local hangouts such as the mall or coffee shops, and at volunteer centers.

In an effort to understand how young people live as citizens and understand citizenship (see Lister, Smith, Middleton, & Cox, 2003), I sought a broad range of students in terms of race, socioeconomic status, high school, and extracurricular activity. My sampling strategy was to use a stratified-purposive sample, drawing from different schools representing diverse student populations. To supplement these school-based samples, I also drew from neighborhood centers or other place-based sites that would tend to overrepresent lower income and minority students.

Interviews were transcribed and analyzed through the coding of emergent themes and issues that came out of the interview and observational data. I summarized key themes, discussions, and theoretical issues that appeared in the interviews and tracked patterns through extensive written memos and notes. The qualitative software program NVivo assisted in my analysis of the data and helped me to refine the codes as new patterns and ideas emerged. These methods allowed me to access young people's perspectives on civic participation and citizenship beyond the literature that examines adult perspectives on the causes and correlates of youth civic engagement (see Eder & Fingerson, 2002).

THE RACIALIZED CONSTRUCTION OF CITIZENSHIP AND CIVIC ENGAGEMENT

Race and the Problem of Civic Engagement

For young people today, *any* form of civic activity "counts" as good citizenship. That is to say, young people are eager to "opt-into" service life, largely as a result of policy and educational goals that tout the benefits of engaged citizens (Gordon & Taft, 2011; Nenga, 2010) and fear the decline in social capital and civic life (Levine, 2007; Putnam, 2000; Zukin, Keeter,

Andolina, Jenkins, & Della Carpini, 2006). Research on youth civic engagement emphasizes the positive correlation between civic knowledge, civic activity, and future engagement (Galston, 2001; Levine, 2007; Youniss, McLellan, Yang, & Yates, 1999; Youniss, McLellan, & Yates, 1997; Zukin, et al., 2006).

Complementary research focusing on youth development indicates that there are positive dividends for both the individual and the community when young people are civically engaged (Eccles & Gootman, 2002; Flanagan & Sherod, 1998; Pittman, 1991). Civic and social participation are a means for youth to gain self-awareness and a positive self-concept (Barber, Eccles, & Stone, 2001; Eccles & Barber, 1999; Youniss et al., 1997, 1999; Youniss & Yates, 1997). Moreover, research shows that activities that enhance young people's social skills and participation enable adolescents to act as responsible citizens while exposing them to democratic process and practice (Camino, 2000; Hart, 1992; R.S. Zeldin, 2000; S. Zeldin, 2004).

Given the benefits of civic engagement, scholars express concern over youth of color who seem to have fewer opportunities than white students to engage in school-based civic activity (Kahne & Middaugh, 2008). For example, a recent survey of over 2,000 California high school students showed that access to civic education and service-learning programs vary by race, ethnicity, and socioeconomic status (Kahne & Middaugh, 2008). Indeed, to take advantage of civic activities, students often need specific classes, teachers, and/or access to limited and selective elective tracks – all of which correlate with race, ethnicity, and class (Kahne & Middaugh, 2008). This is, in part, attributed to disadvantaged students being in lower tracks at school and the overall "civic achievement gap" between middle class and lower class students (Flanagan & Levine, 2010; Levinson, 2007). Less affluent schools are also less likely to offer service learning to their students (Hart & Atkins, 2002; Spring, Dietz, & Grimm, 2007). Accordingly, there are disparities between white youth and low-income minorities in the rates of school-based engagement.

These debates point to race as the problematic variable in levels of youth civic engagement, invoking the larger frame of normative debates about citizenship rights and obligations (see Janoski, 1998). While such narratives are proscriptive about the health of American democracy and youth civic engagement, they tell us little about how young people themselves understand and act as democratic citizens. As Harris (2001) points out, conventional narratives of citizenship can overlook the ways young people enact and articulate alternative visions of citizenship. Moreover, since citizenship can have both exclusionary and inclusionary implications, understanding how youth invoke their identities to understand the fluid nature of citizenship informs the shape of the polity (Lister et al., 2003). Accordingly, rather than looking at rates of citizenship as a problem delineated by race, below I discuss how race emerges in the ways young people engage in their communities and informs their understanding of citizenship as a privilege.

Privileged Citizenship and Emergent Racial Identity

Race informs both young people's understanding of citizenship as a privilege and the ways youth engage in their communities. This is not surprising, since as Milner (2004) argues, although social scientists have gone to great lengths to show that race is socially constructed rather than biologically based, "from the point of view of most – if not all – high school freshmen, this is irrelevant. For them, race and ethnicity seem inalienable" (124). Although citizenship constructed as a privilege excludes youth of color who lack that privilege, minorities resist or push up against this exclusion by: (1) expanding the domain of citizenship; (2) connecting to youth like them from within the community; or (3) civically engaging to avoid being perceived of as "at risk."

Citizenship for young people, therefore, is constructed intersectionally through racial identity and class position. As a domain of privilege, citizenship is enacted through advantages that are socially reproduced. Lareau (2003) shows that middle- and upper-class families cultivate their children, equipping them with both the abilities and sense of entitlement that reproduces their privileged position. Working class children, in contrast, develop on their own and lack privileges as adults. Social class dominates race in the patterns of reproduction that Lareau finds (Choo & Ferree, 2010). MacLeod (1995), likewise, argues that class position shapes aspirations and constrains opportunities for youth who grow up in a low-income neighbor-hood, attend a low-status high school, and where teachers and administrators have limited expectations of them. Importantly, therefore, socioeconomic advantage is a privilege associated with ease, success, and ambition.

While social class drives the reproduction of privileged economic status, youth are actively engaged in constructing and negotiating race and other categorical identities (Best, 2006; Wilkins, 2004). For example, in her study of racial identity among whites, Perry (2002) argues that for youth in a racially and ethnically mixed school, whiteness becomes a distinct category symbolized through dress, tastes, and manners. In contrast, for whites in a predominantly heterogeneous school, whiteness is normalized and youth take the privileges of whiteness for granted. As such, the distinction of whiteness is reinforced when boundary lines are drawn. Race and identity are also central in a black urban school where cultural frames are constantly negotiated between a school culture that emphasizes achievement and black urban culture that teachers perceive as disruptive and rebellious. Students who can effectively straddle cultural frames ("multicultural navigators") are more successful in school and have a better sense of self (Carter, 2005). As with school-based negotiations, as I discuss further below, when citizenship delineates privilege, youth act around their racial identities to reinforce or renegotiate these borders.

However, while class and privilege are reproduced at a structural level, youth navigate the terrain of identity through interaction as an individual process. Since boundaries are constantly in shift (Beck, 1992; Giddens, 1991), youth must negotiate their own identities and "think of the self as a willful project of inventing, reinventing, and refining" (Best, 2011, p. 917). Moreover, conventional markers of identity are no longer clear, so young people must individually navigate not only their own identities but also the information and institutions that comprise the context for their entry into adulthood (Morimoto & Friedland, 2011).

With both identity and context in flux, therefore, race and economic status emerge as youth articulate their notion of citizenship and act as citizens. For many young people, being a U.S. citizen is contrasted with immigrant and disadvantaged minority status. In this way, the privileges of citizenship become the domain of the advantaged white middle class. With that privilege, therefore, the obligations of citizenship are translated into helping those outside this privileged arena. Minority students counter this privileged narrative by seeking to expand the civic domain and find ways for a more diverse engaged citizenship. Race thus emerges as central to the forms of civic engagement among young people on the cusp of full incorporation into the American polity (see Gordon, 2009). Accordingly, rather than discussing a crisis of disengagement particular to racial minorities, I next turn to the data to show how racial identity shapes the discursive and enacted meaning of citizenship for young people.

THE PRIVILEGE OF AMERICANISM

Young people interviewed for this study offered a variety of definitions and meanings for citizenship. Interestingly, however, they often understood citizenship as a *privilege*, rather than a set of rights or responsibilities (Janoski, 1998). McIntosh (1988) conceptualized privilege through her discussions of race, arguing that privilege consists of undeserved and unmarked resources that whites in American society can exchange for various advantages. More generally, privilege is "an unearned, invisible, systemic resource" (Nenga, 2011, p. 266) that is conferred on some groups without individual group members personally securing that privilege. Indeed, because privilege is a lack of barriers and a feeling of ease (Khan, 2011; Nenga, 2011), we can neither gain privilege nor give it away (Kendall, 2006).

By discursively constructing their understanding of citizenship as a privilege, young people valorize the benefits of Americanism rather than pursing rights and grievances against the state. As a result, young people are not interested in changing structural inequality, yet race emerges as important in anchoring citizenship. Considering the public and political attention to immigration, perhaps it is not surprising that so many young people constructed citizenship in this way.[2] For example, since immigration is conflated with race, young people discussed citizenship with attention to legal standing and in ways that uphold the value of citizenship, and also indicate that the benefits of citizenship are benefits of whiteness. Isabelle (white), for example, when asked about the meaning of U.S. citizenship, made the following comment: "I really think that we live in one of the best countries you can live in – in the world. I'm happy that I live here and not Africa or something. Other than that, I'm not sure."

Isabelle appreciates her citizenship, but not for the rights and obligations that accompany her legal standing. Instead, it makes her feel lucky and she is thankful for her good fortune of being a citizen. For Isabelle, the ease of Americanism stands in contrast to being from Africa. Isabelle thus implicates not just the status of citizenship but also the advantages of race, economic development, and socioeconomic status.

Rachel, an opinionated and loquacious white high school junior, spoke at length about the privilege of U.S. citizenship. Like Isabelle, Rachel invokes race and economic advantage in discussing American citizenship. With great faith that the United States was the best country in which to be a citizen, Rachel explains:

> Being a citizen ... being able to come to this country, into this country, is basically like a privilege. As you can see, a lot of people come here and they migrate and immigrate here, you know, and, it's something that you should be proud of here. I have citizenship here. I was born here, you know? Like when people get citizenship in the United States, it's like, "Oh my God! I am free!"

According to Rachel, being born into privileged citizenship should make us proud. Because citizenship is her birthright, it is an individual advantage that is beyond her capacity to change (Nenga, 2011). As with class position (Nenga, 2011) and race (Khan, 2011), immigration and the desire to change citizenship status is an individual struggle. When individuals who are not born into this privilege get citizenship, they will express gratitude for and enjoy their new status. Framing citizenship as pride and gratitude that comes out of an individual struggle, however, divorces social justice questions or political content from immigration as a social issue (Khan, 2011).

Amber (white) expressed similar thoughts, emphasizing her gratitude and the ease she experiences as a citizen. However, Amber goes further and extends the privilege of citizenship more broadly to include barriers that all people of color face. For Amber, citizenship is about privilege and privilege is about race:

> Everybody says it's good to be a citizen because we're like one of the best countries, I guess .... I'm happy I was born in the US [and] I wasn't born in other countries because a lot of people have problems coming in. Or even if you are in you're still not accepted, so ... it kinda sucks that everybody is racist, but that's just the way it is. I'm just happy I was here.

Rachel and Amber accept that the United States is the "best" place to live and suggest that they are fortunate to be part of this country. At the same time, however, while acknowledging inequalities associated with race, and that race and citizenship are connected, they do not see this as something that they have the capacity to remedy about the United States, but instead as a reflection on their own fortune. Instead of being color-blind, young people are aware of race, but only as it stands for relative ease or struggle. In this way, whiteness entails gratitude and ease while people of color struggle in striving for the privilege of citizenship.

Boua, a Hmong immigrant, also discusses the privileges of citizenship, but reflects on the struggle of citizenship and thinks in terms of the specific rights that citizenship offers. In a more active and engaged view of citizenship, for Boua, privilege is the ability to take advantage of the rights of citizenship, not a status that is automatically given and enjoyed:

> Freedom of speech, Freedom of religion .... I guess basically able to live to the fullest. I think education is a really big thing for citizens, you know? Like aliens and stuff like that, they don't have the privilege ... .

Just as class privilege allows elites to sequester themselves into a "bubble" of socioeconomic advantage (Kendall, 2010; Nenga, 2011), citizenship privilege creates a bubble bounded by legal status and race. While students acknowledge racial discrimination and favor diversity (Khan, 2011), they do not take the privilege of citizenship as a rallying cry to change immigration laws or shift the legal standing of racial minorities. Instead, race is inherently connected to citizenship and outside the realm of their ability to change. By being open and sympathetic to the struggle that non-citizens face, however, white youth can appreciate their citizenship status, but distance themselves from the contention of politics (Khan, 2011). Allison's (white) remarks are typical of the young people interviewed for this study:

> [P]olitics – they don't interest me. I really don't want to get involved. I think it's scary to get involved in politics cause, people are just so, I don't know, just, yelling at each other. I don't like that. Like, I'm one of the people thinking: why can't we all just get along? I mean, I know that's not realistic, but I wish that was more how it was.

Although Allison is not interested in engaging in formal politics, her comments demonstrate her idealism and wish that "everyone get along." Like Amber, who says it "kinda sucks that everyone is racist," both girls decry conflict, but neither feels in a position to fight for social justice. While Amber takes comfort in being in the bubble of citizenship and harmony, Allison admits that her perspective not "realistic." Citizenship is envisioned as privilege and ease, effectively setting aside contention over social justice and social causes.

ENACTING THE PRIVILEGE OF CITIZENSHIP: WHITE YOUTH AND THE BUBBLE OF CIVIC ENGAGEMENT

Although individual young people do not have the ability to change their privilege, according to Khan (2011), privilege is embodied and thus has implications for social action and interaction. As such, youth embody and act on their citizenship in race-specific ways. White, college bound, middle and upper-middle class youth – that is, youth who produce the majority of service-based volunteerism – offer a variety of reasons for their civic engagement, including building resumes for college admissions, altruistic motives, religious affiliation, and supporting their political beliefs.

Importantly, in discussing civic engagement, white middle class youth often draw on discourses of helping those who are less fortunate. The privilege of citizenship, therefore, is translated into racial and economic advantage and enacted as an obligation to the disadvantaged. From the bubble of privileged citizenship, this leads to "helping" as a form of civic engagement, and "othering" those who do not have access to citizenship privilege. Unlike the exclusionary practices of socioeconomic elites, privileged status is not inherited or obtained through organizational gatekeeping (Kendall, 2002, 2010), but instead demarcated through the actions of citizenship. In this way, the privilege of citizenship is reified as the domain of whites (Glenn, 2002) and upheld through volunteerism (Kendall, 2002).

White middle class youth invoke the privilege of being an American as an obligation to help "others" while also couching their activities in terms of their future privileged positions, including college and middle class life. Elizabeth, for example, is a high achieving, upper-middle class white senior. She attends a private school where service is part of the curriculum and necessary for graduation. For Elizabeth, this makes sense, since she has advantages that other students do not. She explains:

> I'd say maybe sometimes people can get a little too caught up in what's going on in their own lives and just focus on that a lot. But, especially people that come to [this school] should realize that there's a lot of people out there who have a lot less and just the littlest thing can help someone a great deal ... And if you start now, it's easier to keep doing it in college, and once you are exposed to it, you realize how beneficial your work can be for other people.

While Elizabeth does not talk about race specifically, her reasons behind fulfilling the obligations of citizenship – that is, her civic engagement – are related to her sense that she has privileges and she should help "others." She discusses her plans to go to an urban college, for example, where "they have really good programs for helping inner-city kids and that kind of thing." Implicitly, therefore, "others" are likely to be lower income minority students. In her organizational ethnography of community-based empowerment organizations, Eliasoph (2011) finds a similar pattern among the mostly white youth who are "helpers" in volunteer organizations, and those being "helped" who tend to be racially diverse and from lower socioeconomic backgrounds.

As with the privilege of citizenship, volunteer and civic activity are individually based. Helping the disadvantaged is the primary form of being civically effective rather than working toward institutional change or on social justice causes that give rise to social movements (Fisher, 2012). Lacking strong ties to social institutions or rights-based organizations (Beck, 1992; Best, 2011; Giddens, 1991), white youth do not articulate a strong civic identity or a sense of civic purpose. Thus, short of acting as the *noblesse oblige* and helping the disadvantaged, white students expressed little efficacy in their communities. Justin, for example, says the following about his service learning class project:

Q: How do you feel about service-learning?

A: Well, my algebra class is a service-learning project.

Q: How does that work?

A: We're trying to get [the city] to recycle plastics one through six, not just one and two.

Q: So how are you doing this through your algebra class?

A: We calculate things like volume and cost efficiency and how much people will pay for recycled plastics. We present to City Council in June.

Q: How do you think it's going to go?

A: Not well. It's not going to fly at all.

For middle class white students, therefore, they can be most effective as citizens through helping "others" who are less fortunate. Helping "others" conforms to the notion that being an American is a privilege, but that privilege is constructed along racial lines – not according to legal status. For advantaged youth, civic activity is thus implicated in the process of "othering," while it lacks power to make an impact on the community. Because levels of civic engagement are high overall, civic activity becomes a normative and unmarked process of helping, particularly for those who are college bound (Eliasoph, 2011; Morimoto, 2010). Thus, youth want "everyone to get along," through helping others rather than pursuing social justice activities fostering social change.[3]

EXPANDING THE BOUNDARIES OF CITIZENSHIP: YOUTH OF COLOR AND CIVIC ENGAGEMENT

Just as middle class white youth embody the action of citizenship through privilege, youth of color also act as citizens in race-specific ways. Since youth attach the privilege of citizenship to whiteness, non-whites who lack this privilege are constructed as the "helped" group. Non-white youth, even if they are among the elite, understand that privilege is the domain of whites (Khan, 2011). Youth of color, however, challenge the boundaries of privileged citizenship, demonstrating that they deserve to be part of the civic sphere like their white peers. In order to not be "others" in the civic sphere, they wrestle with civic action that is, at once, effective citizenship, but also entails making connections to the community. Jackson, a middle class African American, explains the civic work of his peers as follows:

> I think you have like several different categories of kids in terms of involvement .... You have people who are just doing it for college, you know? And there are a lot of those types of people. Then you have a lot of people who are like, "I don't want to do it because I am not getting paid and blah blah blah." But ... if you get them out there to actually meet those people then they'll start to see the benefits of it and the rewards of the community.

Jackson discusses the ways youth civic action is divided. Among those with privilege, civic engagement helps with college admission. This type of engagement often emerges as volunteerism that helps "others," and also reinforces privileges for those with advantages. Indeed, the expectation of college admission is indicative of this privilege. However, civic engagement can also expand the boundaries of citizenship and build relationships in the community. Thus, for young people without privilege, civic engagement can legitimate their position as actors in the civic sphere.

Aie, for example, a Hmong immigrant, is a high school senior who is very active in her community and spends a lot of time doing volunteer work through her local community center and the United Way. Aie became involved in community activities as she spent time at the neighborhood center sponsored by the Urban League and aimed at building self-esteem and academic skills for girls of lower socioeconomic background. Aie's desire to increase awareness for other disadvantaged youth about opportunities for community engagement drives her own involvement. She explains:

> If I didn't get [involved with the neighborhood center] and be a part of the Pre-employment Program, I would have never known about youth opportunities. So my biggest thing was I wanted to let other people know about youth opportunities and how they can stay positive and how they can make an impact on the communities and the schools and their family and a lot of people talk about there being nothing for youth or all you hear about in the media is negative images of youth and so that's basically why I really want other people to join.

For Aie, making connections to the community and getting others involved is a top priority. Rather than other Hmong or lower income students being written off, she encourages them to take advantage of what the community has to offer. Moreover, she suggests that immigrants and disadvantaged youth deserve citizenship privilege. Aie tirelessly participates in civic activity and actively recruits others to do the same. She constantly wants to make an impact on the community and increase other young people's awareness of opportunities for civic involvement. In short, Aie wishes to open the "bubble" of privileged citizenship to minorities, but doing so involves a tremendous commitment to volunteer activity and engagement.

For socioeconomically disadvantaged youth, however, expanding citizenship can also be contradictory, involving acting from a position of disadvantage, and also resisting the stereotypes that assign them to the position of "other." Young people who grow up in urban areas, where they regularly witness drug dealing and use, death, lawlessness, and overall despair, have a complex relationship with civic participation. Indeed, while they wish to improve their communities, they are also keenly aware of the deep problems their communities face, and the failure of existing community institutions to begin to address these issues (Rubin, Hayes, & Benson, 2009). Specifically, urban students express low levels of trust in government, feel unsafe in their schools and neighborhoods, and indicate having experienced and witnessed class- and race-based social injustices (Rubin et al., 2009). As such, integrating into institutions that represent citizenship is not always the aim. One avenue disadvantaged youth of color pursue is to "give back to the community" (Charles, 2005). Jared (black) discusses "giving back to the people that have helped you" as part of his commitment to being a reading mentor at an elementary school. When asked why he is interested in helping kids, Jared explains:

A: Well, it's like ... I know where I'm from ... know what I'm sayin'? ... the kids ain't got much there.

Q: Where?

A: [Urban area] ... I know kids ain't got much. I feel like, when I came up here, teachers started helping me, so I can help other people too, know what I'm sayin'? But if there's something they need, if I've got it, I'll give them what they need.

Q: Pass it on?

A: Yeah, treat them like they want to be treated .... Because I don't like to see kids struggling either.

Q: You don't like to see them struggling?

A: Like when kids be walking around with tore up shoes ... Like, I like to see them with good haircuts. Sometimes I just want to go over and buy them a haircut, buy them some new shoes or somethin'. I don't like to see kids dirty.

For Jared, the children he helps are not "others," but they are, in fact, a reflection of his own experiences. Jared acts as a citizen not by trying to access or extend the boundaries of privilege, but by trying to alleviate barriers. Jared finds a place where he can act as a member of society from within a position of disadvantage. Thus, through his action, citizenship is not sealed off by lines of race and class, but informed by his experiences. Having benefited from the mentorship he received when he moved from an inner-city, Jared knows he can help change the position of young children. As Harris (2001) finds with youth in the zine movement, Jared can "better understand how young people are both positioned in and problematize the post-industrial state" (p. 197). His experience puts him in a position to provide assistance and guidance. He feels good about his doing this work because he is alleviating the struggles he experienced.

Other youth of color resist the process of "othering" and engage in civic activity to avoid the stereotypes that are associated with their "other" status (Carter, 2006; Eliasoph, 2011). In resisting being "others," these youth offer their own perspective on the narrative of citizenship being a privilege (Harris, 2001). Drawing on discourses that construct minority youth as "at risk" for incarceration, dropping out, pregnancy or other social problems, volunteerism is a way to avoid this fate while also demonstrating that white students have advantages that youth of color cannot access.

For example, Rona, a Latina freshman, explains that young people of color volunteer to demonstrate that they are not involved with drugs, alcohol, and sex. In contrast, she says white students do not have to worry about staying out of trouble through volunteering because their parents do things for them. She continues, "those rich white kids .... They be gettin' everything [handed to them]." Race determines not only young peoples' access to civic opportunities but also how those civic opportunities are perceived and motivated. To Rona, the privilege of white citizenship means not having to worry about negative stereotypes, and being able to succeed because their parents provide the means for them to do so. Aerial, a black high school student, explains further "you wouldn't believe this, but rich kids are also into crystal meth." She continues, "the white kids are out there doing that as much as black kids but it is the black kids that get caught."

For youth of color, therefore, race is critical not only in who they are personally but also how they negotiate their status as citizens. In contrast to white students, for students of color, civic engagement involves negotiating rather than reifying the boundaries of the civic sphere. While some youth try to expand the boundaries of civic life to include them, others engage civically to give back to the community or expose privilege and resist the boundaries reinforced by white students. The racialized meanings they construct through civic engagement, therefore, puts them in a position where they work hard at being citizens and expanding the notion of citizenship. Paradoxically, this reinforces the sense that the ease of citizenship belongs to white students and the struggle for privilege belongs to youth of color. However, boundaries are contested through individual acts of engagement rather than group mobilization.

CONCLUSION

For the students I interviewed, race emerged as important to constructing citizenship, both in terms of viewing abstract U.S. citizenship as a racialized category and how students behaved as citizens. Interestingly, for students considering the privilege of Americanism, citizenship standing informed their understanding of race and civic engagement issues. At the same time, however, this did not translate into attempting to expand the rights of citizenship, but instead made them think of themselves as lucky.

In contrast to white privilege (Bonilla-Silva & Foreman, 2000; McIntosh, 1988), or class privilege (Nenga, 2011), young people recognize and appreciate citizenship privilege. However, discursively, this positions youth with the privilege of citizenship as having a resource that others do not. Since citizenship consists of both rights bestowed by the state and obligations to the state (Janoski, 1998), articulating citizenship as a privilege has implications for the agency of young people. Young people articulate, embody, and act upon this resource along racial lines rather than strictly along the lines of legal status. Thus, the privilege of citizenship becomes translated into the advantages of invisible racial privilege. Conversely, lack of privilege belongs to people of color, particularly those from socio-economically disadvantaged backgrounds.

By conceptualizing the privilege of citizenship as racialized, white youth engage civically by helping those without privileges. This reifies the domain of citizenship as white, but it appears that youth access civic space through their individual meritorious civic action. For youth of color, acting as citizens means deflecting stereotypes that they are in need of help while also working to diversify civic space (see Kao & Thompson, 2003). However, since civic engagement is an individual undertaking, politics around rights discourses and collective engagement are diluted.

Thus, middle class white youths' understanding of racial inequity and desire for everyone to get along are not incidental to their ideals of citizenship.

We are an increasingly open society, with underrepresented minorities having greater access to schools and careers that were closed to prior generations (Khan, 2011). Openness, however, does not mean equity, but instead occurs alongside rising gaps between the poor and the wealthy (Hooks, 2010). For youth of color, this informs the class-specific ways they negotiate citizenship and civic engagement. Rather than acting as the *noblesse oblige* like their white peers (Kendall, 2002), youth of color challenge the boundaries of privileged citizenship and demonstrate that they deserve citizenship equally to their peers. At the same time, however, they offer a counter-narrative to what engaged citizenship looks like by those who are often overlooked or underrepresented as social and political actors (Harris, 2001). While the hard work of civic engagement refutes stereotypes about who are members of the polity, it also reinforces that the privilege – or ease – of citizenship belongs to those who are helping rather than the helped (Eliasoph, 2011).

Of course, not all young people fit neatly into patterns of citizenship and civic engagement as defined by race. Certainly, regardless of race, youth make contributions to their communities, are richly involved in democratic processes, consider building their resumes the ultimate goal, or try to find a way to avoid trouble by getting involved in youth activities. The contribution of this study, however, is to show how race is emergent and important for youth in both how they define and act as American citizens. Moreover, looking deeply at youth civic engagement allows us to develop an understanding of the forms and meanings of civic engagement over and above what we know about levels of participation, types of engagement, and outcomes of civic involvement. Indeed, it provides a window into youth as they create new and emergent understandings of race and democracy. In an era of shifting boundaries and negotiated status, youth are involved in the process of (re)inventing both citizenship and race.

NOTES

1. All names of locations, organizations, schools, and participants have been changed.

2. Although a number of students indicated that they at least scan the news, very few expressed an interest in partisan political issues. For those concerned with politics, some discussed race and racism, but none mentioned immigration as a major issue of concern.

3. Of course, there are many activist youth who formally engage in political activities. For an ethnographic account, see Gordon, 2009; Taft, 2006.

ACKNOWLEDGMENTS

I am grateful to Karen Gober for her careful reading of the manuscript.
I also wish to thank Sandi Kawecka Nenga, Jessica K. Taft, and anonymous
reviewers for their insightful feedback and advice.

REFERENCES

Barber, B. L., Eccles, J. S., & Stone, M. R. (2001). Whatever happened to the jock, the brain
    and the princess? Young adult pathways linked to adolescent activity involvement and
    social identity. *Journal of Adolescent Research, 16*, 429–455.
Beck, U. (1992). *Risk society: Towards a new modernity.* London, UK: Sage.
Best, A. (2006). *Fast cars, cool rides: The accelerating world of youth and their cars.* New York,
    NY: NYU Press.
Best, A. (2011). Youth identity formation: Contemporary identity work. *Sociology Compass,
    5*(10), 908–922.
Bonilla-Silva, E., & Foreman, T. A. (2000). "I'm not a racist, but … ": Mapping white students'
    racial ideology in the USA. *Discourse & Society, 11*(1), 50–85.
Burawoy, M. (1991). Introduction. In M. Burawoy (Ed.), *Ethnography unbound: Power and
    resistance in the modern metropolis* (pp. 1–7). Berkeley, CA: University of California
    Press.
Burawoy, M. (1998). The extended case method. *Sociological Theory, 16*(1), 4–33.
Camino, L. (2000). Youth-adult partnerships: Entering new territory in community work and
    research. *Applied Developmental Science, 4*(2, Suppl.), 11–20.
Carter, P. L. (2005). *Keepin' it real: School success beyond black and white.* Oxford, UK: Oxford
    University Press.
Carter, P. L. (2006). Straddling boundaries: Identity, culture, and school. *Sociology of
    Education, 79*, 304–328.
Charles, M. M. (2005). *Giving back to the community: African American inner city teens and civic
    engagement.* Working Paper No. 38. Center for Information and Research on Civic
    Learning and Engagement, College Park, MD. Retrieved from http://www.civicyouth.
    org/PopUps/WorkingPapers/WP38Charles.pdf
Choo, H. Y., & Ferree, M. M. (2010). Practicing intersectionality in sociological research: A
    critical analysis of inclusions, interactions, and institutions in the study of inequalities.
    Sociological Theory, 28, 129–149.
Eccles, J., & Gootman, J. A. (Eds.). (2002). *Community programs to promote youth development.
    National Research Council and Institute of Medicine, Board on Children, Youth and
    Families, Committee on Community-Level Programs for Youth.* Washington, DC: National
    Academies Press.
Eccles, J. S., & Barber, B. L. (1999). Student council, volunteering, basketball or marching
    band: What kind of extracurricular involvement matters? *Journal of Adolescent
    Research, 14*(1), 10–43.
Eder, D., & Fingerson, L. (2002). Interviewing children and adolescents. In J. F. Gubrium & J.
    A. Holstein (Eds.), *Handbook of interview research: Context and method* (pp. 181–201).
    Thousand Oaks, CA: Sage Publications, Inc.

Eliasoph, N. (2011). *Making volunteers: Civic life after welfare's end*. Princeton, NJ: Princeton University Press.

Fisher, D. R. (2012). Youth political participation: Bridging activism and electoral politics. *Annual Review of Sociology, 38*, 119–137.

Flanagan, C., & Levine, P. (2010). Civic engagement and the transition to adulthood. *The Future of Children, 20*(1), 159–179.

Flanagan, C., & Sherod, L. R. (1998). Youth political development: An introduction. *Journal of Social Issues, 54*, 447–456.

Friedland, L. A., & Morimoto, S. A. (2005). *The changing lifeworld of young people: Risk, resume-padding and civic engagement.* Working Paper No. 40. Center for Information and Research on Civic Learning and Engagement, College Park, MD. Retrieved from http://www.civicyouth.org/PopUps/WorkingPapers/WP40Friedland.pdf

Galston, W. A. (2001). Political knowledge, political engagement, and civic education. *Annual Review of Political Science, 4*, 217–234.

Giddens, A. (1984). *The constitution of society: Outline of the theory of structuration.* Oxford: Polity.

Giddens, A. (1991). *Modernity and self identity: Self and society in the late modern age.* Oxford, UK: Polity.

Glenn, E. N. (2002). *Unequal freedom: How race and gender shaped American citizenship and labor.* Cambridge, MA: Harvard University Press.

Gordon, H. (2009). *We fight to win: Inequality and the politics of youth activism.* New Brunswick, NJ: Rutgers University Press.

Gordon, H. R., & Taft, J. K. (2011). Rethinking youth political socialization: Teenage activists talk back. *Youth & Society, 43*(4), 1499–1527.

Harris, A. (2001). Dodging and weaving: Young women countering the stories of youth citizenship. *Critical Psychology, 4*(1), 183–199.

Hart, D., & Atkins, R. (2002). Civic competence in urban youth. *Applied Developmental Science, 6*, 227–236.

Hart, R. A. (1992). *Children's participation: From tokenism to citizenship.* Florence, Italy: UNICEF International Child Development Centre.

Hooks, B. (2010). Class and race: The new black elite. In M. S. Kimmel & A. L. Ferber (Eds.), *Privilege: A reader* (pp. 169–178). Boulder, CO: Westview Press.

Janoski, T. (1998). *Citizenship and civil society: A framework of rights and obligations in liberal, traditional, and social democratic regimes.* Cambridge: Cambridge University Press.

Kahne, J., & Middaugh, E. (2008). High quality civic education: What is it and who gets it. *Social Education, 72*, 34–39.

Kao, G., & Thompson, J. S. (2003). Racial and ethnic stratification in educational achievement and attainment. *Annual Review of Sociology, 29*, 417–442.

Kendall, D. (2002). *The power of good deeds: Privileged women and the social reproduction of the upper class.* Lanham, MD: Rowman & Littlefield Publishers, Inc.

Kendall, D. (2010). Class: Still alive and reproducing in the United States. In M. S. Kimmel & A. L. Ferber (Eds.), *Privilege: A reader* (pp. 145–152). Boulder, CO: Westview Press.

Kendall, F. E. (2006). *Understanding white privilege: Creating pathways to authentic relationships across race.* New York: Routledge.

Khan, S. R. (2011). *Privilege: The making of an adolescent elite at St. Paul's School.* Princeton, NJ: Princeton University Press.

Lareau, A. (2003). *Unequal childhoods: Class, race and family life.* Berkeley, CA: University of California Press.

Levine, P. (2007). *The future of democracy: Developing the next generation of American citizens.* Medford, MA: Tufts University Press.

Levinson, M. (2007). *The civic achievement gap.* Working Paper No. 51. Center for Information and Research on Civic Learning and Engagement, College Park, MD. Retrieved from http://www.civicyouth.org/PopUps/WorkingPapers/WP51Levinson.pdf

Lister, R., Smith, N., Middleton, S., & Cox, L. (2003). Young people talk about citizenship: Empirical perspectives on theoretical and political debates. *Citizenship Studies, 7*(2), 235–253.

MacLeod, J. (1995). *Ain't no makin' it: Aspirations and attainment in a low income neighborhood.* Boulder, CO: Westview Press.

McIntosh, P. (1988). *White privilege and male privilege: A personal account of coming to see correspondences through work in women's studies.* Working Paper No. 189. Wellesley College Center for Research on Women, Wellesley, MA.

Milner, M., Jr. (2004). *Freaks, geeks and cool kids: American teenagers, schools and the culture of consumption.* New York, NY: Routledge.

Morimoto, S. A. (2010). Networked democracy: School based volunteerism and youth civic engagement. *Research in Political Sociology, 18,* 129–149.

Morimoto, S. A., & Friedland, L. A. (2011). The changing lifeworld of youth in the information society. *Youth & Society, 43*(2), 549–567.

Myrdal, G. (1944). *An American dilemma: The Negro problem and American democracy* (Vol. 1). Piscataway, NJ: Transactions.

Nenga, S. K. (2010). The value of volunteering: Comparing youths' experiences to popular claims. In H. B. Johnson (Ed.), *Sociological studies of children and youth: Children and youth speak for themselves* (Vol. 13,, pp. 295–318). Bingley, UK: Emerald.

Nenga, S. K. (2011). Volunteering to give up privilege? How affluent youth volunteers respond to class privilege. *Journal of Contemporary Ethnography, 40*(3), 263–289.

Perry, P. (2002). *Shades of white: White kids and racial identity in high school.* Durham, NC: Duke University Press.

Pittman, K. J. (1991). *Promoting youth development: Strengthening the role of youth serving and community organizations.* Washington, DC: Academy for Educational Development, Center for Youth Development and Policy Research.

Putnam, R. D. (2000). *Bowling alone: The collapse and revival of American community.* New York, NY: Simon and Schuster.

Roediger, D. (1991). *The wages of whiteness: Race and the making of the American working class.* London: Verso.

Rubin, B. C., Hayes, B., & Benson, K. (2009). "It's the worst place to live": Urban youth and the challenge of school-based civic learning. *Theory Into Practice, 48,* 213–221.

Shklar, J. (1991). *American citizenship: The quest for inclusion.* Cambridge, MA: Harvard University Press.

Smith, R. M. (1997). *Civic ideals: Conflicting visions of citizenship in U.S. history.* New Haven, CT: Yale University Press.

Spring, K., Dietz, N., & Grimm, R. (2007). *Leveling the path to participation: Volunteering and civic engagement among youth from disadvantaged circumstances.* Washington, DC: Corporation for National and Community Service.

Strauss, A., & Corbin, J. (1998). *Basics of qualitative research: Techniques and procedures for developing grounded theory* (2nd ed.). Thousand Oaks, CA: Sage Publications.

Taft, J. K. (2006). "I'm not a politics person": Teenage girls, oppositional consciousness, and the meaning of politics. *Politics & Gender, 2*(3), 329–352.

Wilkins, A. C. (2004). Puerto Rican wannabes: Sexual spectacle and the marking of race, class, and gender boundaries. *Gender & Society, 18*(1), 103–121.

Youniss, J., McLellan, J. A., Yang, S., & Yates, M. (1999). The role of community service in identity development: Normative, unconventional, and deviant orientations. *Journal of Adolescent Research, 14*, 248–261.

Youniss, J., McLellan, J. A., & Yates, M. (1997). What we know about engendering civic identity. *American Behavioral Scientist, 40*, 620–631.

Youniss, J., & Yates, M. (1997). *Community service and social responsibility in youth: Theory and policy.* Chicago, IL: University of Chicago Press.

Zeldin, R. S. (2000). Integrating research and practice to understand and strengthen communities for adolescent development. *Applied Developmental Science, 4*(2, Suppl.), 2–11.

Zeldin, S. (2004). Youth as agents in adult and community development: Mapping the processes and outcomes of youth engaged in organizational governance. *Applied Developmental Science, 8*(2), 75–90.

Zukin, C., Keeter, S., Andolina, M., Jenkins, K., & Della Carpini, M. X. (2006). *A new engagement? Political participation, civic life, and the changing American citizen.* New York, NY: Oxford University Press.

MEXICAN IMMIGRANT CHILDREN AND YOUTH'S CONTRIBUTIONS TO A COMMUNITY *CENTRO*: EXPLORING CIVIC ENGAGEMENT AND CITIZEN CONSTRUCTIONS

Jocelyn Solís[†], Jesica Siham Fernández and Lucia Alcalá

ABSTRACT

Purpose – *The present study looks at the dynamic process of Mexican immigrant children and youth's civic engagement through their participation in community and family activities. In particular, it explores how their collaboration in a grassroots, immigrant community-based* Centro *in New York City allows for civic engagement. We demonstrate how active community participation, in the form of civic engagement, shapes children and youth's citizenship constructions.*

Methodology – *Based on extensive participant observations and focus group interviews, this article demonstrates how children and youth's civic*

[†]Dr Solís passed away in 2004.

Youth Engagement: The Civic-Political Lives of Children and Youth
Sociological Studies of Children and Youth, Volume 16, 177–200
Copyright © 2013 by Emerald Group Publishing Limited
All rights of reproduction in any form reserved
ISSN: 1537-4661/doi:10.1108/S1537-4661(2013)0000016012

engagement is mediated by their integration and contributions to family and community civic activities and how these activities inform children and youth's knowledge of citizenship discourse. We present evidence that demonstrates that children and youth's involvement and participation in protests, rallies, volunteer activities, as well as the creation of a booklet, associated with immigration, human rights, and social justice, organized through the Centro Guadalupano, *facilitated their knowledge about illegality and citizenship issues.*

Findings – *Findings suggest that when indigenous Mexican children and youth are integrated into the important activities of their community, as active and engaged members, they develop a deeper understanding of civic engagement and what it means to be a participatory "citizen."*

Research implications – *The present study provides a starting point for future research on the importance of and possibilities for child and youth civic engagement in grassroots community organizations. For example, children and youth learn that through active civic participation and community contributions, they are able to challenge dominant discourse on immigration, human rights, and citizenship. This study sheds light on the value of involving children and youth in civic engagement opportunities – a process that can facilitate the construction of citizenship among marginalized groups, particularly undocumented Mexican immigrants from indigenous regions.*

Value – *The findings presented extend broader discourses on the politics of immigration and citizenship, and also challenge, to some extent, mainstream constructions of children and youth. More research in these areas is needed; our paper is a small contribution to the emerging field of indigenous and immigrant children and youth's political socialization and activism.*

Keywords: Civic engagement; citizenship construction; Mexican immigrant youth; community involvement

In the United States, approximately 1.5 million children and youth[1] under the age of 18 years are undocumented immigrants (Passel & Cohn, 2009). Another 4 million children and youth are U.S. citizens in mixed families (e.g., one parent is undocumented) or have family members who are undocumented (Passel & Cohn, 2009). The children of immigrant and/or undocumented parents are directly and strongly affected by anti-immigration sentiment and discourse. Children and youth's political socialization becomes rooted in their experience as immigrants, and is devoid of legal rights and privileges by virtue of both their age and the anti-immigration nativist sentiments that perpetuate the exclusion of people born outside of U.S. borders. These formative experiences may have life-long detrimental effects, such as poor sense of belonging, social exclusion, and political marginalization (Passel & Cohn, 2009).

Active community involvement, however, can counter experiences of exclusion and marginalization, and can help shape children and youth's sociopolitical engagement (Cammarota & Fine, 2008; Flanagan, 2009; Kirshner, Stroble, & Fernandez, 2003; Watts & Flanagan, 2007). Engaging children and youth in civic engagement opportunities affords them a different set of experiences and perspectives from which to interpret different social constructions of citizenship (Lister, Smith, Middleton, & Cox, 2003). Mexican immigrant children and youth in the United States, for example, can gain some understanding of citizenship, what it means to be a citizen, and what counts as civic engagement through engaged community participation (Lopez & Marcelo, 2008; Perez, Espinoza, Ramos, Coronado, & Cortes, 2010).

Focusing on the community inclusion and civic contributions of Mexican immigrant children and youth in a grassroots nonprofit community center, we examine how community participation facilitates the development of citizenship practices among immigrant children and youth whose families are from predominantly indigenous rural parts of Mexico. Our analyses are twofold. First, we document how *Centro Guadalupano*,[2] located in the South Bronx of New York City, serves as a setting for learning opportunities in developing and facilitating civic engagement and participation among these children and youth. Second, we explain how engaged civic participation, through involvement in family and community activities supported by the *Centro Guadalupano*, shapes children and youths' understanding of citizenship practices in the United States.

CONSTRUCTING CITIZENSHIP THROUGH CIVIC ENGAGEMENT PRACTICES

Although there are multiple definitions of civic engagement, it is most commonly associated with voting and electoral participation (Flanagan,

2009). Yet, equating civic engagement with electoral participation is too narrow a view, and cannot help us understand civic engagement among children and youth who are too young to vote. Therefore, it is necessary to broaden the definitions and characteristics associated with civic engagement when describing the experiences of children and youth.

Approaches to defining civic engagement as a developmental process are especially helpful for understanding children and youth's experiences, as is research characterizing youth civic engagement as activism and transformative civic participation in the community (Flanagan, 2009; Watts & Flanagan, 2007). Civic engagement as a form of activism has been characterized as a developing process that emerges with critical awareness of structural and institutional inequality, and when the motivation to make socially just change in civil society is greater than withstanding injustices – a process facilitated through supportive learning opportunities (Cammarota & Fine, 2008; Kirshner et al., 2003; Youniss, 2009). Often such opportunities are provided by youth programs or centers focused on youth empowerment and civic participation (Cammarota & Fine, 2008; Kirshner et al., 2003). Others describe civic engagement as engaging in community service work and/or contributing to society by, for example, disseminating information about a political issue (Flanagan, 2009; Seif, 2009; Watts & Flanagan, 2007).

Notably, civic engagement of underrepresented minority children and youth is often excluded from these definitions of civic engagement. We argue that civic engagement can be usefully characterized as a developmental process often encouraged through interactions with children and youth's communities (Kirshner et al., 2003; Youniss, 2009). Although this view suggests that community members – children, youth, and adults alike – can contribute to their community's empowerment and well-being, little research has explored the civic engagement trajectory of indigenous Mexican immigrant children and youth in the United States. The limited research that exists often compares civic engagement patterns across different generations of Latino youth in high school or college, or in comparison to European American youth (Seif, 2009). For example, the research by Perez et al. (2010) on the civic engagement patterns of undocumented Mexican high school students defines civic engagement as the process of taking advantage of social opportunities, such as community-based services, with the intent of improving their community environment. By this definition, civic engagement entails individuals and community members identifying and pursuing means of improving community well-being, often through productive social interactions (Perez et al., 2010).

Moreover, it involves not only self-beneficial action but also collective beneficence.

Indeed, our understanding of civic engagement must be ontologically broad enough to capture child and youth's civic engagement, which may not be recognized under the mainstream definitions. This is because these definitions are often limited to adult forms of civic engagement, such as voting, from which children are legally proscribed. Therefore, our conceptualization of civic engagement incorporates informal community-mediated practices that are often excluded from adult-centric definitions.

LEARNING THROUGH INTENT: COMMUNITY PARTICIPATION IN CIVIC SETTINGS

Children in many indigenous communities of the Americas are present for and participate in almost all the activities available in their community such as work, ceremonies, and resistance movements (Corona & Fernández, 2000; Corona & Linares, 2007; Rogoff, Moore, Najafi, Dexter, Correa-Chávez, & Solís, 2007; Rogoff, Paradise, Mejía-Arauz, Correa-Chávez, & Angelillo, 2003). Mexican indigenous-heritage children and youth also spend a great deal of time in household work, including sibling caregiving and work that benefits the entire family. Mothers reported that their children (6–8 years old) contributed to a wide range of complex household work and did so under their own initiative, without having to be asked or convinced to help (Alcalá, Rogoff, Mejía-Arauz, Roberts, & Coppens, under review). Children at this age expressed that they should help their families; their responses indicated feelings of shared responsibility and a desire to help as responsible members of the family (Coppens, Alcalá, Rogoff, & Mejia-Arauz, under review). These findings suggest that children and youth develop initiative and sense of shared responsibility as they contribute to household work, which might relate broadly to their civic engagement and involvement in the community.

Children and youth in many indigenous and indigenous-heritage communities of the Americas are expected and allowed to contribute to their community by taking part in important rituals, community celebrations, as well as in political events (Bolin, 2006; Gaskin, 2000; Medina, 2003; Nájera-Ramírez, 1997; Orellana, 2001; Ramírez Sánchez, 2007; Rogoff et al., 2007). In fact, among some indigenous communities in Mexico, children and youth's presence is seen as crucial and necessary for the community's cultural and political future and the children's own cultural development (Linares & Velez, 2007). Children participate with their parents in resistance movements and are seen as important agents of social change (Corona, 2003; Corona & Fernández, 2000; Corona & Linares, 2007; Corona & Pérez-Zavala, 2007; Linares & Velez, 2007; Salles, 1995; Smith, 2007). From an early age, children develop an understanding of the political relations between their community and the Mexican government, which is characterized by distrust and abuse toward indigenous communities (Corona & Pérez-Zavala, 2007). Furthermore, children and youth in these communities often organize action plans to address community social problems such as drug use, violence, and environmental issues, commonly implementing new practices (Linares & Velez, 2007).

Community-wide activities, including resistance movements and cultural celebrations, provide complex opportunities for children and youth's civic engagement and citizenship practices – they participate as contributors and agents of social change (Corona & Pérez-Zavala, 2007; Ramírez Sánchez, 2007; Smith, 2007). Children's integration into the community allows them to *learn* by being present, side by side with their families, taking the initiative to make responsible contributions to their community, even as they learn the skills necessary to do so (Paradise & Rogoff, 2009).

With the increase of migration to the United States from traditionally indigenous regions of Mexico, it is important to look at how immigrant children and youth continue to participate in the receiving community as they encounter new political and economic challenges in their new environment. This paper addresses the need for more research on the civic participation of immigrant children and youth, examining in particular the experiences of Mexican immigrant families from indigenous backgrounds, and their arrival to non-traditionally receiving regions of the United States, such as New York City.[3]

METHOD

This study explores Mexican immigrant children and youth's civic engagement process through their involvement in a grassroots community *Centro*. We examine instances where some of the active adult or parent members of *Centro Guadalupano* discuss with children and youth the intricacies of illegality, immigration, and citizenship. Most importantly, we examine how children and youth's active contribution and participation in the *Centro* is a form of civic engagement and how this shapes their understanding of citizenship practices.

Research Site

Given its strong presence and value to the Latino and immigrant community in New York City, the *Centro Guadalupano* served as the setting for this interdisciplinary research project conducted between 1999 and 2001 by the first author. During the development of this research at the *Centro*, Solís established a relationship of mutual trust, familiarity, and reciprocity with key stakeholders. She gained direct understanding of the way the *Centro* operated, the services and resources it offered, as well as past and future programs and projects. Solís' involvement and commitment to the *Centro*, and her emerging career as a Mexican American researcher and scholar, led her to develop this research project.[4] Thus, Solís' participation and subjectivity in the *Centro* is an important component in understanding the production of this research.

Centro Guadalupano, the largest Mexican umbrella community center in New York City, was founded in 1997 to help Mexican immigrants defend their human and legal rights, and advocate for changes to immigration laws. The *Centro* has been an active and essential resource to the Mexican community since its inception. The mission of the *Centro* is to unify, educate, and provide service to Mexican immigrants in need. The mission includes an explicit stance on successful immigrant adaptation to life in the United States. The *Centro* positions itself within a non-assimilationist discourse, advocating "integration without assimilation" as an important developmental indicator of immigrant success.

The *Centro Guadalupano's* mission is guided by principles of social justice, which they define as unearthing abusive treatment against Mexican immigrants; building community among those who share similar difficulties and struggles; joining people together along cultural, religious, and national backgrounds; and increasing public knowledge and visibility of Mexican immigrant families in New York City. Despite its short existence, the *Centro* has become the largest and most public Mexican organization in the city, with transnational connections to human rights' organizations, churches, labor unions, and political supporters in the United States and Mexico. It is important to mention that despite the *Centro's* affiliation with the Catholic Church, its events, political activism, and civic engagement are not tied to any religious agendas. Rather, the *Centro's* affiliation with the Catholic

Church affords Mexican immigrants a sense of trust and familiarity. Many constituents of the *Centro* were informed about the *Centro's* resources and services via the Catholic Church.

Although the *Centro* makes no clear statements or assumptions about its constituents' capacities for citizenship, neither are direct assumptions made about children and youth's citizenship. It does encourage and provide opportunities for community members to engage civically in political manifestations, particularly around immigration and citizenship issues (e.g., General Amnesty). All members, regardless of their age, are encouraged to participate in events organized and sponsored by the *Centro*. Many of these events include providing counsel, resources, and services to immigrant families.

The *Centro* disseminates information through a Spanish monthly bulletin that reaches more immigrants than its membership includes. The bulletin teaches undocumented immigrants that they need not be silent about injustices they face, and that as a unified community they are capable of creating a safe space to make public demands that improve the quality of their private lives. The bulletin includes a variety of writing genres, with a wide range of topics such as immigration, human/legal rights, education, health, violence, Mexican folklore/traditions, religious/spirituality, sports, events in Mexico, and community activity. Themes that run through the publications include injustice, solidarity, individuality, resistance, progress, success, transformation, struggle/fight, loss, and hope. Below is an example of an expository piece illustrating a typical Mexican immigrant story, as well as the intervening role of the *Centro*. It was published in the April 2000 bulletin and was written by a male *Centro* member. The piece is entitled *En la Lucha por Nuestra Dignidad* ["In the Struggle for Our Dignity"]:

> Poverty obligates us to emigrate to this country with the hope of earning good money and taking our families out of crisis in our beloved Mexico. And we risk our life when we cross the border. From there, on the border, our suffering begins as it is not so easy to cross. Our hope is to soon pay off the money we brought that is often loaned at a high credit rate. That is what obligates us to work at the first job we find, without caring about the hours, nor the low salary, nor how one will be treated. On some occasions, all of this [labor abuses and physical mistreatment] has to be reported to the police or to the *Centro Guadalupano* so that help will come from our office. Do not be afraid of denouncing all of these violations, because even as undocumented immigrants we have rights! We are humans, not animals to be treated in such an unfair manner by those children of arrogance and money. If you are one of those workers, denounce those atrocities. The *Centro Guadalupano* is here to help us. It teaches us how to defend ourselves from those abuses. Remember that we are not alone. The *Centro Guadalupano* is there to help us.

The activities of the *Centro* are always simultaneously political, religious, and cultural. The major civic and political activities include feast day of *la Virgen de Guadalupe* on December 12; *ViaCrucis* of immigrants on Good

Friday; and a festival of artistic expressions such as folkloric dance, song, and photography. Other activities include the celebration of Mexican Independence day on September 16, the Day of the Dead on the first two days of November, and a march for unconditional General Amnesty usually taking place in New York City and Washington, DC, on various days.

In order to observe Mexican immigrant children and youth's civic engagement, our project used in-depth group interviews with parents as well as participant observation with children and youth. Observations included rallies, marches, religious and cultural events, a 10-week writing workshop, and a booklet-making activity. The booklet-making activity served two purposes. First, it provided children and youth with opportunities to discuss their lived experiences in the city through creative artistic and writing activities that allowed full participation regardless of age and language ability (e.g., English or Spanish proficiency). Second, the booklet was intended as an informational resource for families planning to migrate or recently arriving to New York City. The booklet would tell the children and youth's stories and experiences in their own voice.

The booklet was developed during 10 writing workshop meetings. The writing workshop functioned as a meaningful activity for children and youth to explore and illustrate their experiences in the city. The children and youth participants were asked to write and illustrate stories about their lives in New York. During the writing workshops, 90-minute focus group interviews were facilitated and supervised by the first author in the *Centro's* main office on Friday afternoons, between February and April 2000. Framing the meetings as workshops, with a focus on the creation of the booklet, allowed for issues of illegality to emerge during the meeting discussions. Throughout the booklet-making process, children and youth were encouraged by the adult facilitator to make suggestions or changes to the type and presentation of information provided in the booklet. The completed booklet was a product of children and youth's engaged participation in the *Centro* and their experiences as migrants to New York City.

Participants

A total of 16 children and youth participated in the making of a booklet over the course of 10 meetings. A core group of five children and youth participated consistently until the booklet was completed (see Table 1). The participant sample was diverse in age, country of birth, and number of years residing in the United States. Demographic reports of families and community members affiliated with the *Centro* indicated that participating children and youth

Table 1. Children's Demographic Information.

Participant	Age	Place of Birth	Years in the United States	Place of Residence	Meetings Attended
David	14	Mexico	10	Manhattan	8
Karina	12	Mexico	10	Manhattan	7
Marcos	9	United States	9	Bronx	7
Margarita	6	United States	6	Bronx	8
Ariel	5	United States	5	Bronx	8

were predominantly Mexican immigrants from rural agricultural areas of the southern state of Puebla, approximately 60 miles south of Mexico City.

The children and youth participating in this study were recruited through the *Centro* by word of mouth and by placing informational flyers at the entrance of the central office. Interested participants were told that the writing workshop was part of a research project exploring how Mexican families, specifically children and youth, come to identify themselves in a new country. All participants consented to having their writing and graphic illustrations used in the making of a booklet for children and youth whose families intended to migrate to New York City or who had recently arrived.

RESULTS

In this section, we present the social transformation of children and youth's civic engagement, emphasizing how through active community involvement at the *Centro* they were able to engage and challenge citizenship discourse in ways that promoted their participation. Then, we describe how children and youth's participation in political events led them to greater engagement with their community. Finally, we provide evidence showing how the creation of an informational booklet guided children and youth in reflecting on and challenging discourse on immigration, citizenship, and politics of belonging in New York City.

Children and Youth's Participation in Political Events:
Contributions to the Centro Guadalupano

In the *Centro*, it was common for community members of all ages to participate in public rallies and other events. Children, youth, and adults alike participated as a collective community, and the presence of the *Centro* was strongly shaped by the solidarity of its participating and active community members. Children and youth, for example, were immersed in these forms of participation and discourse directly through their families' experiences of immigration, as well as indirectly through their parents' participation in the *Centro*. This level of participation exemplifies the notion that Mexican immigrant families' existence in the city is a personal and a political struggle for rights claiming citizenship, belonging as community members, and participating in civic transformation.

We posit that indigenous Mexican immigrant children and youth's learning and civic engagement stems from their own and their family's contributions, engagement, and participation in the *Centro Guadalupano*. Families participating in the *Centro* share a political identity based on their immigration experiences and/or undocumented status. This shared identity, one often conceived as *othering* (e.g., "illegal" and "alien"), becomes an identity of struggle and collective action toward creating socially just change. In the *Centro*, collective action was aimed at challenging the meaning of illegality via the (re)construction of citizenship as a form of active collective civic participation.

Children and youth at the *Centro* were exposed to immigration discourse on the politics and experiences of being undocumented by accompanying their mothers to meetings, political demonstrations, and other public events. Children and youth's participation in public events such as marches and rallies is acknowledged and welcomed by members of the *Centro*, but especially by mothers, who often guided their children during these social and political events, socializing them to enact a particular type of civic engagement rooted in principles of citizenship as an embodied process of rights claiming and belonging (Rosaldo, 1994).

In an interview with two mothers, Lucero (mother of Marcos, Ariel, and Margarita) and Mercedes (mother of David and Karina) reported on how their children learn about the political events and activities:

Interviewer: [Children] hear you when you're talking…

Lucero: They hear when we–, why we're here, when we have meetings, you see, we bring them.

Mercedes: Sometimes on the street they say: "Here we are and we won't go!" [laughter] They repeat one of the chants.

Interviewer: Yes, once they did that here (meeting room)! [laughter]

Lucero: In other words, they already know, but he tells me, "*Mami.*" Marcos has asked me. "*Mami,*" he told me, "why do you do this?"… And he says, "Can I do it?" I tell him, "Yes, you're going to help me. You're supporting us because of your mother, because you don't have a problem. You were born here."

In the above example, the mothers mentioned how their children demon-strated some familiarity with their mothers' activities within the *Centro*. Based on statements made by both mothers and their children, it seemed that even the youngest child, although not fully conscious of the meaning of immigration and illegality, was being socialized and exposed to discourse on illegality through family and *Centro* practices. Marcos, one of the oldest participants, was already beginning to question the reasons for his mother's (Lucero) actions and his own involvement within the *Centro*. Lucero's reply to Marco's questions demonstrates how political involvement is closely tied to Mexican immigrants' sense of family unity, respect for one's parents, and children and youth's initiative in contributing to their family's well-being. Through his involvement, Marcos learns that the goals of his actions are not necessarily personal benefit, but rather are in support of his mother and other undocumented immigrants. Marcos' participation allows him to acknowledge his own rights as a legal citizen, realizing that he can contri-bute to his family and community's well-being through his civic engagement and commitment to make social change and justice possible for immigrant families like his.

Older participants, like Karina and David, did not accompany their mothers to every event. Yet, they were all familiar and aware of the importance of collectively participating and having their voices be heard. Part of their political socialization stemmed from their access to other sources of information on immigration and citizenship at the *Centro*, as well as their own migration experiences and/or that of their family members. David, for example, spent much of his time as a volunteer in the *Centro's* office where he was exposed to its everyday activities and social justice philosophy. Indeed, the more political events children and youth partici-pated in with their mothers, the more cognizant they were of the purpose of the protests, marches, and political manifestations that the *Centro* helped organize to advocate for immigrants' rights.

Civic engagement and participation opportunities provided through and supported by the *Centro* were essential in mediating children and youth's knowledge about immigration and citizenship discourse. Such collective actions were often represented institutionally at public rallies where children and youth accompanied their parents carrying picket signs that read: "I am an American citizen but my mommy is not. She deserves Amnesty now." In this way, children and youth's involvement and collaborative participation in shared activities alongside their mothers and the *Centro* taught them informal ways of being civically engaged. Even children who were legal U.S. citizens eagerly participated in social and political events as a way of being in solidarity with their families' struggle. As we will expand on in the sections that follow, through this process children and youth learned to construct their own ways of being young citizens, advocating for General Amnesty and legal rights, as well as challenging misconceptions about citizenship and illegality.

Creating an Informational Booklet for Immigrant Families, Children, and Youth: Community Activities as Civic Participation

The booklet project was framed as a writing workshop in which youth were asked to write and illustrate stories about their lives in New York (for a description of the writing workshop meetings, see Table 2). Participants were constantly reminded that they could suggest information they believed should be included in the booklet. The booklet project, drawing on children and youth's experiences and struggles as new immigrants to the United States, explored issues of illegality and was a resource the *Centro* provided to other families who were planning to migrate or newly arriving families. The booklet project's elicitation of bilingual and bicultural knowledge positioned the children and youth as cultural brokers who could use their diverse knowledge and skills to mediate or "translate" the expectations of future migrants and facilitate their integration into life in New York City.

Mission Statement
The participants developed a mission statement about the purpose of the booklet and the motivation for its creation. The mission statement gives voice to the children and youth's desire to inform other families, children, and youth about their experiences in New York City. Participants stated:

> Our purpose was to make a booklet about our experiences as Mexican children who live in New York and give it to other children and youth and their families who are in Mexico and who are thinking of coming to live here in New York.

The mission statement demonstrates the concrete purpose in making the informational booklet. As well, through the creation and dissemination of this information, participants opened opportunities to transform discourse on immigration and illegality. During the booklet meetings and through text revisions for the booklet, participants talked about the processes of illegality and citizenship.

In the last booklet-making session, participants had an opportunity to examine the working group's politics and negotiate personal understandings

Table 2.   Outline of Meetings.

Meeting	Topic/Activity
Introductory meeting	The children and youth who attended the first meeting were told what the research involved: audiotaping discussions of one's experiences in New York, and writing and illustrating a booklet for future immigrant families. Parental consent forms were distributed and informed consent from each participant was later collected. This information was repeated every time a new participant joined the group.
Meeting 2	This meeting entailed a discussion about information that new immigrants should be familiar with, and led to a conversation of the participants' life experiences and knowledge about the city. By the end of the meeting, they had produced texts and drawings based on these conversations.
Meeting 3	Interviews were conducted between participants about their experiences in U.S. schools, at home, in their neighborhoods, and in Mexico. Each participant took turns audiotaping themselves as both interviewer and respondent.
Meeting 4	Participants were asked to brainstorm and write advice for new Mexican immigrant families, children, and youth. Some of them completed drawings they felt could be included in the booklet. The group present during this meeting co-authored a piece of fiction about a typical afternoon in the lives of a Mexican brother and sister living in New York City.
Meeting 5	Participants produced more drawings, and added to the advice columns from previous texts. They also discussed spontaneously their personal experiences of political manifestations.
Meeting 6	The youngest participants who were not yet literate were asked to make illustrations about themselves; the rest of the participants were asked to write a letter describing themselves to the children and youth in Mexico who would read the booklet. The texts compiled for the booklet were reviewed and edited by the group. Our discussions on this day were audiotaped.
Meeting 7	Participants discussed their experiences of life in Mexico before migrating to the United States, and produced illustrations based on their narrations.
Meeting 8	Participants audiotaped interviews with each other about their own and others' beliefs about immigrants. The questions included: (1) What do other people think about immigrants? and (2) What do you think about immigrants? They also produced more illustrations.
Meeting 9	Participants were audiotaped as they reviewed and edited texts to be included in the booklet. They also made decisions about the booklet's layout and sequence of texts and illustrations. Some participants were questioned further about the possibilities of future programs or projects that the *Centro* could implement for children and youth who were already living in New York and who were members of the *Centro*.
Concluding meeting	The final session of the workshop was dedicated to reflect on the process of compiling a booklet for other children and youth, and to devising a title that the group collectively decided would be New York, *Nueva York para niños y familias mexicanas* [New York for Mexican children and families].

of the societal history of Mexican immigrants in New York City. The children and youth's discussion also functioned as a reflection about the purpose of their booklet, its audience, major topics, and the central message for their potential readers – immigrant families, children, and youth.

Selecting a Title

By living in the United States, participants were exposed to mainstream politics, which to some extent socialized them into certain kinds of political life. Some of these politics involved voting. In the process of creating and deciding on a title, both having a voice and voting were important. The process entailed a number of strategies, including but not limited to persuasion and critical thinking about the meaning they wanted the title to convey.

All the participants, except Ariel and Margarita, were vocal about their title and tried to persuade the other members of the group into voting on behalf of their offered title. For example, Karina engaged in coercive tactics using conditional negotiations, like making unrealistic promises, if the other participants were to vote for her proposed title. But David and Marcos used Karina's conditional negotiation tactic to suppress her and win votes against her. At times, David's rejection of his sister's proposed title were more explicit and authoritarian. For example, any decisions made in favor of Karina's proposed title were encouraged to be rejected or ignored. In the following excerpts, we demonstrate how some titles were proposed and consequently rejected.

David: What about *Vida en Nueva York*? *Vida en Nueva York* [Life in New York]

Marcos: Yeah!

Jorge: *La Vida en Nueva York*? What else can we say?

David: Well, we got our title?

Jorge: How about, *La Vida Loca*? [The Crazy Life]

Karina: *La Vida Loca en Nueva York*! [The Crazy Life en New York]

Solís: That's another option...

David: No, anything Karina says is a rejection. That's it.

The following conversation illustrates how participants were asked to use the purpose and audience of the booklet as criteria for creating and deciding a title.

Jorge: How about *La Vida Loca?* [The Crazy Life]

Karina: *La Vida Loca en Nueva York!* [Crazy Life en New York]

Solís: That's another option. Others?

Karina: *El Estilo Nueva York!*

David: No, no! *El Estilo Nueva York?* (New York Style)

Karina: *El Estilo AND Nueva York!* (Style & New York)

David: No, they [immigrants] are not coming here for fashion reasons, man!

Solís: So, *work* in Nueva York?

David: No, not that either! [laughter] El *trabajo,* la *vida...* (work, life)

Solís: Well this is for kids; so should we say something about that in the title?

Karina: *Los Niños en Nueva York!* (Children in New York).

After several of these titles were proposed, each one was written on the white board, and participants were asked to vote for a title. By the end of the session, the group had combined Karina and David's proposed titles, and elected by majority vote *"Nueva York para Niños y Familias Mexicanas"* (New York for Mexican Children and Families) as the winning title.

Creating a title for their booklet challenged participants because embedded in the title were the politics of their lived experiences in New York City, and how to best represent them. The entire group was involved in a political socialization process that involved decision making based on collaboration and reciprocal dialogue. Through these processes and a majority vote, participants learned about democratic practices at the cornerstone of American values.

Creating a Maze
During the making of the booklet, Karina suggested that the booklet should contain games for children and youth. She proposed to include a maze leading from Mexico to New York illustrating the migration trajectory of the booklet's potential readers. In subsequent sessions, David drew the maze himself and added a twist to Karina's suggestion by inserting two dead ends in the middle of the path, which he labeled *"la migra,"* a colloquial term for the Immigration and Naturalization Services (INS), now under the name U.S. Citizenship and Immigration Services.

In this study, participants transformed the severity of illegality into a humorous and challenging game for their readers. Both humor and challenge are embodied in David's title for the maze: "Can you get to

New York without running into *la migra?*" David, unlike other participants in the group, could remember crossing the U.S.–Mexican border with his sister and mother 10 years ago when he was 4 years old, but disliked talking openly about this experience. We argue that activities like drawing the maze for inclusion in the *Centro's* booklet provide an acceptable and safe means to explore relations of power and oppression that immigrants experience. Through this activity, a possible world was created where clever children and youth could outsmart a higher authority (e.g., the immigration officials, *la migra*), whom they perceived as threatening their lives and that of their families. Such an activity served to reaffirm their identity as Mexican immigrants in a new country seeking greater opportunities, and give some closure to the traumatic experience of crossing the border.

Overall, participants showed initiative and responsibility in their participation and contributions to the *Centro*. By being integrated in the community *Centro*, children and youth learned about the importance of their political activities and took the initiative to contribute to their family's involvement in such events. Their civic engagement included learning about politics and policies that affected their community, and making real contributions to their community, the *Centro*, and their own learning and development (Paradise & de Haan, 2009; Rogoff, 2003). Similar to some indigenous communities in Mexico, Mexican immigrant children in New York City were integrated into activities valued by their community such as protests, marches, and community-wide civic activities. In contrast to other communities where children's involvement is limited to age-segregated settings and child-focused activities, children in this study both actively participated in the activities of the *Centro* and showed agency in their family and community contributions.

Learning about Politics, Citizenship, and Civic Processes through Civic Engagement

The sessions for the development of the bulletin served as an opportunity to examine several topics that included the construction of "citizenship" and "illegality," reasons for immigrating to New York City, mainstream conceptions of Mexicans in the United States, and how undocumented immigrants and their families (or anyone presumed to be a foreign-born Latino) are treated by other people. These critical and controversial conversations were brought up spontaneously in the context of the booklet-making project and in reference to participants' experiences. When telling about these experiences, Solís often followed through with questions to further the participants' thinking and learning process. In some cases, conversations were emotional and triggered bad memories of, for example, encounters with immigration law officials.

At times, participants showed resistance to discussing the material, and at other times discussions were able to mediate children's knowledge about citizenship and migration. For example, during one of the booklet-making sessions, David (14 years old) seems to be unengaged with Solís' request for them to write about or interview each other about what they and other people think about immigration and immigrants. David's perspectives on citizenship and immigration were summarized in Solís' fieldnote in the following way:

> By the time our group meeting was nearly over, David had barely written a few words amounting to "I think that people who are citizens think that they are better than immigrants" and "I think that immigrants are just as equal as non-immigrants." In my attempt to understand how, why or on what basis he had made these statements, I continued to question David. At this point, David simply added a phrase to his first statement: 'They [citizens] think they have more rights.' [Fieldnote, week 5, Solís]

In a later session, David expanded on his views and argued for a mainstream definition of citizenship construed as a birthright and not as civic practice consisting of community service and involvement, and effecting social structures to improve social conditions. David offered that his U.S.-born youngest sister is a U.S. citizen and perhaps also a Mexican immigrant, and stated that he was also a citizen simply because he lived in the United States. This stirred a debate between he and Karina, who reverted to her original understanding: "No, that's not a citizen! A[n] immigrant is a person who doesn't have ten years over here who came from another country." David ended this discussion by widening the range of what constitutes a U.S. citizen, integrating both legality and residence as criteria. He stated, "Karina, I didn't say I was a legal citizen!" He identifies himself as a citizen because he resides in the United States, and could also be qualified as an "illegal" citizen according to Karina's understanding.

David's citizenship definition and views on illegality were challenged by his younger sister, Karina, because they did not include legality and residency (number of years living in the United States). Karina questioned David's assumptions by suggesting that citizenship is constructed via a social and historical context of immigration, rather than as dictated by dominant hierarchical structures that perpetuate power and status quo. During this discussion, Karina defined citizenship as an outcome of an immigration process. According to Karina's understanding, an immigrant was a person who had not lived more than ten years in the United States: "cause in order not to be an immigrant you gotta have at least ten years here, then you could become citizen. Right?" Karina insists that: "an undocumented person could make the papers [file application for legal documentation], and after ten years you could be citizen." Karina was alluding to the legal conditions needed for a one-time amnesty afforded by the Immigrant Reform and Control Act of 1986, in which legal residency was granted to undocumented immigrants who could demonstrate that they had lived continuously for 10 years in the United States prior to 1982.

Through such discursive strategies as defining, challenging, and offering counter arguments, "citizen" was understood in relation to "immigrant," where immigrants were defined under legal/illegal categorizations. When asked what other people thought about immigrants, Karina and David's responses revealed that their identification of immigrants was not only expressed in terms of illegal citizenship but also in terms of other social structures of power. The participants recognized being an immigrant, aside from being a non-citizen, in terms of class and language inequalities and differences. Karina identified "other people" as "Americans," as those that were legal citizens and permanent residents of the United States. Specifically, she referred to those who arrived in the United States without having to cross the border as people who think they are better than immigrants because they mistakenly think of immigrants as "different" and "less American."

As reflected in the above statements, after several discussions about citizenship both Karina and David engaged in an interrogative process of reciprocal and critical learning regarding their different understandings of citizenship, immigration, and illegality. David and Karina's understanding of citizenship processes evolves within experiences and interactions happening through the *Centro*, and the civic opportunities that were provided to the families and their children and youth.

The data presented show how Mexican immigrant children and youth, through their active participation in the *Centro*, gained valuable civic engagement experience. This early exposure and active community involvement – in marches, protests, and the making of an informational booklet – afforded children and youth opportunities to engage in citizenship practices to effect social change. The booklet was a culmination of participants' experiences as Mexican indigenous immigrants, and indicated a desire to inform, educate, and welcome newly arriving or prospective immigrant families to a land of opportunities for some. The booklet was both an informational product, wherein their civic engagement and day-to-day experiences are documented, and also a testament to their struggle for equality, justice, and General Amnesty.

GENERAL DISCUSSION AND IMPLICATIONS

Our findings suggest that civic engagement, as an active form of community participation in the *Centro*, helped shape children and youth's understanding of citizenship practices, illegality, and immigration. Within the context of an anti-immigration discourse, challenging a sense of belonging among first-generation undocumented immigrant families in New York City, civic engagement in the *Centro*'s activities afforded many families, children, and youth a sense of community. The *Centro Guadalupano* served as a mediating setting for civic engagement opportunities. Indigenous Mexican immigrant children and youth who volunteered and participated in the *Centro* demonstrated a deep and broad understanding of concepts such as "citizen" and "illegality," challenging and in some situations rejecting those concepts when defining themselves and their family. Some children and youth created new categories that would more accurately conceptualize their situation as undocumented people.

Mexican immigrant children and youth in this study challenged the concept of citizenship to include undocumented citizens. In some instances, participants did this by talking about human rights and their experiences as members of society. This resembled Rosaldo's (1994) concept of cultural citizenship that all people have the right to belong to a social community, and thus participate in the social, historical, and political reproduction of civil society in ways that allow for self-expression and equality. Children and youth actively participated in the cultural events that the *Centro* organized, and their participation in the *Centro* allowed them to affirm their identities, membership, representation, and space.

By taking part and contributing to important activities in the *Centro*, for individual and community benefit, Mexican immigrant children and youth developed a critical awareness of structural inequality that undocumented immigrants experience. This process was facilitated by first-hand learning opportunities available through the *Centro* and by the inclusion and welcoming of children and youth's contributions to their community. By being present for public civic activities and the creation of the booklet, participants learned by engaging in those specific activities, listening to important discussions, and observing how others organize and work together.

The findings gathered from the participants involved with the *Centro* demonstrate how illegality as an identity, with a focus on the meaning of citizen, is co-constructed and mediates citizenship understanding via civic engagement in immigration and human rights discourse. Previous research has shown that Latino children and youth can navigate invisibility within schools, overcome challenges in school settings, and move beyond being passive recipients of knowledge to active and engaged citizen learners that advocate for social justice and change (Seif, 2009; Valenzuela, 1999). Among the participants in this study, active community involvement and engagement was evident in their conversations and activities, like the making of a booklet for newly arrived Mexican immigrant families. A greater understanding of how undocumented children and youth experienced the protests, marches, and political manifestations for General Amnesty was observed through informal conversations. Children and youth's discussions and conversations arose out of a series of events and political activities supported by the *Centro* and allowed for an awareness of immigration and citizenship discourse. Indeed, collective participation and civic engagement can directly empower and inform immigrant families and communities.

Future research should look at how institutions facilitate children and youth's civic engagement process. For example, schools and community centers similar to the *Centro*, as institutions for learning and socialization into civic life, shape immigrant children and youth's conceptions of belonging, citizenship, civic engagement, and illegality. Additional research should explore the role of these institutions as mediators in the civic learning process of children and youth from historically underrepresented backgrounds, such as those from immigrant and indigenous communities.

Research on children and youth's civic participation and engagement with citizenship and immigration discourse is necessary, given current demographic shifts and increases in the number of undocumented and/or mixed-status families in the United States. Many of the undocumented or immigrant children and youth will become important members of society; research should explore the implications of children and youth's civic engagement in early years of life for later adult citizenship and participation. When children and youth are seen as agents of social change (Linares & Velez, 2007) and contributing members of their community, more opportunities to engage in important activities to effect social change are created. This research provides evidence of children and youth's civic engagement as a social change process, specifically toward challenging and advancing the processes by which children and youth understand illegality, citizenship, immigration, and civic engagement.

NOTES

1. In using the term *children*, we do not imply that there is one unitary or monolithic age that sets them apart from youth (Qvortrup, 1995). Children and youth are subject to the norms, discourses, and age-based social and legal policies that underpin their construction as nonadults. Thus, we refer to children as those between the ages of 5 and 11 years, and use the term youth to describe participants 12–17 years old (Qvortrup, 1995).

2. The grass-roots community center is given the pseudonym of *Centro Guadalupano* to maintain the confidentiality and privacy of the organization. Throughout the paper, we will refer to *Centro Guadalupano* as *Centro*.

3. Historically, New York City has been a receiving region for Puerto Ricans and Dominicans, but only recently for Mexican communities. At the time of this study, in 2000, Latinos accounted for 27.8% of New York's population; 8.4% were Mexican (Bergad, 2011).

4. At first, Solís' work consisted of meeting with the executive director, staff, volunteers, and center beneficiaries, as well as attending meetings and events sponsored by *Centro Guadalupano*. The initial collaboration was geared toward locating and applying to grant foundations that would provide financial support for educational activities and social services resources at *Centro Guadalupano*. In the process, Dr. Solís had also been involved in a range of other activities. One of her main tasks was to translate *Centro Guadalupano's* pamphlets and brochures, as well as the executive director's press releases. In addition, Solís was asked to participate as a member of *Centro Guadalupano's* advisory board in May, 2000. After completing the data collection phase of her dissertation, she became coordinator of Research and Development in January, 2001.

REFERENCES

Alcalá, L., Rogoff, B., Mejía-Arauz, L., Roberts, A. D., & Coppens, A. D. (under review). Children's contributions to family work: Cultural comparisons in México. (Submitted manuscript).

Bergad, L. W. (2011). The Latino population of New York City, 1990-2010. *Latino Data Project Reports CUNY*. Retrieved from http://web.gc.cuny.edu/lastudies/latinodata projectreports/The%20Latino%20Population%20of%20New%20York%20City%2019 90%20-%202010.pdf. Accessed on 8/1/2012.

Bolin, I. (2006). *Growing up in a culture of respect: Child rearing in highland Peru*. Austin, TX: University of Texas Press.

Cammarota, J., & Fine, M. (2008). *Revolutionizing education: Youth participatory action research*. New York, NY: Routledge.

Coppens, A. D., Alcalá, L., Rogoff, B., & Mejía-Arauz, L. (under review). Children's views on their contributions to family work across two communities in Guadalajara, México. (Submitted manuscript).

Corona, Y. C. (2003). Reproducción cultural y generación de relaciones comunitarias alrededor de la niñez [Cultural reproduction and generation of community relations around childhood]. *Anuario de Investigacion, 1*, 230–247.

Corona, Y. C., & Fernández, A. M. (2000). Infancia y política [Infancy and politics]. In Y. C. Corona (Ed.), *Infancia, Legislación y Política* (pp. 61–67). México, MX: Editorial U.N.A.M.

Corona, Y. C., & Linares, M. E. (2007). Promoting child and youth participation in the creation of citizenship. *Children, Youth and Environment, 17*(2), 1–10.

Corona, Y. C., & Pérez-Zavala, C. (2007). Infancia y cultura política en una comunidad rural [Childhood and political culture in a rural community]. *Foro de Educación Cívica y Cultural Política Democrática, 10*, 383–393.

Flanagan, C. A. (2009). Young people's civic engagement and political development. In A. Furlong (Ed.), *International handbook of youth and young adulthood* (pp. 293–300). New York, NY: Routledge.

Gaskins, S. (2000). Children's daily activities in a Mayan village: A culturally grounded description. *Cross-Cultural Research, 34*(4), 375.

Kirshner, B., Strobel, K., & Fernandez, M. (2003). Critical civic engagement among urban youth. *Penn GSE Perspectives on Urban Education, 2*(1), 1–20.

Linares, M. E., & Velez, H. (2007). Children as agents of social change. *Children, Youth and Environment, 17*(2), 217–255.

Lister, R., Smith, N., Middleton, S., & Cox, L. (2003). Young people talk about citizenship: Empirical perspectives on theoretical and political debates. *Citizenship Studies, 7*, 235–253.

Lopez, M. H., & Marcelo, K. B. (2008). The civic engagement of immigrant youth: New evidence from the 2006 Civic and Political Health of the Nation survey. *Applied Developmental Science, 12*(2), 66–73.

Medina, M. P. (2003). Niños mayos: Movimientos, danza y formas de apropiación de las prácticas festivas [Mayan children: movements, dances, and forms of appropriating festival practices]. *Tramas: Diversidad de Infancias, 20*, 121–148.

Nájera-Ramírez, O. (1997). *La fiesta de los tastoanes: Critical encounters in Mexican festival performance.* Albuquerque, NM: University of New Mexico Press.

Orellana, M. F. (2001). The work kids do: Mexican and Central American immigrant children's contributions to households and schools in California. *Harvard Educational Review, 71*(3), 366–390.

Paradise, R., & de Haan, M. (2009). Responsibility and reciprocity. *Anthropology & Education Quarterly, 40*(2), 187–204.

Paradise, R., & Rogoff, B. (2009). Side by side: Learning by observing and pitching in. *Ethos, 37*(1), 102–138.

Passel, J. S., & Cohn, D. (2009). A portrait of unauthorized immigrants in the United States. *Pew Hispanic Center.* Retrieved from http://www.pewhispanic.org/files/reports/107.pdf. Accessed on 7/12/2012.

Perez, W., Espinoza, R., Ramos, K., Coronado, H., & Cortes, R. (2010). Civic engagement patterns of undocumented Mexican students. *Journal of Hispanic Higher Education, 9*, 245–265.

Qvortrup, J. (1995). From useful to useful: The historical continuity of children's constructive participation. In A.-M. Ambert (Ed.), *Sociological studies of children* (Vol. 7, pp. 49–76). Bingley, UK: Emerald.

Ramírez Sánchez, M. A. (2007). 'Helping at home': The concept of childhood and work among the Nahuas of Tlaxcala, Mexico. In B. Hungerland, M. Liebel, B. Milne & A. Wihstutz (Eds.), *Working to be someone: Child focused research and practice with working children* (pp. 87–95). London, UK: Jessica Kingsley Publishers.

Rogoff, B. (2003). *The cultural nature of human development*. New York, NY: Oxford University Press.

Rogoff, B., Moore, L., Najafi, B., Dexter, A., Correa-Chávez, M., & Solís, J. (2007). Children's development of cultural repertoires through participation in everyday routines and practices. In J. E. Grusec & P. D. Hastings (Eds.), *Handbook of socialization* (pp. 490–515). New York, NY: Guilford.

Rogoff, B., Paradise, R., Mejía Arauz, R., Correa-Chávez, M., & Angelillo, C. (2003). Firsthand learning through intent participation. *Annual Review of Psychology, 54*, 175–203.

Rosaldo, R. (1994). Cultural citizenship and educational democracy. *Cultural Anthropology, 9*, 402–411.

Salles, V. (1995). Ideas para estudiar las fiestas religiosas: Una experiencia en Xochimilco. [Ideas on how to study religious celebrations: An experience in Xochimilco]. *Alteridades, 5*(9), 25–40.

Seif, H. (2009). The civic education and engagement of Latina/o immigrant youth: Challenging boundaries and creating safe spaces. *Latino Immigrant Civic and Political Participation*. Retrieved from http://www.wilsoncenter.org/topics/docs/Hinda%20Seif%20 Challenging%20Boundaries%20and%20Creating%20Safe%20Spaces.pdf. Accessed on 1/3/2011.

Smith, A. M. (2007). The children of Loxicha, Mexico. *Children, Youth and Environments, 17*(2), 33–55.

Watts, R., & Flanagan, C. (2007). Pushing the envelope on youth civic engagement: A developmental and liberation psychology perspective. *Journal of Community Psychology, 35*, 779–792.

Youniss, J. (2009). Why we need to learn more about youth civic engagement. *Social Forces, 88*, 971–975.

Valenzuela, A. (1999). *Subtractive schooling: US-Mexican youth and the politics of caring*. Albany, NY: SUNY Press.

"MY MOTHER AND FATHER ARE AFRICAN, BUT I'M NORWEGIAN": IMMIGRANT CHILDREN'S PARTICIPATION IN CIVIC SOCIETY IN NORWAY

William A. Corsaro, Berit O. Johannesen and Lily Appoh

ABSTRACT

Purpose – *To examine children and youth's participation in civic society in Norway with a particular focus on immigrant children's participation in May 17 (Constitution Day).*

Methodology – *We observed May 17 activities in Trondheim, Norway, over several years and conducted in-depth interviews with immigrant children about their participation in May 17 activities. We also relied on archival data and statistical reports of youth participation and immigration policy as well as attitudes toward immigrants to provide context for the observations and interviews.*

Findings – *We found three clear patterns in the data. First, the children continually expressed their enjoyment of traditional intergenerational*

Youth Engagement: The Civic-Political Lives of Children and Youth
Sociological Studies of Children and Youth, Volume 16, 201–225
ISSN: 1537-4661/doi:10.1108/S1537-4661(2013)0000016013

activities and in the discussion we see how certain activities helped to integrate themselves and their families into their communities. Second, the children displayed a keen knowledge of the 17th of May traditions, their history, and their symbolic value in Norwegian society. Third, especially the older children and youth often discussed their feelings of being Norwegian while also expressing an awareness of their immigrant status and cultural heritage. Their reflections on these dual identities provide more general insights into immigrant status, assimilation, and multiculturalism in Norway.

Keywords: Civic society; children and youth; Norway; immigrant policy; immigrant experiences and identity

INTRODUCTION

After marching in the May 17 children's parade in Oslo, Norway, a young boy from African heritage was interviewed on national television. He was holding a Norwegian flag and smiled broadly as he announced into the microphone that his father was from one country in Africa and his mother was from another, but he was Norwegian!

On July 22, 2011, 69 members of the Labour Youth organization were shot to death by a domestic terrorist at a party retreat camp on Utøya Island outside Oslo. Of the 69 victims, 8 were immigrant youth ranging in age from 15 to 20. One of the victims, Bano Rashid's story was recounted in an article in the *New York Times*. She is described as an Iraqi Kurd who came to Norway as a child and "wanted to stretch the limits of the country's blond and blue-eye identity, to help redefine what it means to be Norwegian" (Schwirtz, 2011). Bano Rashid was very politically active and wrote articles and gave speeches in which she denounced racism and discrimination against immigrants in Norway. She believed that the integration of immigrants into Norwegian society was both possible and vital. She argued in 2010 in the Norwegian newspaper *Aftenposten*: "Let Norway use the resources of its immigrants. Give us time to integrate, preferably without discrimination" (Schwirtz, 2011).

In this paper, we draw on archival data, statistical reports, observational data, and in-depth interviews to examine the participation of immigrant children and youth in civic society in Trondheim, Norway. Our focus is in particular on these children's perception of and participation in May 17 activities in celebration of Norway's Constitution Day, the main national holiday. However, we also explore the immigrant experience, multiculturalism, and civic society in Norway more generally including immigrant children and youth awareness of Norwegian history, their perception of themselves as Norwegians with different cultural and ethnic backgrounds, and their active involvement in their local communities.

Our main focus on immigrant children's participation in Norway's Constitution Day (May 17) is central to our view of civic society. By civic society, we mean in line with Robert Putnam (1993) a collective celebration of civic engagement, people's connection with and participation in the life of their communities. On May 17, the people of Norway collectively celebrate the establishment of their constitution which symbolizes their country as a free and democratic society. Norway's constitution was adopted in 1814 and its celebration was influenced by two important national figures Henrik Wergeland and Bjørnstjerne Bjørnson. The poet, Wergeland, argued early on that the celebration of May 17 be centered on children and not militaristic symbols or political activity. He wrote the lyrics of the song, *Smaagutternes Nasjonalsang*, which celebrates small boys as citizens. Boys sang the song in May 17 parades beginning in 1870 and girls joined the singing in parades in 1889. Lyrics of the song remained the same as they are gender neutral. Since that time, elementary school children and older youth (known as *Russ*) graduating from high school have been the center of May 17 activities which involve a multi-layered set of traditional intergenerational activities. Through their preparation for and participation in the civic celebration of these activities, children collectively construct their identities as Norwegians and acquire a sense of belonging as active citizens through their dress; their collective activities with other children and adults at the national, city, and local level; and their knowledge and embracement of national traditions (Elgenius, 2011). In our data, we repeatedly see that when immigrant children are involved in community practices such as those related to May 17, they also engage their adult family members in activities embedded in the their local schools and neighborhoods. In this way, the children actually contribute to the integration of their families into Norwegian society.

The paper has three sections. First we examine the active nature of children and youth participation in civic and political society in Norway. We also focus on Norway's long tradition of engaging children and youth in civic participation. In the second section, we provide historical, demographic, and political aspects of the immigrant experience most especially how it affects the lives of children and youth in present day Norway. In the final section, we first discuss in general the special role of children and youth in the celebration of May 17 in Norway. We then go on to analyze patterns in our interviews with immigrant children and youth regarding their perceptions of and participation in May 17 activities in Trondheim.

HISTORY AND PATTERNS IN CIVIC PARTICIPATION OF CHILDREN AND YOUTH IN NORWAY

Norway has a long history of granting children basic rights and promoting and valuing the participation of children and youth in civic society. The recognition of children in Norwegian law goes back 700 years to a penal code in the 13th century which decreed that "children should not be punished as harshly as adults" (Council of Europe, 2004, p. 13). By the 17th century, there was provision for the public authority to supersede parental authority. In Norway, there has been a general trend for children and youth to have their own legal rights. For example, "it is the child who has the right to education, a right which in many other countries is given to the parent(s) on behalf of the child" (Council of Europe, 2004, p. 13).

Another long tradition in Norway is the strong political activism of adolescents as members of organizations affiliated with major political parties. The Labour Youth organization, the largest youth party, was established in 1903 (LNU, 2011). With its 10,000 members, in a population of 4.7 million, it is about the same size as the youth wings of all the other major political parties combined. By contrast, the Young Socialists in France has 6,000 members, in a country of 65 million (Saltmarsh, 2011). The other six major youth organizations in Norway also have long traditions dating from 1909 to 1978. While such organizations exist in other European countries, they are almost unheard of in the United States (see Delli Carpini, 2000).

While youth organize and are in full control of their activities, they have important interactions with adult party members. Every election year, the Norwegian Directorate for Education and Training arranges trial or school elections a few weeks prior to national and regional elections. All high school students (aged 16–19) are invited to vote. In conjunction with school elections, there are panel debates where all youth parties are represented. These activities have led to Norway's recent consideration of lowering the voting age to 16 (see Bessant, 2004, for an evaluation of policies to encourage such youth political involvement in Australia). Partisan political activity is purposely not a part of the May 17 celebrations, still youth party members participate to express their national identity in various parades and other activities we discuss in more detail below.

These traditions of children and youth participating in civic society are also expressed in myriad other ways. For example, Norway was the first country in the world to appoint an Ombudsman for Children in 1981. The duties of the Ombudsman are to promote children's interests to public and private authorities and to investigate the developments of conditions under which children grow up and live (Barneombudet, 2011). Regarding the theme of "child participation" in society, the Ombudsman cooperates with other national organizations and ministries and numerous NGOs. In fact, participation "in a voluntary organization is part of the childhood experience of almost all children and young people in Norway, and responds not only to their sporting, musical or other leisure and recreation interests but also supports their involvement in the community and provides an opportunity for them to express their views" (Council of Europe, 2004, p. 40).

We know from other research that youth participation in civic society does relate to political awareness and commitment (see Yates & Youniss, 1998). In the Norwegian context, Kjørholt (2002, 2003) has taken up the question of the discourses which support and justify the nature of the participation of children in civic society. She argues that discourses of the participating child are complex, multi-faceted, and sometimes contradictory. It is her discussion of discourses of the "participating child" in terms of children as resources which has the most bearing on our analysis. Kjørholt (2002) argues that these discourses are deeply embedded in key Norwegian values related to nature and sustainable local communities.

As an example of children's participation related to sustainable communities, Kjørholt (2002, 2003) describes the "Try Yourself" project run by the Norwegian Council for Cultural Affairs in 11 different municipalities in Norway in the early 1990s. The main aim of the project was to empower children as social participants in their local communities. In the process, children had the opportunity to infuse their views and values into their local communities, thereby strengthening a sense of belonging and identity.

In analysis of the children's individual projects, Kjørholt (2002, 2003) found that children often turned to adults for help and guidance and especially valued adult recognition. The latter was important for children positioning themselves in the intergenerational order and as "playing citizens" in the public spaces of their local communities (2003, p. 214). For our purposes, what seems missing in this discussion is the ethnic diversity of children who participated in this project and similar ones. Further, the focus on local community often in smaller towns can miss especially immigrant children or children of families seeking asylum whose everyday lives often take place in communities which are part of large cities or in reception centers (Lidén, 2008). In our data, we repeatedly see that immigrant children are deeply involved in community practices related to May 17. We argue that the understanding of children as national resources and emerging citizens is an integral idea of May 17 celebrations in the tradition initiated by Wergeland. These traditions serve as an arena where immigrant children can and do negotiate their Norwegian identity.

Kjørholt (2002, 2003) sees the participating child as manifested in the "Try Yourself" project and other activities as having the opportunity with peers to produce and share their *barnefellesskap* (children's community). Of central importance is preserving an "imagined community" among children in line with Norwegian values which associate children and nature – children climbing trees and enjoying outdoor life in highly visible ways in their local communities. This notion of an imagined community of children captures children's significant role as symbols in Norwegian culture widely apparent in the celebration of the 17th of May.

In the last section, we explore how immigrant children fit into these discourses and this symbolism. However, first in the next section, we put the immigrant experience into contemporary perspective.

THE IMMIGRANT EXPERIENCE IN NORWAY: PROGRESS AND CHALLENGE

In Norway, immigrants are defined as persons born abroad with two foreign-born parents, but statistics also include information on Norwegian-born persons with two immigrant parents. As of January, 2010, there were 460,000 immigrants in Norway making up 9.5 percent of the total population. Additionally, there were 93,000 Norwegian-born persons with immigrant parents residing in Norway. Overall, immigrants and their Norwegian-born children constitute over 550,000 persons or more than 11 percent of the total population at the beginning of 2010. To apply and receive citizenship in Norway normally requires living seven consecutive years in the country. Norway-born children of two foreign parents usually must wait until age 18 to apply for citizenship. However, it is possible to submit an application for citizenship for a child above the age of 12 (Norwegian Directorate of Immigration, 2011). Among immigrants, 35 percent were Norwegian citizens at the beginning of 2010 (Ellingsen, 2011).

The largest groups of immigrants had country backgrounds from Poland, Sweden, Germany, and Iraq, while among Norwegian-born to immigrant parents the largest groups were from Pakistan, Vietnam, Somalia, and Iraq. A large percentage of the populations of immigrants and Norwegian born to immigrant parents live in the Oslo area including Akershus (42 percent).

Continued high immigration is expected in Norway with a predicted increase of immigrants and Norwegian born to immigrant parents to more than double from 11 percent in 2010 to between 22 and 28 percent of the total population by 2060 (Andreassen & Dzamarija, 2011).

Norway also has been cautiously open to asylum seekers and refugees. In 2009, there were over 17,000 applicants with the highest number from Afghanistan followed by Eritrea, Somalia, Stateless (mainly Palestinians), and Iraq. While awaiting asylum decisions, applicants are offered temporary accommodation in reception centers. Norway also admits a pre-determined number of refugees as part of an annual resettlement quota administered by the United Nations High Commissioner for Refugees. In 2009, five groups were favored for resettlement: Burmese refugees from Malaysia, Bhutanese refugees in Nepal, Afghan refugees in Iran, stateless Palestinians, and Eritrean refugees in Sudan (Thourd, Haagensen, & Jølstad, 2010).

In a recent report, Henriksen, Østby, & Ellingsen (2011) present information on the quality of life of immigrants in Norway. They find that in 2009, immigrants (with considerable variation by country of origin) generally lag behind the rest of the population in terms of employment, income, and education. However, there have been significant advances on all these indicators since 2005. Of special interest regarding education in 2009, both immigrant students (27 percent) and Norwegian-born students of immigrant parents (42 percent) went on to higher education compared to a rate of 25 percent for all students (Nygård, 2011).

For our purposes, the most interesting data in the report relate to patterns in attitudes toward immigrants. Attitudes toward immigrants are generally positive and have become increasingly so, but there are pockets of concerns especially regarding refugees and asylum seekers. Seven out of ten Norwegians appreciate immigrants' culture and labor efforts and highly favor labor immigration from non-Nordic countries. In short, immigration that contributes to the economy is viewed most positively (Bloom, 2011).

Attitudes are more complex on social and political issues. For example, while 9 out of 10 do not mind having immigrants as neighbors, a sizeable minority of 1 out of 4 would feel uncomfortable having an immigrant as a son-in-law or daughter-in-law. As we will see this concern (even though it is a minority view) runs counter to attitudes about assimilation. Sizeable minorities (30 percent) suspect that immigrants abuse the welfare system and 33 percent agree with the statement that most immigrants represent a source of insecurity in society. These levels of more negative attitudes are 10–12 percent lower than they were in 2002 (Bloom, 2011).

There are sharp divisions regarding social policies pertaining to asylum seekers and refugees. Half of the respondents in 2009 thought it should be more difficult to obtain a permit, while 4 out of 10 were of the opinion that the access to residence permits should remain the same as it is today. One out of ten held the view that it should be easier for refugees and asylum seekers to obtain a residence permit in Norway (Bloom, 2011, p. 39).

Bloom (2011) does not mention the possible role of differences in many asylum seekers from native Norwegians that go beyond the usual language and cultural differences of many immigrants who enter on work permits. For asylum seekers, religion (especially attitudes toward Muslims) and race are important. For example, we see very split attitudes regarding assimilation. In 2009, 47 percent thought that "Immigrants in Norway should endeavor to become as similar to Norwegians as possible." On the other hand, 39 percent disagreed with this statement, while 14 percent neither agreed or disagreed or did not know (Bloom, 2011).

This tension regarding assimilation reflects somewhat contradictory positions regarding multiculturalism (see Hylland Eriksen, 1997, 2011). First, there is a general belief that "immigrants should retain key parts of their culture, while simultaneously learning skills, gaining knowledge, and forming attitudes that are necessary to live and take part in Norwegian society" – a form of multiculturalism (Bloom, 2011, p. 138). Second, major qualms about multiculturalism exist from different ends of the political spectrum. From the liberal end, some immigrant customs, values, and practices are seen as undemocratic or male dominated from Norwegian viewpoints and sensibilities. While the very notion of multiculturalism is viewed as threatening to the purity of white, Christian, and nativistic Norwegian values at the conservative end.

However, the issue goes beyond debates about multiculturalism as Gullestad (1997, 2002) has noted in her discussion of a "passion for boundaries" and "invisible fences" related to immigration, egalitarianism, nationalism, and racism in Norway. For Gullestad, "[B]oundary-setting involves, among other things, an image of pure national community inside the boundaries. This involves an attempt to resolve the ambiguities of difference by fixing the boundaries of belonging" (1997, p. 22). This range of boundaries, Gullestad argues, led to Norway's decision to remain outside the European Union and also contributes to a restrictive immigration policy. It is also related to the rise of the right wing progressive party who has an even more restrictive immigration policy as a major aspect of their agenda (see Gullestad, 2002, p. 48).

However, such boundaries go against Norway's values of being a nation with liberal social welfare policies, opposed to militarism, and committed to peaceful negotiations in the world's major long-term conflicts like that between the Israelis and Palestinians. Also Norway's "rate of per capita expenditure on developmental aid is one of the highest in the world" (Gullestad, 2002, p. 59). In struggling with these contradictions, Gullestad argues Norway builds invisible fences to maintain an imagined sameness. This process in terms of immigration policy creates a situation where Gullestad (2002, p. 59) argues: "'Immigrants' are asked to 'become Norwegian', at the same time as it is tacitly assumed that this is something they can never really achieve. 'They' are often criticized without much corresponding consideration of 'our' knowledge of 'their' traditions, or 'our' ability and willingness to reflect critically upon 'our' own."

Although Gullestad (2002) does discuss the actual experience of some immigrants in her analysis, research and discussion from the immigrants' perspective is relatively rare. Recent exceptions are studies involving reflection on immigrant life from the perspective of Somali immigrants in Oslo (Ali, 2010) and of immigrants from Croatia, Bosnia, and Iraq in Trondheim and smaller nearby towns (Valenta, 2008). These studies only indirectly looked at children, while Rusten (2006) looked at the lives of children in families of asylums seekers and argued for their right to be included in appeals for asylum. In our analysis, we examine how immigrant children in discussing their participation in May 17 activities reflect on their identities as immigrants and Norwegians – often running up against invisible fences as described by Gullestad.

"NORWAY WON THE WAR!": PATTERNS IN IMMIGRANT CHILDREN'S PERCEPTIONS OF AND PARTICIPATION IN NORWAY'S CONSTITUTION DAY

We observed and took field notes and pictures of the celebration of 17th of May activities in Trondheim in May 2005–2006 and 2008–2011. We conducted interviews over a five-year period (2006–2012). We interviewed a total of 36 elementary school children and *Russ* individually or in small groups about their participation in May 17 activities and the importance of their participation in their schools, peer groups, and communities. We also interviewed the chairperson (herself an immigrant) and one member of the

17th of May planning committee and seven adults (three who were immigrants).

We mainly relied on convenience and snowball sampling of the children's interviews starting with interviews of friends and neighbors of the second and third authors and then contacting others through these original interviews. For *Russ*, we again relied on convenience sampling, but we also sampled *Russ* from large groups who gathered near the center of the city the night before the May 17. While we do not claim the sample is representative of children and youth in Trondheim, it is diverse in terms of age, gender, and ethnicity.

In this paper, we concentrate on interviews of seven elementary school children and one middle school child in May 2009, all of whom were from immigrant families from African countries and two additional immigrant children from Africa in 2011. We re-interviewed the middle school child when she was a *Russ* in 2012. Parents were present for many of the interviews of the children, but were not formally interviewed. However, in a few cases, parents briefly joined in the discussion.

Our sample of immigrant children is small and given convenience sampling it is made up of children from African countries. There has been an increase of immigrants from African countries to Norway over the last 15 years primarily from Somalia. Somalian immigrants are primarily refugees and Muslim. Our sample represents immigrants from primarily central African countries who were Christians and whose parents immigrated to Norway as refugees or with educational or work visas. The sample, despite these limits, does provide important insights on how the celebration of May 17 relates to the immigrant experience and these children's views about their lives and identities in Norway. In reporting the interview data, we use cover names for all the respondents.

Before turning to the interview data, we recreate typical activities of May 17 based on our detailed observations in Trondheim. Thoughts turn to the 17th of May with the appearance of *Russ* in their traditional clothes usually around May 1. *Russ* have many traditions including a baptism at their high schools which involves each of the youth drinking a shot of liquor (or water if they prefer) and receiving a nickname on their caps which they wear along with special pants (of a color that represents their areas of study – usually red but also blue, green, and black) throughout the period until after the celebrations on May 17. *Russ* engage in a number of traditional pranks (ranging from benign things like sleeping in a tree to more daring drinking and sexual dares) to earn knots on the strings of their caps. *Russ* also purchase special cards (*Russekort*) on which they have their pictures and an often comical sayings or proverbs. They exchange these cards with each other and hand them out to young children who relish collecting as many as possible. Elementary school children begin collecting *Russekort* in early May and by 17, they tend to have a considerable amount. The interest that children hold in these cards is common knowledge and parents and even grandparents approach *Russ* to ask for cards for their children or grandchildren.

Residents of local neighborhoods also know May 17 is close at hand when they hear marching bands practicing their repertoire of national songs. The bands constitute the backbone of the May 17 celebration. A number of schools have such bands which are mainly coordinated and run by parents and other volunteers. Elementary school children can join the band and learn to play an instrument and over the years earn their ranks from aspirants to fully participating musicians. On May 17, the marching bands play from early morning until late afternoon.

During the last couple of weeks before May 17, the elementary school children learn about how the Norwegian constitution was developed during the spring of 1814 by 112 men and signed on May 17. The children also color flags, rehearse traditional songs, and practice how to march in an orderly fashion.

On the big day, children normally gather at their schools to take part in flag raising ceremonies before going to the center of town. Once in town, they join other schools for the children's parade, the main highlight of the day. Each school in the parade is led by a child carrying a banner with an insignia designating the school's name and inception. There are usually flag troops carrying large Norwegian flags made up of boys and girls of different ages. This group is followed by the school band (if the school has one) and the various grades of the schools. The children wear their best clothes or traditional clothes (the *bunad*) and they march waving small flags, singing traditional songs, and shouting "*Hip-hip-hurra.*"

The children's parade is followed by the people's parade in which children, youth, and adults march together in a wide range of groups – sports clubs, choirs, theatre groups, and so on. Any group can join as long as it does not partake in partisan political activity. In Trondheim, we observed immigrant groups from Somalia and the Philippines dressed in native costumes and carrying their own as well as Norwegian flags. The last parade is the *Russ* parade in which the youth march with emblems of their high school and dance and sing to popular music and throw out *Russsekort* to young children.

After the parades, many children return to their elementary schools. Here, they enjoy food prepared by parents as well as games, lotteries to win prizes, and many other entertaining activities that often have long traditions. These local and intergenerational activities normally bring the collective civic celebration to a close. However, children and youth with friends and family often go to traveling amusement parks or Tivoli in the evening of the special holiday.

All of these aspects of the experience of the May 17 celebration appeared in our interviews of the African children, but they were expressed in ways that often resonated with their immigrant experience. We found three clear patterns in the interview data. First, May 17 is fun for the children. They continually expressed how much they enjoyed all the activities they shared with peers and family. Second, the children and youth displayed a great interest and keen knowledge of the May 17 traditions, their history, and their symbolic value in Norwegian society. Third, especially the older children and youth often discussed their feelings of being Norwegian while also expressing an awareness of their immigrant status and cultural heritage. Their reflections on these dual identities provide more general insights into immigrant status, assimilation, and multiculturalism in present-day Norway.

Celebrations and Fun

All of the children we interviewed noted that they looked forward to May 17 as a fun and happy day. Let us consider the different aspects of fun and celebration the children pointed out to us beginning with their fascination with the *Russ*. Young children especially in the early grades of elementary school love to collect *Russekort*. As 12-year-old Ama from the Congo noted " ... 3rd, 4th, or 5th grade, then it is the best time for *Russekort*. And then it is like I must have *Russekort*. I must have at least 500 *Russekort*. It is a priority to get the *Russekort* then." Ama was now in the 7th grade so only collected a few cards from friends she knew. However, in our group interview with four children from the Congo (Alice, 7; Esperance, 8; Dany, 7; and Joel, 6), there was much talk about collecting many *Russekort* and even selling duplicates and rare ones to other children. The kids also were aware of and relished the funny and risqué sayings on the cards:

Esperance: Yes, and on the *Russekort* it says "Poop in my ear"—

Dany: "Poop on my leg, pee in my ear, I can't hear."

Esperance: No. "Poop on my leg, I can't hear, I don't listen to you anyway.

So it is clear these young immigrant children, like the native Norwegian children we interviewed, much enjoyed collecting and reading the cards. They get a thrill from this glimpse into the world of adolescents challenging adult norms.

Like native Norwegian children we interviewed, the immigrant children reported enjoying wearing their best and often new clothes for the May 17 parade. One 12-year-old girl from Tanzania, Jana, reported wearing the traditional *bunad* in the past, but it was now too small. The children reported wearing clothes or ribbons with the red, white, and blue colors of the flag. Lizette, a 7-year-old girl from the Congo, excitedly told us:

> Lizette: Yeah. I am going to wear a yellow dress and a blue sweater. Which is brand new and I am going to wear high heel shoes ... And I am going to have a ribbon.
>
> I: On your sweater? And then high heel shoes, have you tried that before? And do you think you can march a long way with them?
>
> Lizette: Yeah, they're gold.

The immigrant children were also excited about marching in the children's parade, waving flags (and in some cases being in special flag troops), and cheering. They were also looking forward to singing special songs they had practiced, most especially patriotic songs with a focus on children.

The 12-year-old girl, Ama, we quoted earlier discussed her family's tradition of attending the people's parade and cheering for her brother who marched with his youth soccer team. Here, we see how belonging to this local sport club was not only important for her brother, but that her whole family took pride in his skills and participation. They could display this pride and celebrate both the son's and their own participation in their local community, Trondheim, and Norway, through the people's parade.

Another May 17 activity especially important in involving immigrant children and their families into the community were the special activities organized by parents at the elementary schools in the late afternoon after the parades. All of the immigrant children we interviewed expressed how much fun they had engaging in contests like sack and potato races, ring tosses, throwing darts, and fish ponds to win small prizes donated by parents and sometimes local merchants. Parents brought bake goods and traditional hot dogs and ice cream were also available for sale.

In some cases, there were special contests that developed over the years pitting adults against children. This tradition is captured by 16-year-old Fasila from the Congo.

And the tradition is this soccer match between the parents and the children. And then always the ones who win get a prize and a trophy. And that's fun. And then there are different activities at the school and you win prizes. I remember that always ... the 7th grade at school, their parents take care of the food and stuff. Yes. Because I remember in the 7th grade I was some kind of hostess, I and someone else in my class at the party.

Here, we see traditional intergenerational civic routines which foster the integration of children, parents, and relatives into their local communities.

Finally, nearly all the children noted how much they enjoyed going to Tivoli which is always present in Trondheim for May 17. The younger children reported going with parents usually during the evening of May 17 while the older children said they much enjoyed going with friends. Although many children in Trondheim go to Tivoli with family and friends in the May 17 period, few of the Norwegian children we interviewed mentioned it as central to the celebration. It may be that since many of the African children have less experience in participating in May 17 activities and the general history of the children's parade, going to Tivoli is perceived as of equal importance to them and their families.

Knowledge of History and Traditions of 17th of May

Knowledge is always an integral part of social practices and situated learning (Lave & Wenger, 1991). It can be explicit as in factual knowledge, or implicit as embedded in collective routine activities and embodied skills. For children in Norway, much of their knowledge of May 17 is situated and embodied in the practicing of marching and singing songs and the actual performance of these activities collectively on Constitution Day.

This type of situated learning was apparent in our interviews when children performed marching steps and maneuvers and sang songs they had been practicing for us. A group of young children from the Congo (Alice, Dany, and Esperance) we identified earlier gave a spontaneous performance of the "17.*mai-sang for de Minste*" ("17.May song for the small ones") written by Margrethe Munthe in the early 1900s which nicely captures the idea of situated learning. It also strongly conveys the notion of children as resources in line with Kjørholt's (2002) views. The first verse of the song expresses the feelings of joy of a young child on this special day with feelings of national pride as well as anticipation of future citizenry. "*I cheer the day so long, singing for Norway, many a song. And I, I can love you my country, you shall see again.*" The second verse gives a description of the flag as well as a prescription of how to display and care for it: "*Now I want to run, and lift my flag and wave it around, and raise it high against the sky.*" By participating in May 17 and singing this song, the children establish themselves as ideal Norwegian citizens both in words and actions.

The children also reflected on what they had learned about the history and purpose of May 17. Like most of the native Norwegian children we interviewed, the immigrant children often made reference to the May 17 as Norway's birthday. However, the young children from the Congo (Alice, 7; Esperance, 8; Dany, 7; and Joel, 6) went well beyond this general knowledge in that they quickly took over the interview and turned it into a history lesson.

> Esperance: And then we celebrate, and then we celebrate ... We celebrate the 17th of May because it's the National Day. And that England helped Norway win—
>
> Dany: The war.
>
> Esperance: Yes the war. What is the name of those—
>
> Alice: That is not about the 17th of May, Esperance!
>
> Esperance: Yes it is. Norway won the war and then the others gave up. And then—
>
> Dany: And then Hitler killed himself.
>
> Alice: No it wasn't that. It was Norway celebrated because they won the war.
>
> Esperance: Yes the war ... And—there is something else; we have a good country to live in.
>
> Alice: And then it was more than a thousand people who were celebrating and came to Norway.

The children were very excited (often interrupting each other and talking simultaneously) in telling us about Norwegian history and displaying knowledge about World War II and Hitler. The mention of a thousand people by Alice is especially interesting as it is commonly discussed by older Norwegians and in history texts how thousands of people took to the streets in celebration of the May 17, 1945, shortly after the end of World War II and German occupation of Norway. The children came back to this question later when we asked them about the clothes they wear on May 17.

> I: Yes do you usually wear your best clothes?
>
> Esperance: Yes, and we—
>
> Alice: 17th of May is when Norway is celebrating its birthday.
>
> ...
>
> Dany: When Norway won the war then everybody took out their Norwegian flags and marched in the parade in town.

Alice: Yes and they closed the stores to celebrate.

Dany: Yes and everybody in the whole town joined in because we won the war.

Esperance: And then it was a hundred people who celebrated.

Dany: More than a thousand.

...

Esperance: Only men.

Here, the children return to the topic of what is celebrated on May 17 on their own as Alice points out correctly that it is Norway's birthday. Dany, as Alice did earlier, seems to refer to the first celebration of the 17th of May after the end of World War II. Esperance's reference to a hundred men adds a new element in that it is close to the 112 man assembly that drafted the constitution. She is also correct in noting that only men participated. In this example, the children creatively appropriate information from their history classes (which seem very advanced for first and second grade) for use in telling us about the importance, meaning, and celebration of May 17 in their lives. Thus, the children collectively contribute to their own socialization and evolving membership and participation in civic society in line with the notion of interpretive reproduction (Corsaro, 2011). Further, the children identify themselves as Norwegian by their use of "we" and give historical context to their own participation in the May 17 celebration.

Twelve-year-old Ama expressed her knowledge of the importance of May 17 in a more refined way than the younger children. She pointed out: "We celebrate that Norway is a free country and that we are sort of not being ruled – led by another country. But we are our own country with our own laws. And yes that we are a free country." Like the younger children, Ama had spent almost all her life in Norway and through the consistent use of "we" she identifies herself as Norwegian in this quote. Later in the interview, she refers to a speech she was preparing for the activities that would occur after the parades in her school.

Ama: I have calculated that is something like 195 years since we got that constitution. Yes, I am going to give that speech in my school ... . Yes, I and two of my friends. And then we are supposed to calculate how many years ago the constitution was established.

I: This speech, is it given every year by someone?

Ama: Yeah it is sort of either a play or a speech and we chose a speech ... . And it is three of us and we are going to give the speech. Each of us has a part. I am the second one.

...

I: And are you three girls?

Ama: No it is two girls and one boy.

I: From your class?

Ama: Yes. It is one Norwegian, and then it is me, and then it is one boy from Iran.

Here, we see that on the one hand Ama identifies as Norwegian and on the other hand as different from the Norwegian girl as is the boy from Iran. Finally, Ama discusses what she plans to say in her speech.

> Ama: ... I am happy that my parents choose to come to this country. And that I was allowed to go to this school because it allowed me to experience a lot. And I am happy about my friends. And I thank God for this every day. But I think I will re-write some parts of my speech.
>
> I: Are you a bit nervous about it?
>
> ...
>
> Ama: Yeah, my brother and my friends—my brother and his friends are going to be there. And it is sort of—well they did go to [Name of school] as well, so they come to the parties. Yes I will be a bit nervous.
>
> I: So they are older?
>
> Ama: My brother is in the second year of high school and the friends are in the third so they are *Russ*.

In preparing the speech, Ama reflects on what she sees as positive aspects of both Norway and her experience as an immigrant. It is an important type of civic participation in that many such speeches are given on May 17. The choice of the three speakers displays a diversity of ethnicity in the school and in Norwegian society and leads Ama to reflect on her immigrant identity. She is still planning her speech and is nervous because she anticipates the attention of her brother and his friends, some of whom are *Russ*.

Redefining What It Means to Be Norwegian: Identity, Assimilation, and Multiculturalism

In the introduction, we described how Bano Rashid wanted as a young adult immigrant to stretch and redefine what it means to be Norwegian. We later discussed in the work of Gullestad the "invisible fences" immigrants to Norway face given the complexity of immigration policy and Norwegians' attitudes regarding assimilation and multiculturalism. In this section, we present data from three of our interviews that give us insight to these issues.

First consider 12-year-old Jana from Tanzania who has lived in Trondheim for nine years. Jana's school is in an ethnically mixed area of Trondheim. On May 17, children gather at her school and then they march to what is called a receiving school for immigrant children from many nationalities. From there, the children parade around the local community, greeting family, friends, and residents of a retirement center. Especially interesting is a discussion about flags from different countries some children carry in this parade.

> Jana: Well we have—some want to carry foreign flags, the flag where they come from. So we have one student from Somalia. And he carries a Somalian flag. And then we have some from different countries and they have flags from different countries. And then we have Norwegians.
>
> I: Yes. But you are carrying a Norwegian flag? You are not carrying a Tanzanian flag?
>
> Jana: We don't have that at school.
>
> I: But if they had it, you could have carried it?
>
> ...
>
> Mother: I was thinking about. I was thinking about carrying the Tanzanian flag. It has nothing to do with the 17th of May. We are celebrating the constitution which has nothing to do with the Tanzanian flag.
>
> Jana: But if they had it.
>
> Mother: No. We do have the Tanzanian flag here, but we cannot carry it. Because it does not have anything to do with Tanzania on that day.
>
> I: Did you discuss these kinds of issues in class?
>
> Jana: Yes in KRL [a subject about religious beliefs]. And then we learned about the 17th of May and then we wrote how—and then we read how Norway became a free country on that day.
>
> I: And so you discussed if it was possible to carry other flags or not?
>
> Jana: Um—it is possible because we do have other flags.
>
> ...
>
> I: Do people in your class have different opinions on whether it is the right thing or not on the Norwegian national day?
>
> Jana: Well there was a question in class why do those who come from other countries celebrate the 17th of May. Well—I was thinking we are in Norway after all.

We see in this discussion that the children from the schools in this area do not march in the parade in the city center. Rather several schools join up at the receiving school and children march in their neighborhoods. Some children also carry flags from their countries. Jana does not carry a Tanzanian flag, but she indicates she would like to carry one. Her mother (in one of the very few times a parent entered into the discussion in our interviews) disagrees and says they have a Tanzania flag but that it has nothing to do with Norway's constitution day. Jana does not dispute her mother, but she does not show agreement either. She offers up instead a complex response that was clearly affected by discussion in her religion class. She notes that children from different countries like her celebrate May 17 because "we are in Norway after all." This comment could be interpreted that these children celebrate because they are in Norway and not because they identify as Norwegian.

However, Jana's comments here must be put into the context of other things she told us in the interview. For example, she noted that in the past she wore the Norwegian *bunad*, but would not this year as it was now too small. She also said that after the children's parade in her multi-ethnic community she planned as she had in the past to go to the city center with her father to watch the people's parade and the *Russ* parade. In wearing the bunad and watching the people's parade, she embodies knowledge of Norwegian traditions. However, in the people's parade, she witnesses diversity in the participation of ethnic groups as we discussed earlier. These points are important because they suggest Jana's awareness of her dual identity of being Norwegian and an African immigrant. Her comments also in this way support ethnic diversity and multiculturalism.

Earlier we discussed aspects of our interview with 16-year-old Fasila. We interviewed Fasila again when she was 19, a few days after May 17, 2012, shortly after her experiences as a *Russ*. In the first interview, Fasila had discussed her anticipation of being a *Russ* and expressed concern about certain of the *Russ* pranks and how some of them could be "something really bad." In the second interview, Fasila talked about her mixed experiences of being a *Russ* and how they related to her identity both as an immigrant and a Norwegian.

In her class, Fasila was one of three students with an immigrant background. She said she was surprised at how prepared her classmates were for the *Russ* activities and experience and how important the rituals and traditions were for them. She, on the other hand, noted "And I was kind of like okay it's fun but it's not such a big deal. So I don't know I thought it was kind of weird at first." She had anticipated the *Russ*

period and activities as symbolic of finishing high school and entering
adulthood and felt for most of her classmates; on the other hand, "it seemed
like it's kind of just an excuse to be doing whatever we want to do in
17 days."

Fasila did, however, participate in and enjoyed the whole range of
activities from the baptism (where she drank water rather than liquor), to
buying and wearing the special clothes, to going to a large national *Russ*
party by plane in Southern Norway, to staying out all night many times,
passing out *Russekort*, and to engaging in a number of pranks. These
pranks were very mild ones like swimming in a lake before May 1, eating a
hamburger in two bites, among others. One of which was for a group to
surround a stranger and then one yells something and they all fall down to
scare the person. She notes " – and the first lady she was so scared."

On the other hand, she felt somewhat distanced from and did not
fully embrace the experience noting that for her classmates it was "almost
something holy, but I am not there." She did note that her classmate whose
both parents were immigrants reacted much like her while her other classmate with an immigrant father but Norwegian mother was more fully
involved like her Norwegians classmates.

At one point, we asked Fasila directly about being a *Russ* and her
immigrant or ethnic background.

> I: So the fact that you are a little bit less involved or you are less whole heartedly taking
> part in the *Russ* celebration does it have to do with that you have a different background
> do you think?
>
> Fasila: I think so.
>
> I: You don't have the Norwegian background?
>
> Fasila: I think it has a lot to do with that. Because I didn't really—like understand how
> important it was for them until we started out as *Russ*. For me it was kind of like a
> celebration—for finishing the school, but it was more than that for them – yeah it was
> kind of like—I don't know—I can't even explain it—it was yeah—
>
> I: Like a ritual or something?
>
> Fasila: Maybe.

Here, we see that Fasila agrees that the fact that she is not a native
Norwegian is important, but she struggles to explain why it is important and
her response is inconclusive.

Later Fasila talked about her actual activities on May 17 as a Russ. She
noted that she marched in the children's parade with many of her high
school classmates, went to a celebration at her church where there is a yearly

celebration of singing and musical performances and visiting with families and friends. Later she marched with her classmates in the *Russ* parade which is the last of the official May 17 activities in the center of Trondheim. This led us to ask again about her identification of being Norwegian.

> I: When you were a *Russ* and when you were younger, being part of May 17th did this make you feel more part of being Norwegian?

> Fasila: I did not really think about that actually—I—normally I think I would consider myself more Norwegian than Congolese, but at the same time there is a lot of stuff that I just—I don't know I think I get to pick and choose between the two ones—I just pick what suits me the best—but at the same time I would say that I am more Norwegian than Congolese.

Fasila has been a citizen for five years and sees herself as more Norwegian than Congolese, but she embraces both identities and picks and chooses what suits her best. It would be good to have more information on how she picks and chooses, but her description aptly fits the idea of multiculturalism and an appreciation of ethnic diversity. We saw in the earlier discussion about attitudes toward immigrants and Gullestad's (2002) notion of invisible fences that concepts of national identity, ethnicity, assimilation, and multiculturalism are complex and evolving in Norway. Fasila's discussion of her experiences in the collective celebration of May 17 reflects her implicit struggle with these invisible fences immigrant children encounter with their increased participation in Norwegian society. Her reflections also capture both her individual agency in this process and the evolving nature of her national and personal identity.

CONCLUSION

We began this paper with two stories from the media. In the first a young boy, who after marching in the May 17 parade and collectively sharing the embodied knowledge of being an active citizen on this special day, declares that while his parents are African he is Norwegian. The second story of Bano Rashid and her death at the hands of a domestic terrorist is tragic but deeply inspiring. Deprived of her activist goals to break through the invisible fences Gullestad (2002) describes and to contribute to her new homeland as not simply an immigrant but as an Iraqi-Norwegian, Bano Rashid's story serves as model for all members of Norwegian society.

Patterns in our observations of the participation of immigrant children in May 17 celebrations and in intensive interviews fit both of these stories in important ways. The younger children in our sample (Alice, Esperance, Dany, Joel, and Lizette) actively embraced and clearly enjoyed their participatory roles in the multi-faceted activities of the 17th of May. In marching and waving Norwegian flags in the children's parade, wearing their best clothes, singing patriotic songs centered around children's perspectives, learning and sharing their knowledge of Norwegian history, playing games and winning prizes in parent-coordinated activities at their schools, going to Tivoli, and collecting *Russekort*, these children actively acquired an embodied knowledge of being Norwegian. In the process, the children in line with Corsaro's (2011) concept of interpretive reproduction collectively contribute to their own socialization and involving membership in civic society. Of key importance of these children's participatory role for the immigrant experience were those activities communally shared and produced with family members that contributed to their own and their families' integration into their communities and Norwegian society more generally. These findings add to Kjørholt's (2002, 2003) discourse on children as resources by providing evidence on immigrant children's participation and sense of belonging on Norway's most important day of national celebration.

The participatory roles of the older children in our sample (Ama, Jana, and Fasila) and these children's reflections on their participation were more complex and nuanced. These older children (outside of collecting *Russekort*) participated in most of the same May 17 activities as the younger children. In addition, we interviewed Fasila at two points in time with the second interview capturing her experiences as a *Russ*. In our interview with Ama, we saw that she went beyond the embodied knowledge of the younger children's participation as she was given the task of writing a speech which she was to present at gathering in her school after the parades. Planning for this task impelled her to reflect on her life as an immigrant in both a retrospective and projective fashion. Retrospectively, she, in a somewhat formulaic way, stresses the positive aspect of her parents "bringing her to this country" which allowed her to attend her school and "experience a lot" and "have good friends." But in prospecting to actually giving her speech along with another immigrant from Iran and a Norwegian, Ama becomes more aware of the very fact that she is not a native Norwegian. She also, in this projective way, expresses a certain nervous pride of this very fact of her African ethnicity which she will display and share with members of her family when she gives the speech. Here, we see how this civic act (one of many speeches given on May 17) displays the complex interweaving of citizenship and ethnic identity.

For Jana, there is again the embodied knowledge in marching in a parade and waving a flag on May 17. However, Jana points out that some children she marches with carry flags from their home countries and that she would as well if there were a Tanzanian flag at her school. When her mother challenges this idea as inappropriate (an implicit endorsement of assimilation), Jan deftly sidesteps a bald disagreement, but offers an answer that one can honor Norway as a citizen and still display one's ethnic identity (a more direct endorsement of multiculturalism).

Fasila reports both her full involvement in *Russ* activities while at the same time expressing a clear ambivalence in their meaning for her compared to her Norwegian classmates. She sees herself as more Norwegian than Congolese, but she embraces both identities and "picks and chooses" what suits her best. In this way, she also endorses multiculturalism, but in doing so she struggles to navigate her way around or over the "invisible fences" Gullestad argues Norway places before all her immigrants.

Overall, all the children expressed positive feelings about their participation in the children's parades and their involvement in civic activities celebrating May 17 in their local communities and schools. They were aware of and embraced the historical significance of May 17 and clearly expressed feelings of being Norwegians. However, we found a pattern with the younger children having an embodied knowledge of identity and citizenship through participation that may be challenged with their experiences as they mature and participate more widely in a society new to rapid immigration. The older children, on the other hand, having experienced the invisible fences which Gullestad (2002) has described, displayed a more nuanced and tempered view of being Norwegian while clearly aware of and identifying with their African heritage. In the end, although our sample is small, we believe the patterns in our findings shed important light on the immigrant children's participation in civic society in Norway and their identities as African-Norwegian citizens. However, the findings are far from definitive and display the same complexity and evolving nature as Norway's policies, attitudes toward, and embracement of her growing immigrant population. More research is clearly needed on this important topic for Norway and much of Europe. We hope that our study will spur on such research.

ACKNOWLEDGMENTS

The research on which this paper is based was supported by funds from an endowed chair at Indiana University, Bloomington, to William A. Corsaro. The authors would like to thank Jason Blind, Ann-Magritt Jensen, Jens Qvortrup, and two anonymous reviewers for very helpful comments and suggestions on earlier drafts of the paper.

REFERENCES

Ali, A. (2010). The rough road to integration: The case of Somali immigrants' integration in Norway. *MSc thesis. Noragric.* Norwegian University of Life Sciences.

Andreassen, K., & Dzamarija, M. (2011). Population. In K. Henriksen, L. Østby & D. Ellingsen (Eds.), *Immigration and immigrants* (2010, pp. 9–14). Oslo, Norway: Statistics Norway.

Barneombudet. (2011). Retrieved from www.barneombudet.no/english

Bessant, J. (2004). Mixed messages: Youth participation and democratic practice. *Australian Journal of Political Science, 39,* 387–404.

Bloom, S. (2011). Attitudes towards immigrants and immigration. In K. Henriksen, L. Østby & D. Ellingsen (Eds.), *Immigration and immigrants* (2010, pp. 133–149). Oslo, Norway: Statistics Norway.

Corsaro, W. (2011). *The sociology of childhood.* Thousand Oaks, CA: Pine Forge Press.

Council of Europe. (2004). *Youth policy in Norway: Report by the international team of experts appointed by the council of Europe.* Strasbourg, France. Retrieved from http://www.coe.int/youth

Delli Carpini, M. (2000). Gen.com: Youth, civic engagement, and the new information environment. *Political Communication, 17,* 341–349.

Elgenius, G. (2011). The politics of recognition: Symbols, nation building and rival nationalisms. *Nations and Nationalism, 17,* 396–418.

Ellingsen, D. (2011). Statistics of importance. In K. Henriksen, L. Østby & D. Ellingsen (Eds.), *Immigration and immigrants* (2010, pp. 9–14). Oslo, Norway: Statistics Norway.

Gullestad, M. (1997). A passion for boundaries: Reflections on connections between the everyday lives of children and discourses on the nation in contemporary Norway. *Childhood, 4,* 19–42.

Gullestad, M. (2002). Invisible fences: Egalitarianism, nationalism and racism. *Journal of the Royal Anthropological Institute, 8,* 45–63.

Henriksen, K., Østby, L., & Ellingsen, D. (Eds.). (2011). *Immigration and immigrants 2010.* Oslo, Norway: Statistics Norway.

Hylland Eriksen, T. (1997). Multiculturalism, individualism and human rights: Romanticism, enlightenment and lessons from Mauritius. In R. Wilson (Ed.), *Human rights: Culture and context* (pp. 49–69). London: Pluto.

Hylland Eriksen, T. (2011). Individets frihet *(Individual's freedom). Aftenpoften,* August 1. Retrieved from www.aftenposten.no/meninger/kroniker/article4188856.ece

Kjørholt, A. T. (2002). Small is powerful: Discourses on 'children and participation' in Norway. *Childhood, 9,* 63–82.

Kjørholt, A. T. (2003). 'Imagined communities': The local community as a place for 'children's culture' and social participation in Norway. In K. Olwig & E. Gulløv (Eds.), *Children's places: Cross-cultural perspectives* (pp. 197–216). New York: Routledge.

Lave, G., & Wenger, E. (1991). *Situated learning: Legitimate peripheral participation.* Cambridge, UK: Cambridge University Press.

Lidén, H. (2008). Common neighborhoods – Diversified lives: Growing up in urban Norway. In K. Olwig & E. Gulløv (Eds.), *Children's places: Cross-cultural perspectives* (pp. 119–137). New York: Routledge.

LNU. (2011). *Factsheet: Norwegian youth party organizations.* Retrieved from http://www.regjeringen.no/upload/UD/Vedlegg/FN/Factsheet_Norwegian_Youth_Party_Organisations.pdf

Norwegian Directorate of Immigration. (2011). Norwegian citizenship for children by application. Retrieved from http://www.udi.no/Norwegian-Directorate-of-immigration/Central-topics/citizenship

Nygård, G. (2011). Education. In K. Henriksen, L. Østby & D. Ellingsen (Eds.), *Immigration and immigrants* (2010, pp. 47–76). Oslo, Norway: Statistics Norway.

Putman, R. (1993). *Making democracy work*. Princeton, NJ: Princeton University Press.

Rusten, H. (2006). *Making children visible to the immigrant administration: A study of the right of the child to participate in Norwegian asylum proceedings.* Submitted in partial fulfillment of the MA in the Theory and Practice of Human Rights, Norwegian Centre for Human Rights, University of Oslo, Department of Law.

Saltmarsh, M. (2011, July 27). Young survivors find their faith in Norway's system is even stronger. *New York Times.*

Schwirtz, M. (2011, July 29). Norway displays unity at attack victim's funeral. *New York Times.*

Thourd, E., Haagensen, E., & Jølstad, F. (2010). *International migration 2009–2010: SOPEMI-report for Norway.* Retrieved from www.regjeringen.no/AD/.../SOPEMI_Report_2010_pdf

Valenta, M. (2008). *Finding friends after resettlement: A study of the social integration of immigrants and refugees, their personal networks and self-work in everyday life.* Ph.D. thesis, Department of Sociology and Political Science, Norwegian University of Science and Technology, Trondheim, Norway.

Yates, M., & Youniss, J. (1998). Community service and political identity development in adolescence. *Journal of Social Issues, 554,* 495–513.

LEARNING FROM EACH OTHER: COLLECTIVE PRACTICES IN MAKING INDEPENDENT YOUTH MEDIA

Rachel Kulick

ABSTRACT

Purpose – *This paper explores how the interactive dynamics of peer education models within independent youth media outlets facilitate and impede youth engagement in media activism and social change work, more broadly defined.*

Design/methodological approach – *Ethnographic and participatory action research methods are used with the youth media hub, Youth Media Action (YMA), to examine the possibilities and challenges that peer media educators confront in cultivating a noncommercial space for the collective production of oppositional media. YMA specifically seeks to involve youth from marginalized communities.*

Findings – *The results suggest that peer-to-peer education models do act as vehicles for political engagement as youth experience shared ownership, cultivate solidarity, and acquire community organizing skills through the collective production of oppositional media. At the same time,*

Youth Engagement: The Civic-Political Lives of Children and Youth
Sociological Studies of Children and Youth, Volume 16, 227–251
Copyright © 2013 by Emerald Group Publishing Limited
All rights of reproduction in any form reserved
ISSN: 1537-4661/doi:10.1108/S1537-4661(2013)0000016014

challenges can surface when peer educators juggle multiple roles and participating community youth groups espouse differing organizational values and pedagogical sensibilities.

Research limitations/implications – *This study offers a potential pathway for further research on how peer education and collective media making models influence youth citizenship and social change work.*

Originality/value – *The focus on the organizational and social dynamics of peer education models is useful in understanding youth citizenship and digital access as a collective experience for youth living in disenfranchised communities that seek out these spaces for not only media making but also community building.*

Keywords: Media activism; youth media; independent media; peer education; prefigurative practices; collective production practices

INTRODUCTION

A common expression at Youth Media Action (YMA) is "anything is possible." Ina, a YMA peer media educator, college student, and young woman of Russian descent, dedicates her Saturdays to leading community media trainings for youth. Starting at age 16, Ina has participated in youth media organizations making videos. A few years later, she became a youth producer for the YMA's news show, and akin to many YMA participants, her initial experience led to increased involvement and an interest in working with and teaching youth how to produce media content on issues that they care about. Now, as a peer media educator, Ina leads media training programs with youth living in communities where equity, fairness, and inclusion have historically been compromised or altogether absent. Ina's motivation in working as a peer media educator is to help youth develop skills in filmmaking as a critical vehicle for social change work. In a slight Russian accent she explains, "Despite all the perceptions that modern youth are careless and stupid, per se, young people actually have a lot to say and they just feel neglected so they don't say anything; it's not like they don't have opinions. My personal reason for doing this is just to let the young people know that people want to hear you, you just need to speak up, don't be afraid to speak up and we are going to help you voice your opinions to change this society because it is possible. Don't give up." Independent youth media spaces such as YMA offer us a lens into the ways in which collective production practices enable and hinder youth engagement in media activism and other forms of social change work.

Since the beginning of the new millennium, independent youth media outlets have been increasing in numbers within the United States and around the world (Buckingham, 2011; Chavez & Soep, 2010). These outlets are part of a larger movement that seeks to ensure communication rights and power for everyone regardless of age, social class, race, ethnicity, gender, sexual orientation, and other social forces. Most groups and individuals participating in the movement share a collective critique of the mainstream media system, including the vast corporate consolidation and commercialization of media as well as the multiple forms of racism, sexism, classism, homophobia, and other forms of discrimination embedded in mainstream media structures, practices, and content (Hackett & Carroll, 2006; Kidd & Rodriguez, 2010). Participation is grounded in the belief that these media injustices significantly undermine the open communication of diverse cultural perspectives about important social issues and concerns.

Independent youth media outlets attempt to transform the structural, social, and representational arrangements of the current media system by creating noncommercial spaces – that is, media that are distributed without advertising dollars supporting them, framing them, or determining their value or content – for groups to produce alternative media on multiple platforms including television, film, Internet, radio, and print. Most media outlets seek to foster youth engagement in social change work through the collaborative process of producing "activist," "oppositional,"[1] or "socially conscious media." These spaces often look to peer-to-peer education models, collaborative production practices, and other informal mentoring approaches for youth to make media but also to cultivate a sense of belonging within a larger youth community or culture.

This paper draws from ethnographic and participatory action research with the independent youth media hub, YMA,[2] a division of a public access media center that operates as a central hub of media education, production, and distribution for youth groups and schools across an urban area in the northeastern United States. YMA looks to a peer-to-peer education model as a cultural platform for political engagement as youth look to each other to collectively produce media to bring into public view their perspectives about local and global issues that concern them. The intent of YMA is to conduct community media trainings in a participatory, collective, informal fashion, but this approach can also become a juggling act for peer educators as they oscillate between the roles of educator and peer. The peer approach can also engender challenges with community youth groups, especially those with differing pedagogical sensibilities that do not complement the peer education model. My goal is to analyze how peer media educators, participants, and community youth group staff negotiate these dilemmas in the day-to-day practices of producing oppositional media, and how they work with and against their goals and values to realize an alternative youth-centered media system.

The field of independent media making is a fertile and contentious terrain to examine these dilemmas as actors bring differing backgrounds and tools to engage in social change work. Youth media outlets such as YMA are highly representative of this terrain, as one single racial, ethnic, religious, gendered, or class-based community does not subsume this network. Rather, YMA represents a fairly diverse network of participating youth and youth groups that reflect a wide range of identities, values, political orientations, and structural arrangements. Rethinking youth media with an emphasis on the collective organizational dynamics of producing independent media across a diverse organizational field of participating youth groups allows me to conceptualize how these spaces mobilize within themselves and their constituencies in an effort to engage youth in media activism and social change work more broadly. Before I turn to the empirical discussion of the peer education model, I present some theoretical reflections on the connections between youth media practices and political activity as it relates to media literacy, civic engagement, and movement building, and then I briefly summarize the methods for this research.

LOCATING YOUTH MEDIA IN SOCIAL CHANGE WORK

The growing numbers of independent youth media spaces represent a shift in how youth engage not only in production practices but also more broad engagement with social change work. We see a changing citizenship in the digital age in which youth are moving away from notions of "dutiful citizenship" of civic obligation – based on voting and partisan, professional, and religious participation in formal politics – to an ethos of "actualizing citizenship" in which "citizenship is not merely inherited as found, but made through creative experience" (Bennett, 2008; Coleman, 2008, pp. 204–205). Notions of the "dutiful citizen" correspond to traditional assumptions about political socialization and what Gordon and Taft (2011) refer to as "citizenship in the making" with an emphasis on the role of adult intervention in informing the political orientations of youth (p. 1500). The notion of "citizenship in the making" stems from a deficit model, "youth are socially constructed as citizen participants only in future tense; ill-equipped to participate in social and political decision-making as youth, only capable of this participation as adults" (Gordon, 2010, p. 9).

We see this protective stance toward youth within the historical and the contemporary context of adult perceptions of youth consumption of media and popular culture. Adult concerns with these consumption practices points to a long, contentious history traceable to Plato who proposed to censor certain dramatic poets from *The Republic* on the premise of potentially corrupting the minds of young people (Buckingham, 2000; Plato, 1987). Prior to television, in the time of predominantly print media, adults could control youth access to information. Youth knowledge of and access to larger society occurred gradually depending upon one's literacy skills and opportunity for travel and mobility (Meyrowitz, 1985). Over time with the circulation of new modes of media, adults have become increasingly concerned about youth access to the "outside" world, including their engagement with comic books, poetry, novels, theater, radio, or on the screen (e.g., television, movies, video games, web sites, etc.).

More recently, a growing public discourse has emerged on the dangers of media consumption for youth (Buckingham, 2000; Meyrowitz, 1985; Postman, 1994). Parents, academics, educators, administrators, and politicians have expressed concern regarding the negative effects of media including hypersexualized imagery and pervasive violence in films, the "dumbing down" of television, excessive video game playing, and cyber bullying. Youth are often portrayed as "passive" receivers of messages embedded in media. Some adults respond to this contested arena of youth and media with a largely protective and authoritative stance (Buckingham, 2000, p. 4). As such, youth themselves, especially those living in disenfranchised communities, are frequently left out of the conversation (Buckingham, 2000; Fisherkeller, 2000).

At the same time, we see an increased presence of independent youth media spaces across the country and globally from which youth engage "actualizing citizenship" practices as critics of mainstream media and active producers of socially conscious media. These spaces, especially those with a focus on peer education, correspond to more recent understandings of political socialization in which youth development of political identities and consciousness "is not something that adults do to adolescents, it is something that youth do for themselves" (Youniss, Bales, Diversi,

Christmas-Best, McLaughlin, & Silbereisen, 2002, p. 133). In other words, political socialization does not occur in a vacuum as youth are "active agents of their own socialization" collectively and creatively engaging in peer cultures and processes of negotiation by way of peer relations and activities that differ from dominant adult culture (Corsaro, 2003, p. 4).

These spaces can evoke considerable collective negotiation in figuring out how to represent an identified social issue at the intersection of gender, race, class, and citizenship. Akom, Cammarota, and Ginwright (2008) use the term "youthtopias" to denote traditional and nontraditional educational spaces that overtly aim to understand how race intersects with other axes of social oppression and resistance; challenge conventional norms and messages used to characterize youth of color; privilege their experiential knowledge; and commit to cultivating critical consciousness in the service of social justice work (p. 12). Many youth media spaces enact "youthtopian" principles in their missions to provide an open space from which "young people depend on one another's skills, perspectives, and experiential knowledge, to generate original, multitextual, youth-driven cultural products that embody a critique of oppression, a desire for social justice, and ultimately lay the foundation for community empowerment and social change" (Akom et al., 2008, p. 3). Many scholars and media educators frame the collective production of media as a way for youth to encode their lived experiences, personal challenges, and hopes into expressive media pieces that activate dialogue and change in their communities (Chavez & Soep, 2005; Jenkins, Clinton, Purushotma, Robinson, & Weigel, 2008).

Media literacy education (MLE) acts as a backbone for many independent youth media spaces to begin considering what it means to produce an alternative to mainstream media. Media literacy trainings typically involve examining power structures of media systems, developing critical tools to decode messages transmitted in media content, and cultivating skills to counter dominant media and messaging through the production of independent media (Carlsson, Tayie, Jacquinot-Delaunay, & Manuel Perez Tornero, 2008; Hobbs & Jensen, 2009; Kellner, 1995).

Over the years, MLE has evolved in multiple directions.[3] In the 1990s, we see the conflation of media activism and MLE, with many media educators asking the question, should MLE have a more explicit political agenda? More recently, a school of thought has emerged within the movement for media change arguing that the only way to truly understand and challenge mainstream media is by making your own media (Hackett & Carroll, 2006). Rodriguez (2001) refers to alternative media as "citizens media" for disenfranchised groups to colonize public spaces for media production. They begin to rupture existing power structures by reappropriating tools of representation and rendering visibility to a diverse set of social struggles, oppositional targets, and agendas of resistance and social change (Rodriguez, 2001).

With varying degree of success, these spaces mediate multiple interests, perspectives, and identities through the development of inclusive media structures and content that privilege stories and perspectives of marginalized populations that often go unheard or misrepresented in mainstream media. Many youth participating in these spaces start with exercises in "bricolage," tinkering with and reappropriating dominant objects, practices, and ideas in order to subvert conventional meanings and begin to impose youth-centered ideological beliefs on them (Hebdige, 1979). The act of picking up a camera or editing a news piece helps youth realize that every aspect of producing media involves choices, that very little is by accident, and that all media-making choices have their own biases (Chavez & Soep, 2005; Gitlin, 2003). Yet the experience of producing socially conscious media is not just creative, it is also a collective experience that involves the negotiation of multiple agendas and interests that do not always fit neatly into a standardized rubric.

METHODS

This analysis is based on an 18-month ethnographic study and 2-year participatory action research project with YMA Center. Founded in 2000, YMA has built a strong youth-centered learning environment within the larger public access center. It is a multiracial independent youth media hub composed of staff, peer media educator, and youth participants from varying ethnic, racial, and class backgrounds. The full time staff, all in their late twenties, is composed of five positions – the director, education coordinator, outreach coordinator, production coordinator, and programming coordinator. In addition, there are six part-time peer media educators (sometimes called peer trainers), ages 16–25 who facilitate the educational and production workshops for community youth groups throughout the city. Most of the peer trainers are college students or recent college graduates that have experience as participants or interns at YMA or another independent youth media outlet in the area.

YMA offers peer-to-peer media trainings that teach youth in community and school settings how to produce activist media from experienced peer media educators of their own age and background. YMA specifically seeks to involve youth from disenfranchised communities, including, but not limited to, youth of color, youth who struggle in traditional education programs, immigrant youth, lesbian, gay, transgender, bisexual, and questioning (LGTBQ) youth, and youth from low-income families. The network of youth participating in YMA ranges in age between 14 and 35.

The ethnographic design included participant observation at YMA with in-house programs, community media trainings, and other related events such as media democracy conferences and public access hearings.[4] I participated in, observed, and sometimes filmed sessions from the life history of four community media trainings[5] that were led by YMA peer media educators. The trainings were longer term trainings that typically ran for three to four months, and included a focus on media literacy, preproduction planning, storyboarding, filming, editing, and screening sessions. In addition, I conducted fifteen 30–60-minute semi-structured interviews with peer educators, staff, and youth who participated in the longer term trainings. The majority of the interviewees were youth of African American and Latino descent between the ages of 15 and 25. Focusing on the peer education and the conversations of production, I paid particular attention to three key themes: (1) the role of shared ownership in the media making; (2) the role of solidarity as youth negotiate their values, views, and interests through media making; and (3) the role of bridging as the peer trainers attempt to connect youth to the larger movement for media justice.

In addition, there was a participatory action research (Cornwall & Jewkes, 1995) component to this study that was funded by the Social Science Research Council (SSRC) in the United States. My colleague Amy Bach and I worked with YMA to recruit a research team composed of YMA staff as well five youth researchers that worked with us to design and implement a community needs assessment to examine the media needs and interests of urban youth. The youth researchers conducted 15 semi-structured interviews and 15 focus groups with YMA participants, peer trainers, community youth groups, schools, parents, and media activists that support YMA programs. We sought to create a youth-centered research process, which meant multiple feedback loops along the way. One pivotal feedback loop was a pilot focus group with YMA alumni who provided invaluable suggestions on ways to avoid academic jargon and make the focus group questions more accessible and compelling for the participating youth. These feedback loops were critical for the team to surface the inherent messiness of collaborative research in a manner that contributed to building a sense of trust and engagement in the research process (Castellanos, Bach, & Kulick, 2010, p. 170).

With a grounded theory approach (Charmaz, 2005), I developed an analytical framework that examines the "collective" nature of media making as this lens gets to the crux of this project: the organizational dilemmas of peer-to-peer education within the larger context of social change work. After coding to identify emergent themes and accompanying thick description, I engaged in a series of feedback loop sessions with YMA staff, peer educators, and participants in which I presented the themes and framework for the findings, and YMA responded with comments, corrections, and suggestions to enrich the overall analysis.

HORIZONTAL EXCHANGES OF KNOWLEDGE: PRIVILEGING YOUTH LEADERSHIP AND JUGGLING MULTIPLE ROLES

Similar to Chavez and Soep, I am leery of presentations of independent youth media that idealize this work as emancipatory just because it represents youth speaking their minds. They contend that scholarship on "youth voice" tends to bracket an isolated, highly desirable outcome when all too often these accounts are "divorced from any social, relational, or political context" (Chavez & Soep, 2005, p. 4).[6] They frame social relations in youth media as a "pedagogy of collegiality" in which "youth and adults mutually depend on one another's skills, perspectives, and collaborative efforts to generate original, multitextual, professional-quality work for outside audiences" (Chavez & Soep, 2005, p. 3).[7]

While there is some adult involvement at YMA in the form of support from other departments at the public access center, the pedagogy of collegiality does not accurately reflect the YMA experience. Instead I use the term, *horizontal exchanges of knowledge* to represent the peer-to-peer media education model as youth learn from each other with much less adult influence. During the popular uprising in Argentina in 2001, the concept *horizontalidad* was used to reflect "direct democracy to create horizontal, nonhierarchical social relationships that would allow participants to openly engage with each other" (Sitrin, 2012, p. 74). De Angelis (2005) uses the concept "horizontality" to connote a "mode of doing ... based on participatory, open, and inclusive democracy" by which participants engage a continuous relational process to attain agreement on both their desired goals as well as their processes and strategies to achieve them (p. 195). In the case of YMA, horizontal exchanges of knowledge reflect youth-centered modes of doing wherein peer trainers and participants cultivate solidarity and peer trainers assume a bridging role as they support youth in making media that opens up dialogue in their communities in real and tangible ways.

The following section outlines some key dilemmas that surface as YMA deploys a peer education model with a changing cast of youth groups. On the one hand, we see how the peer-led education model promotes "a do it yourself" space from which youth can uncover, challenge, and, in some cases, transform existing assumptions about specific issues of interest through the collective production of socially conscious media. On the other hand, we see how horizontal exchanges of knowledge can pose obstacles for peer educators including insufficient training; role confusion; challenges in navigating the expectations, values, and practices of community youth groups; and problems with participant engagement and commitment.

Cultivating Youth Centered, Collective Modes of Media Making

I begin this section with a brief summary of a successful community media training to distill some of the horizontal strategies that peer media educators deploy to engage young people in a youth-centered experience of social change.

In the spring of 2008, I attended a community media training in which YMA peer educators, Ina and Majida, teamed together to work with a small group of urban scholars to develop, produce, and air a live studio show at the public access center. The group devoted the first two sessions to identifying a topic for the show. During the second session, Ina read aloud from the large newsprint a long litany of possible topics that the scholars had brainstormed for the live show – relationship problems, mental and physical abuse, gang violence, drunk driving, arranged marriages, child brides, school conditions, Iraq war, global warming, poverty, pedophilia, materialistic society, alienation and friendship, sex education, racism, stereotyping, gossiping, and self-esteem. There was no shortage of ideas. After reading the list, Ina reiterated what she had said the first day, "As I said, we can go as controversial as we want, like, we can express our own opinions, we can do it, basically, we don't have any censorship here at all, so we can do whatever we want." To which Lee, a male teen of Chinese descent, responded, "So we can curse?" Ina said, "We can curse" and proceeded to share examples of live shows in which young people brought their own views and vernacular to live shows on controversial issues.

Toward the end of this session after a lengthy discussion about different themes, Ina tried to move the group toward selecting a topic by asking "so what issues are you personally concerned with?" Lee explained, "Right now … I'm a little less concerned with political issues … like the recession or whatever … that's important, but I don't feel like, it's not on my mind, I don't wake up every morning and be like, oh my God, we're in a recession … I guess something that has to do with peers, relationships, that concerns me the most." After much back and forth, the students decided to focus their production efforts on "relationship problems" as it links to gender, race, and media. Even though the group did not choose to focus on an explicitly political issue, their decision to connect the topic to gender, race, and media did introduce a fairly political lens.

The planning and production phase for the show involved conducting street interviews and a survey as well as producing a series of three short vignettes that the audience would watch and respond to as a part of the live show. During these discussions, Ina and Majida made a point to encourage the discussion of controversial issues by saying, "I love debates, arguing … . yeah, lets go" and "Okay I love that argument, let's go ask people [on the street] their different perspectives, one perspective of a guy that plays video games and one from the perspective of a girl who gets annoyed by that?" This legitimation of controversy encouraged the urban scholars to elicit and interrogate differing perspectives about teen relationships.

Their work yielded strong dividends during the live show. The urban scholars invited young people from their organization to attend – every seat was occupied. Drawing from the skills that they had developed through public speaking, street interviews, and critical inquiry, the scholars sat on tall director's chairs in a semicircle in front of the audience hosting and engaging the audience in a wide range of controversial conversations. Lorenzo, one of the scholars, remarked that the live show opened the door for young people to talk to one another about the pressures that they feel from their families to date and marry within their cultures, the pressures that young women and men experience to uphold traditional gender roles, as well as ways to subvert and challenge these pressures.

YMA community-based media trainings, such as the one described above, operate as a space where peer trainers and participants enact social relations that expand the boundaries of who can be a media educator and producer. The trainings with their focus on peer-to-peer learning, the inclusion of differing perspectives, and the direct hands-on experience of filmmaking serve as a model or a way for young people to prefigure a youth-centered space to collectively make media about issues they care about from their perspectives. Prefigurative spaces support individuals and groups to engage in social, cultural, political, and/or economic efforts of direct action in which they are modeling or realizing an alternative vision for themselves and their communities.[8] These spaces lend themselves to the incubation of new ideas and visions where people "envision alternative futures and plot strategies to realize them" (Polletta, 1999, p. 3).[9] YMA fits with this characterization as youth shape alternative media structures, practices, and experiences that begin to enact what is possible (Maeckelbergh, 2011).

A number of participants noted the importance of YMA as a youth-centered space. They expressed frustration with the unsolicited power that adults in their day-to-day lives wield in their attempts to get youth to conform to their rules and expectations. Gio, YMA peer trainer and media producer, framed how this overbearing weight of authority plays out:

> I think the barriers that young people face are a lot of voices denying that youth can do anything. I think the big thing that stands in youth's way is the constant vision that other people give them. Let's say you go to school, and there's this specific way that that institution works, where youth are basically in a space where the teacher says this is how its done, this is how you should be, you should act this way, not this way because you'll be punished, you'll be reprimanded ... But a lot of people get in the way whether it be adults, whether it be officials, whether it be the cops, because they don't believe that youth have that knowledge to bring up that perspective, or say these things that they have to say.

Gio's account illuminates how youth are schooled to think that they need to mold themselves according to the rules of authority figures. According to Gio, "mainstream thought of what a youth is or what a youth thinks or what a youth should be" sets up norms that discourage and sometimes criminalize youth for challenging the system.

In addition to adult rules, young people contend with negative societal perceptions of youth – particularly poor urban youth of color as uninterested, self-involved, problems to be fixed – that reinforce existing disconnects between youth and adults. Akom et al. (2008) assert that these characterizations overlook the "relevance of youth agency – young people's ability to analyze and respond to problems impeding their social and economic advancement" (p. 2). These depictions also point to a cultural tendency to "adultify" youth of color in a manner that denies them the "protections of childhood innocence often accorded to white, middle-class children" while also precluding them from the privileges of adult political participation and power (Gordon, 2010, p. 9).

But these misrepresentations and stereotypes about urban youth also fuel YMA's interest in and commitment to the peer education model. The shared ownership of the production process enables YMA peer educators and participants to challenge and break out of the molds of authority that define what they are supposed to do and say. Gio likes to think of YMA as a space in which young people can share their discontents on a peer-to-peer level and leverage whatever it is that is "riling them up to make a video opposing whatever these forces are … . It creates a space where youth tend to take on that power that film is art and art is an expression, and their expression is what's inside them."

The hands on nature of YMA peer-led trainings reflects Bennett's notion of "actualizing citizenship." Quentin, YMA production coordinator, describes the hands on sensibility:

> How many places can you actually man the cameras as a high school student, be in the control room, you know what I'm saying? And then you have a network. And most likely you'll be an intern if you're in high school. You'll be an intern getting coffee for the reporter that's coming in late somewhere. But here, it's hands-on. It's true. It's real. And the possibilities are endless, pretty much.

Niko, a YMA participant, explained:

> [YMA] has impacted me and my community because it makes us stronger and bold to express our ideas. And then, to say, to speak our minds, and yeah, to say what's right, what's wrong.

Kevin, YMA intern, remarked:

> As far as I'm concerned being the youngest black male, like, at this age to be here, you know, you don't hear stuff like this everyday. I'd rather be out there controlling the media … about kids like me going out and doing things like this, than seeing me come home … on the 10 o'clock news with a kid looking like me got shot for some girlfriend foolishness. As far as, like, any race, like, any minority race, you don't see much of us in the media.

We see in these accounts how the participants draw from their grievances about adult-centered education models and mainstream media practices to articulate the importance of spaces like YMA.

The hands on and youth-centered culture can invoke youthtopian principles as youth develop skills in media production and media literacy to resist and challenge negative portrayals of youth of color as "problems" or "disengaged." Kevin asserted, "people are getting tired of seeing stereotypical bad and sad news all over TV … and nowadays people want to become the media." Kevin identified "becoming the media" as a vehicle for autonomy that is particularly important for youth like himself to get a "chance to speak about what they see and what they do and things they go through, things that are important to them … . A good chance to really express and really get a really good hand on technology and get into the world of media." Like Kevin, many YMA participants identify hands-on media making as a source of public power and control.

Cultivating solidarity among YMA participants is another key dimension of the peer education model. At YMA, creating a culture of solidarity invokes a sense of belonging, a shared critique of mainstream media, "the promotion of intercultural dialogue," and a "culture of hope" that staff, peer educators, and participants can actively construct a more just media system (Bandy, 2004, p. 412). Peer trainer, Gio, explained, "I think it's just a really powerful dynamic of being able to work with another youth to build yourself and teach that person at the same time, so it's like the learner is also the teacher and the teacher is the learner." The peer-to-peer connection in age, background, and interest can facilitate rapport and trust between the peer media educators and participants that are difficult to achieve in conventional teaching and learning arrangements between teachers and students. Gio explained the importance of establishing common ground:

> If there's somebody that's 19 teaching somebody that's 19, I think there's an easier common ground to find, and I think in education that's the biggest, biggest, biggest thing, that's really important with education is finding where that similarity is within people ... Its even better than the teacher model because the teacher model, its like taking a curriculum based on whoever wrote it, it's usually European history that doesn't have to do with any history with an immigrant youth here and a lot of that stuff is just fed ... Well what I'm trying to say is that the teacher model in schools isn't as involved. Not to say that all teachers don't get involved with their youth but ... a lot has to do with following that job, following that curriculum that says this is the European history but where is the African history, where is the Latino history? ... And I think that's a big thing with the peer to peer model is that these [peer media educators] are from the communities of these youth ... . it's like having that same struggle.

This common ground and identification with "that same struggle" combined with the absence of a teacher-like figure opens up leadership positions for youth to assume. Gio explains, "not having somebody that be the end all be all director, the surveyor of what should happen and what shouldn't happen, it just goes back to youth." These connections between peer trainers and participating youth can also lead to the formation of production groups and other career opportunities.

The peer educators assume a bridging role as they seek to transfer communicative power and skills to youth. The YMA participants often frame the peer educators as mentors, which in turn leads to a shift in how youth view each other. Andrea, the YMA director, explained:

> I definitely see the peer trainers as foot soldiers in what we do. And we see them as a way to find a larger cadre of peer trainers ... on the premise that ... especially if we're

working with at-risk youth … it becomes easier to create safe space[s], when one young person talks to another young person. And I also think it creates role models that you may not have always seen, or may not have always aspired to see in someone that is your peer, you know, doing something different. And I think it's all about exposure, you know, creating filmmakers, but also creating critical thinkers, and a community of young people where they see themselves as resources. And so that's the kind of guiding philosophy of our work.

In many ways, the peer media educators operate as "foot soldiers" for new media making ideas and practices within the media justice movement. This role is akin to Robnett's (2000) study of bridge leadership in the civil rights movement. The bridge women (and some men) occupied an intermediate tier of leadership bridging individual politics to the larger politics of the movement. The peer media educators assume a similar bridging role as they introduce and connect youth and youth groups to the larger principles and goals of the media justice movement.

The peer educators also gain a wide range of organizing skills. Gio noted some of these skills: "finding my own language, how to work with youth, how to work within the production field, how to be a director, how to communicate different things." Many peer media educators also articulated a sense of passion for their work. Vianka remarked:

You have to have dedication to love what you do, because if I didn't love what I do it, like, the stress alone could like kill me, like just all the things, all the trainings that I have to do here, all the people that I have to work with, constantly in and out of the office … If I didn't love what I do it would be very stressful. But it's good stress because I love being here and I love the people that I work with.

This dedication to teaching and media making is critical in enduring the many responsibilities associated with facilitating media trainings for a changing cast of community youth groups. We see Bennett's notion of actualizing citizenship at play with the peer-to-peer focus on hands-on production practices, shared ownership, and solidarity that enables youth to begin to prefigure an alternative media system, a path toward direct democracy wherein participants can render their visible grievances, values, and visions through a youth-centered platform.

The Other Side: Challenges of Juggling Multiple Roles

Yet the peer-to-peer model is not in and of itself emancipatory, as it also poses challenges that can surface when YMA and community-based groups uphold differing organizational goals, arrangements, and power relations.

The community media trainings tend to fall into two broad categories: the *all-encompassing training* by which the YMA peer trainers assume full responsibility for facilitating the production of a media piece and the *add-on training* by which the YMA trainers insert themselves into a youth group with already existing facilitators. The following observations of a not so successful community media training illustrate the challenges of the add-on approach.

During the spring of 2008, I attended a 3-month YMA training that peer educators, Wanda and Jamal, facilitated with youth journalists from "Youth Power Press." The press is part of a larger organization, City Organizers, a citywide advocacy/activist network for low-income and immigrant communities focused on issues of equity, economic justice, environmental justice, fair housing, and immigration rights. The training was intended to produce a set of videos to accompany online articles that the youth journalists were publishing about the war in Iraq and school budget cuts.

Wanda, the YMA peer media educator, experienced frustration throughout the training as a result of ineffective communication between her and the peer trainer and staff at City Organizers. Before the training began, Wanda emailed the staff a weekly outline of the planned agendas and activities for the three-month training. Invariably the day before each training, one of the educators would email or call her, "what are we going to do tomorrow" without recognizing that Wanda had already provided them with this weekly outline.

This oversight was compounded by a lack of respect that she experienced at City Organizers. The training was initially scheduled to meet once a week from 4 PM to 6 PM but things shifted fairly quickly when the City Organizers peer educator gathered the students at 4:30 on the first day, facilitated an icebreaker, talked about upcoming events, and Wanda, who already had limited time with the group wondered, "can't you do this another time? They [City Organizers staff] are like, well the students only come in once a week so [you] can keep them longer." Wanda was annoyed with this assumption that she was expected to accommodate their changing needs and schedules. Her frustration down spiraled into a series of difficult interactions whereby she occasionally lost patience with some of the youth participants in the training.

Leah, a City Organizers educator in her forties, had another perspective on the matter. While she recognized that the peer educators were in college with multiple responsibilities, she felt that some time needed to be carved out for planning. She explained:

> I think to do anything well, the model of someone coming in with all sorts of skills and popping in and popping out, I don't think it is the most effective. And I think just my

experience working in public schools, writing in private schools, working in CBOs [community based organizations], the planning time, the extra time it takes to plan, I just think it would bear so much fruit. Like two planning meetings, one in the beginning and one debriefing meeting in the end that is all it takes just to get on the same page to know this is the ethos here, these are the values of how we work, we really respect everyone, we try to be really patient, sometimes it's really crazy .... But I actually think that a lot of the problems could have been dealt with by one planning meeting but the leader refused to do it and she refused to even talk on the phone and that's just hard, we are all busy. She said email me, email me and then, she wouldn't email back.

Leah also acknowledged, "our site is very chaotic." City Organizers, like many community-based organizations (including YMA), operates with some degree of dysfunction as Leah explained, "we are in a too small space, we have different kids sometimes, so it is not like we are perfect because we are not, we are far, far from perfect." The lack of planning, ambiguity in roles and expectations, and differences in organizational culture led to disappointment for Leah and Wanda. In addition, Wanda ended up taking on the brunt of editing for the videos because she did not have the patience or time at the end of her college semester to provide the necessary training for the participants to edit the raw footage into coherent videos for their online articles.

A number of the peer media educators recognized the struggles with the "add-on" approach because youth group staff and YMA peer trainers who work together often end up "stepping on each other's toes." In addition to breakdowns in communication, some peer educators discussed the hierarchical nature of some community media trainings in which existing relations between young people and staff can subsume the YMA principle of power sharing especially when YMA was solely an "add-on." Overall, the YMA peer educators were more adaptable to differing organizational dynamics when they were facilitating "all encompassing" media trainings, because even if it did end up being more work on their part, they established better connections with participants when they did not have to share facilitation and planning with adult staff or peer educators from the community groups.

The peer-to-peer education model can also be overwhelming for incoming peer trainers when they have limited experience facilitating groups and teaching media production skills. Some YMA peer trainers encountered a "trial by error" culture when they first started. Gio recalled his first few months on the job:

They hired me as a peer trainer, I was like what, now I gotta teach people, it was freaking me, it really was freaking me out. So [the] first day I tried and I literally was like you know had a very shaky voice and I was like what the fuck is going on, I didn't know what was going on with anyone that's in this room and I felt all these very, very uncertain things about myself and I did feel like it was a lot ... I think what worked for me was, kind of just having my own space to really learn how to do things through, again, trial by error.

Another YMA peer trainer, Vianka, likened learning how to peer educate to learning how to ride a bike. She recommended that YMA assume a "training wheels" approach for newcomers that combined the distribution of resources including training materials, facilitations tips, and YMA curricula with mentoring from YMA staff and more seasoned peer educators. With this approach, Vianka noted:

You know what you have to do. And then you go with a peer trainer and not only you see what is being done on paper, but, you actually probably get to participate a little bit and be involved in it. So that when you do go on your own, you kind of get the training wheels off. It's, like, when you first learn how to ride a bike, you got training wheels to help you balance. And then once you really get the hang of it, you can just go.

Many peer educators lamented that they wished they had received this combination of resources and support. But most would also add the disclaimer that there is not "one way" to facilitate community media trainings as each one is different depending on the composition, learning styles, and aims of the group. Given the variation in training needs among incoming peer educators, it has been challenging for YMA to develop an orientation that takes into account this mix of needs for support and autonomy.

A third underlying dilemma within the peer education model is how to negotiate the closeness in age between trainers and participants. Although this age similarity can foster a sense of connection, it can also present challenges for peer trainers who are not always taken seriously by the participants. Ina discussed the first few times that she worked with Urban Thinkers:

I was trying to be really friendly with them and [then] they would lose complete respect for you kind of. Like you would tell them to do something and the group would disregard it and keeping doing their thing. They would not be taking you seriously. So what I mean is be friendly but at the same time, make sure that they know that you are an educator and that [they] have a task.

Many YMA peer trainers try to cultivate this sense of shared common ground with groups that can backfire especially with large groups or groups that do not have a specific focus for their community media projects.

In mediating this closeness in age, the peer trainers often used the term, "flip flop" or "balance" to characterize the oscillation between friendship and leadership that they invoke in their interactions with participants. Vianka remarked:

> I flip flop. I be like, be quiet [and then], okay you want to hang out tomorrow. Yah I really flip flop because I understand that I am not that much older than them but it's kind of like a big sister, big brother role. It's much easier if you put it that way ... because I am a big sister. I know that even though I still like to hang out and talk to my sister but I am still the big sister and there is still a level of respect that she has to have for me but at the same time I have to have it for her. So that's how I kind of see it, I put myself in a big sister role with the young people.

In negotiating the balance between connection and leadership, the peer educators identified strategies including the development of flexible lesson plans, strong facilitation skills, and the delegation of leadership responsibilities to participants.

Peer educators also bump into some salient challenges with respect to youth engagement. Andrea explained that when groups and schools reach out to YMA to plan a workshop, "the connection is between two adults ... and not necessarily at the urges of the students to bring [YMA] in." Leading up to a community media workshop, staff from youth organizations often expressed excitement about the prospect of the training but the participating young people do not always share this enthusiasm. Soledad, YMA peer educator, recounted a training that she did with Vamos, a Latino youth empowerment group, in which the adult staff were excited about working with YMA on the development of a public service announcement, but in practice, the participants were not particularly interested in the project. Soledad stated, "I felt like I was pushing a rock up a hill." Working with community youth groups and schools, attendance can also be challenging as the peer media educators do not have control over who shows up from week to week. At the same time, the peer trainers also lead busy lives. One peer educator explained, "one of the inherent problems with [YMA] probably is because we're all so young, we have other things."

This juggle of differing goals, roles, and responsibilities has interesting implications for spaces such as YMA that seek to engage youth from disenfranchised communities in social change work. Narrow definitions of civic engagement linked to participation with formal government and institutions do not square with the diversity of interests that youth bring to YMA. We need to consider that "the economic, social and cultural resources that young people ha[ve] access to shap[e] their experiences and these in turn shap[e] their definitions of politics and views of political institutions" (Marsh, O'Toole, & Jones, 2007, p. 212). Many participants do not consider themselves activists, as Karl, one media educator, explained, "because ... if you ask about activism, they'd be like it's rich white kids who are outside yelling." Karl's account illustrates how YMA youth often enter these spaces with racialized and class-inflected ideas about activism. As such, many YMA youth do not see themselves fitting into this particular rubric. Therefore, part of the challenge for peer trainers is creating a space where YMA constituencies can feel a sense of collective ownership in the media-making process. This can be especially challenging given the part-time commitment that youth from disenfranchised communities tend to make with the many other competing family, work, school, and social obligations on their plate.

The changing cast of community groups and the lack of engagement within certain groups can also present challenges for peer educators in ways that facilitate burn out, lack of professionalism, and frustration with inconsistent attendance, and so forth. At the same time, the demand, pace, and diversity of this work can operate as a catalyzing force for the peer educators to develop skills in navigating the politics and practices of differing community youth groups. Many of the trainers gain experience and knowledge that allow them to advance to staff positions either at YMA or other independent media groups. In looking at the current staff at YMA, three of the five staff started as YMA peer media educators. This high level of retention of peer trainers at YMA reflects a fairly enduring model for youth to connect with peers in ways that cultivates an alternative system for media education, production, and distribution. The skill-building model of peer leadership provides opportunities for youth to grow within the organization and build important life skills in a gradual manner, assuming continued commitment on the part of the participating youth.

CONCLUSION

This case examines the role of collective production practices as a vehicle for youth participation and leadership in media activism. Akin to recent works that privilege more youth-centered experiences of citizenship (Akom et al., 2008; Bennett, 2008; Coleman, 2008; Gordon, 2010), this case shifts our attention to the organizational dilemmas of peer media education as a model for youth engagement in social change work.

Peer-to-peer education facilitates the development of youth-centered spaces from which youth from disenfranchised communities can begin to prefigure alternative media systems, practices, and content on their own terms. The focus on informal training and mentoring at YMA allows youth to see one another as resources, which in turn facilitates connections, dialogue, and common ground among and between peer educators and participants. Additionally, the absence of an adult or authority figure enables youth to assume a significant amount of power as decision makers and leaders within their alternative space and throughout the larger movement.

At the same time, YMA peer media educators indicate tensions that can surface in doing community media trainings. It can be especially taxing for YMA peer media educators when YMA and community group goals and values differ. This tension is even further amplified when the YMA training becomes an "add-on" to an existing program. Many peer educators find themselves juggling multiple roles and responsibilities as they "flip-flop" between the role of mentor, facilitator, and friend. Additionally, some community groups express a desire for more professionalism on the part of the peer trainers.

This discussion of peer education points to broader questions about the implicit citizenship practices embedded in the collective production of socially conscious media. What is the promise of peer education in sparking social change? Throughout the course of this research, I began to realize that youth participation in independent media spaces is not only about securing additional pipelines for youth to make media. Rather, we need to recognize a complex set of factors that inform the internal dynamics of peer education and collective social change projects, more generally defined.

First, the tendency to frame the persistence of the digital divide in terms of youth access overlooks collective and community-driven experiences of digital participation and citizenship. This shift in framing digital access, involvement, and citizenship from an individual to a collective experience is particularly indicative of the peer education model as youth look to each other to collectively negotiate the politics of producing media. Additionally, YMA staff noted that youth living in disenfranchised communities seek out independent youth media spaces as a platform for not only media making but also community building and organizing.

Second, horizontal exchanges of knowledge are particularly indicative of peer education models as the absence of an authority figure opens a space for youth to assume more power as decision makers and leaders. Maeckelbergh (2011) notes that horizontality is both a value and a practice for movement actors to actively work toward equality (p. 10). However, horizontality also leans on the premise that inequality infuses every interaction to the extent that constant vigilance is necessary to recognize these inequalities and establish "structures that hold each person responsible for continuously challenging inequalities at every step of the democratic decision-making process" (Maeckelbergh, 2011, p. 10).

Third, the peer-to-peer education model facilitates a social environment for youth to cultivate a sense of solidarity. The physicality of youth media spaces is critical for youth to convene and experience face-to-face encounters that enable youth to transmit their experiences and knowledge to each other in ways that build skills in collaborative problem solving and community engagement. Kellner (2010) notes that a primary challenge of contemporary education is the separation between student experiences with technoculture and the classroom environment based in print culture and conventional individualized learning methods. Jenkins et al. (2008) identify "collective intelligence" as a key skill of participatory culture in the digital age wherein individuals and groups have an increased capacity to pool knowledge, elicit participation, and interact with larger communities. In spaces such as YMA, collective intelligence is a valuable resource as youth look to the peer educators and each other as informal mentors and sources of guidance and validation throughout the collective process of making oppositional media.

Finally, the peer media education model opens up a space for creativity, experimentation, and imagination. Scholars like to theorize youth as agents who invoke disjunction, disruption, and sometimes rupture between the conventional social order and subversive acts of resistance (Melucci, 1996). The ongoing influx of new images and information provide a diversity of possibilities unforeseen in previous eras (Fornas, 1995; Giddens, 1991). The frequent antipathy of youth to constructing an identity that resonates with dominant culture opens a unique space for hybridized or activist media production.

In many ways, peer media education model lends itself to experiences of "actualizing citizenship" as challenging mainstream media involves active engagement, experimentation, constant redefinition, and a slurred belonging in which youth recognize dominant culture without being entirely subsumed by it. In the case of independent media spaces, youth represent the majority generation that is tinkering with dominant systems and open software sources to model noncommercial, inclusive, oppositional systems and practices of producing media. Longitudinal research tracking the life courses of the participating youth is needed to better understand how involvement in leadership positions in youth media production impacts their life, education, and work trajectories over time.

NOTES

1. Williams (2005) contends that someone who possesses an "alternate point of view ... is someone who simply finds a different way to live and wishes to be left alone," whereas "someone [with oppositional views] finds a different way to live and wants to change the society in its light" (p. 42).

2. YMA Center is an assigned pseudonym for the primary site of research.

3. See Hobbs and Jensen (2009).

4. My fieldwork amounted to 810 hours over the course of 18 months.

5. I assigned pseudonyms to represent the four groups – Vamos, City Organizers, Urban Thinkers, and the Palestine Israel Collective for Education (PICE).

6. See Fleetwood (2005) and Ellsworth (1989).

7. See Freire's (1994, 1973) theory of emancipatory education.

8. Most conceptualizations of prefigurative work pulls from a larger body of work on *free spaces* introduced by Sara Evans and Henry Boyte (1986) to connote public spaces in which "people are able to learn a new self-respect, a deeper and more assertive group identity, public skills, and values of cooperation and civic virtue" (p. 17).

9. See Maeckelbergh (2011), Polletta (1999).

REFERENCES

Akom, A. A., Cammarota, J., & Ginwright, S. (2008). Youthtopias: Towards a new paradigm of critical youth studies. *Youth Media Reporter*, 2(4), 1–30.

Bandy, J. (2004). Paradoxes of transnational civil societies under neoliberalism: The coalition for justice in the maquiladoras. *Social Problems*, 51(3), 410–431.

Bennett, L. (2008). Changing citizenship in the digital age. In W. Bennett (Ed.), *Digital media and youth civic engagement*. Boston, MA: MIT Press.

Buckingham, D. (2000). *After the death of childhood: Growing up in the age of electronic media*. Malden, MA: Polity Press.

Buckingham, D. (2011). Afterword. In W. Fisherkeller (Ed.), *International perspectives on youth media: Cultures of production and education* (pp. 375–380). New York, NY: Peter Lang Publishing.

Carlsson, U., Tayie, S., Jacquinot-Delaunay, G., & Manuel Perez Tornero, J. (2008). *Empowerment through media education: An intercultural dialogue*. Goteborg University, Sweden: The International Clearinghouse on Children, Youth and Media, Nordicom.

Castellanos, I., Bach, A., & Kulick, R. (2010). Youth channel all-city: Mapping the media needs and ideas of urban youth. In P. M. Napoli & M. Aslama (Eds.), *Communications research in action: Scholar-activist collaborations for a democratic public sphere* (pp. 157–176). New York, NY: Fordham University Press.

Charmaz, K. (2005). Grounded theory in the 21st century: Applications for advancing social justice studies. In N. Denzin & Y. Lincoln (Eds.), *Sage handbook for qualitative research* (3rd ed., pp. 507–536). Thousand Oaks, CA: Sage.

Chavez, V., & Soep, E. (2005). Youth radio and the pedagogy of collegiality. *Harvard Educational Review*, 75(4), 409–434.

Chavez, V., & Soep, E. (2010). *Drop that knowledge: Youth radio stories.* Berkeley, CA: University of California Press.

Coleman, S. (2008). Doing it for themselves: Management versus autonomy in youth e-citizenship. In W. Bennett (Ed.), *Digital media and youth civic engagement* (pp. 189–206). Boston, MA: MIT Press.

Cornwall, A., & Jewkes, R. (1995). What is participatory action research? *Social Science and Medicine, 41*(12), 1667–1676.

Corsaro, W. (2003). *We're friends, right? Inside kids' culture.* Washington, DC: Joseph Henry Press.

De Angelis, M. (2005). PR like PRocess! Strategy from the Bottom-Up. *Ephemera, 5*(2), 193–204.

Ellsworth, E. (1989). Why doesn't this feel empowering? Working through the repressive myths of critical pedagogy. *Harvard Educational Review, 59,* 297–324.

Evans, S., & Boyte, H. (1986). *Free spaces: The sources of democratic change in America.* Chicago, IL: University of Chicago Press.

Fisherkeller, J. (2000). The writers are getting kind of desperate: Young adolescents, television, and literacy. *Journal of Adolescent and Adult Literacy, 43*(7), 596–606.

Fleetwood, N. (2005). Authenticating practices: Producing the "real" in youth videos. In S. Maira & E. Soep (Eds.), *Youthscapes: The popular, the national, the global* (pp. 155–172). Philadelphia, PA: University of Pennsylvania Press.

Fornas, J. (1995). Youth, culture and modernity. In J. Fornas & G. Bolin (Eds.), *Youth culture in late modernity.* London, UK: Sage Publications.

Freire, P. (1973). *Education for critical consciousness.* New York, NY: Seabury Press.

Freire, P. (1994). *Pedagogy of the oppressed.* New York, NY: Continuum.

Giddens, A. (1991). *Modernity and self-identity: Self and society in the late modern age.* Stanford, CA: Stanford University Press.

Gitlin, T. (2003). *The whole world is watching television: Mass media in the making and unmaking of the new left.* Los Angeles, CA: University of California Press.

Gordon, H. (2010). *We fight to win: Inequality and the politics of youth activism.* New Brunswick, NJ: Rutgers University Press.

Gordon, H., & Taft, J. (2011). Re-thinking youth political socialization: Teenage activists talk back. *Youth & Society, 43,* 1499–1527.

Hackett, R., & Carroll, W. (2006). *Remaking media: The struggle to democratize public communication.* New York, NY: Routledge.

Hebdige, D. (1979). *Subculture: The meaning of style.* New York: Routledge.

Hobbs, R., & Jensen, A. (2009). The past, present, and future of media literacy education. *Journal of Media Literacy Education, 1,* 1–11.

Jenkins, H., Clinton, K., Purushotma, R., Robinson, A., & Weigel, M. (2008). Confronting the challenges of participatory culture: Media education for the 21st Century. Chicago, IL: MacArthur Foundation, white paper.

Kellner, D. (1995). Cultural studies, multiculturalism, and media culture. In G. Dines & J. Humez (Eds.), *Gender, race and class in media.* Thousand Oaks, CA: Sage.

Kellner, D. (2010). School shootings, violence, and the reconstruction of education: Some proposals. In Ilan Gur-Zeev (Ed.), *The possibility/impossibility of a new critical language in education* (pp. 367–378). Rotterdam, The Netherlands: Sense Publishers.

Kidd, D., & Rodriguez, C. (2010). Volume introduction. In C. Rodriguez, D. Kidd & L. Stein (Eds.), *Making our media: Global initiatives toward a democratic public sphere 1, Creating new communication Spaces* (pp. 1–22). Cresskill, NJ: Hampton Press.

Marsh, D., O'Toole, T., & Jones, S. (2007). *Young people and politics in the UK*. New York, NY: Palgrave.

Maeckelbergh, M. (2011). Doing is believing: Prefiguration as strategic practice in the alterglobalization movement. *Social Movement Studies, 10*(1), 1–20.

Melucci, A. (1996). *Challenging codes: Collective action in the information age*. New York, NY: Cambridge University Press.

Meyrowitz, J. (1985). *No sense of place: The impact of electronic media on social behavior*. Oxford, UK: Oxford University Press.

Plato. (1987). The republic (D. Lee, Trans.). New York, NY: Penguin.

Polletta, F. (1999). "Free spaces" in collective action. *Theory and Society, 28*, 1–38.

Postman, N. (1994). *The disappearance of childhood*. New York, NY: Vintage.

Robnett, B. (2000). *How long? How long?: African American women in the struggle for civil rights*. New York, NY: Oxford University Press.

Rodriguez, C. (2001). *Fissures in the mediascape: An international study of citizen's media*. Cresskill, NJ: Hampton Press.

Sitrin, M. (2012). Horizontalism and the Occupy Movements. *Dissent, 59*(2), 74–75.

Williams, R. (2005). *Culture and materialism*. London, UK: Verso.

Youniss, J., Bales, S., Diversi, M., Christmas-Best, V., McLaughlin, M., & Silbereisen, R. (2002). Youth civic engagement in the twenty-first century. *Journal of Research on Adolescence, 12*(1), 121–148.

AUTHORS' BIOGRAPHIES

THE SERIES EDITOR

Loretta E. Bass is an Associate Professor of Sociology at the University of Oklahoma. She earned her PhD in Sociology from the University of Connecticut and completed a two-year appointment within the Fertility and Family Branch of the Population Division at the U.S. Census Bureau. Dr. Bass focuses her research on children and stratification issues, and has published her research in *Population Research and Policy Review*, *Sociological Inquiry*, *Sociological Focus*, *Political Behavior*, *Anthropology of Work Review*, *International Journal of Sociology and Social Policy*, *Sociological Studies of Children and Youth*, *Journal of Reproductive Medicine*, *Journal of Sociology and Social Work*, *International Journal of Sexual Health*, and *Current Sociology*. Prior to becoming the *Sociological Studies of Children and Youth* Series Editor, she served as co-editor for two years and as a guest-editor for a special international volume in 2005. She has also published a book, *Child Labor in Sub-Saharan Africa* (Lynne Rienner Publishers, 2004), which offers a window on the lives of child workers in 43 African countries. She currently serves as Past-Chair of the American Sociological Association's (ASA) Children and Youth Section and as the President of Research Committee 53 on the Sociology of Childhood within the International Sociological Association (ISA).

THE GUEST CO-EDITORS

Sandi Kawecka Nenga is Associate Professor of Sociology at Southwestern University in Georgetown, Texas. She earned her PhD in Sociology from Indiana University. Her research is positioned squarely within the sociology of childhood and youth, focusing on the experiences of youth volunteers, the lived experience of social class, and middle school peer cultures. Her work has appeared in several journals, including *Journal of Contemporary Ethnography*, *Childhood: A Global Journal of Child Research*, *Sociological Studies of Children and Youth*, and *Journal of Youth Studies*. Currently she is researching the educational experiences of first-generation Latino high school students in a summer college readiness program.

Jessica K. Taft is Assistant Professor of Sociology at Davidson College. Her research sits at the intersection of the literatures on social movements, transnationalism and globalization, childhood and youth, and gender. She is the author of *Rebel Girls: Youth Activism and Social Change Across the Americas* (NYU Press, 2011) and several articles about high school activists, organizations for girls, and girls' relationships to politics. She is currently conducting research for a new project on relationships between children and adults within the Peruvian movement of working children.

THE AUTHORS

Lucia Alcalá's research focuses on cultural variation in children's learning processes as they contribute to family work and community organizations. Her current projects investigate the relationship between children's participation in mature activities and their development of initiative and collaborative planning skills. Alcalá has served as editor of the University of California Santa Cruz, Department of Psychology Newsletter, as well as a Graduate Teaching Instructor within the Department of Psychology and Teaching Associate in the Latin American and Latino Studies Department. She is the recipient of the 2011 Max Levine Scholarship award, as well as numerous other awards within her field. Alcala is expected to receive her PhD in Developmental Psychology from the University of California Santa Cruz in June of 2013.

Lily Appoh is a Post-Doctoral Researcher at the Department of Psychology, Norwegian University of Science and Technology, Trondheim (NTNU). She earned her PhD from the same University in December 2004. Her research project was on Psychological Consequences of Childhood Malnutrition. Her publications have appeared in *Maternal and Child Nutrition, Journal of Psychology in Africa*, and other journals. From 2005 to 2008, she worked with the United Nations High Commissioner for Refugees in several countries in Africa and Asia. She has also been a part-time lecturer in Community Psychology at the Psychology Department, NTNU. Her current research project is on "Integration of African Immigrants in Norway."

Emily Bent serves as the Executive Director of Sage Girl, a New Jersey based non-profit organization that delivers girl-positive programs to the community. She works with girls to provide experiential-learning opportunities designed to enhance the wisdom and strength of every girl. In addition to her work with Sage Girl, Emily teaches in the Women's and Gender Studies Department at The College of New Jersey and is the UN Representative for Girls Learn International. She also remains an active member of the Working Group on Girls at the United Nations. Emily earned a PhD in Global Women's Studies from the National University of Ireland, Galway in 2012 and holds an MA and BA in Women's and Gender Studies from Rutgers University and The College of New Jersey. Her research is broadly classified within the field of Girls Studies and explores the complexities of *girl* as a subject of feminist inquiry.

Rebecca M. Callahan is an Assistant Professor in the Department of Curriculum & Instruction at the University of Texas at Austin, with a research affiliation in the Population Research Center. Dr. Callahan's primary research interests center on the academic and civic preparation of immigrant, language minority adolescents as they transition from high school into young adulthood. Along with her research on immigrant youths' civic development, Dr. Callahan's work explores educational stratification among immigrant youth, as well as the intersection between language and educational policy. Her work has appeared in *Educational Policy, American Educational Research Journal, Social Science Quarterly,* and *Educational Evaluation and Policy Analysis* among others. Her forthcoming book, *Coming of Political Age: American Schools and the Civic Development of Immigrant Youth* will be available from Russell Sage Publishers in spring 2013.

William A. Corsaro was Robert H. Shaffer Class of 1967 Endowed Chair and is currently Emeritus Professor of Sociology at Indiana University, Bloomington where he won the President's Award for Distinguished Teaching. He earned his PhD from the University of North Carolina, Chapel Hill. He is the author or editor of several books including *Friendship and Peer Culture in the Early Years* (Ablex,1985), *"We're Friends, Right?": Inside Kids' Culture* (Joseph Henry Press, 2003), *I Compagni: Understanding Children's Transition from Preschool to Elementary School* (with Luisa Molinari, Teachers College Press, 2005), and *The Sociology of Childhood 3rd edition* (Pine Forge Press, 2011). His publications have appeared in *The American Sociological Review, Social Psychology Quarterly, Sociology of Education, Human Development, Journal of Contemporary Ethnography, Annual Review of Sociology, Sociological Studies of Children and Youth,* and *Childhood* among others. He served as chair of the Section on Children and Youth of the American Sociological Association.

Shira Eve Epstein entered the field of education as a middle school teacher in New York City. She is presently an Assistant Professor at The School of Education in The City College of New York (CUNY). In her research, she primarily studies different forms of youth civic engagement exploring how teachers and students identify, study, and take action in reference to pressing social problems. Her work can be found in journals including *English Journal, Race Ethnicity and Education*, and *Journal of Teacher Education*. She prioritizes learning from and with teachers and students in urban schools. She has also partnered with community-based organizations that design and enact social justice oriented curricula.

Jesica Siham Fernández is a PhD Candidate in Social Psychology with a Designated Emphasis in Latin American & Latino Studies (LALS) at the University of California, Santa Cruz. Her research centers on examining how institutions, like schools and communities, facilitate and support opportunities for Latino youth to move from a place of invisibility to a place of visibility, via civic engagement, despite the education and citizenship challenges that Latino youth experience. Fernández is a joint Teaching Associate in the Department of Psychology and Latin American and Latino Studies. Currently she is the National Student Representative for the Society for Community Research and Action (SCRA, Division 27 of the American Psychological Association), and editor of The Community Psychologist Newsletter, affiliated with the American Journal of Community Psychology. Fernández is the recipient of the Eugene Cota-Robles Fellowship, and a Graduate Student Fellow of the American Association of Hispanics in Higher Education (AAHHE).

Berit O. Johannesen is Associate Professor at the Department of Psychology, Norwegian University of Science and Technology where she earned her PhD in 2006 and teaches developmental and cultural psychology. Her research interests are in the area of human development and meaning making among children in their everyday lives. She is now working on projects on children in civic society and on integration of African immigrant families in Norway with William Corsaro and Lily Appoh, and a study about children's participation in civic celebrations in Bali. Her publications include: *Norwegian children negotiating cross-gender play* (in *Insights and Outlouds: Childhood Research in the North*, Oulu University Press, 2010); *Production de sens et positionnement moral dans les jeux d'imagination lego* (in *Cultures enfantines*, Presses Universitaires de Rennes, 2010); and *The creation of new cultures in peer interaction* (in *The Cambridge Handbook* *of Sociocultural Psychology*, Cambridge University Press, 2007, with W. Corsaro).

Rachel Kulick is an Assistant Professor in the Department of Sociology, Anthropology, Crime, and Justice Studies at University of Massachusetts Dartmouth. Her research focuses on how social justice movements attempt to prefigure or "be the change" in their organizational structures, practices, and values. She is specifically interested in the social and political dilemmas that groups face as they seek to model social change within the realities and constraints of everyday work. As part of this research, she works with community groups on participatory action research projects exploring questions and issues that are meaningful and useful to the participating communities. She was Co-Principal Investigator on a research project with a youth media group that was funded by the Social Science Research Council collaborative media project. She recently co-authored the article, "Mapping the Media Needs of Urban Youth" in the volume, *Communications Research in Action: Scholar Activist Collaboration for A Democratic Public Sphere*.

Stuart Lester is Senior Lecturer in Play and Playwork at the University of Gloucestershire, UK, and an Independent play consultant, researcher, and trainer. Current research interests include the nature and value of children's play, everyday playful production of time/space and the conditions under which playfulness thrives. Publications include "Play, Naturally" (with Martin Maudsley, 2007), "Play for a Change. Play, Policy and Practice: A review of contemporary perspectives" (2008), and "Children's Right to Play: An examination of the importance of play in the lives of children worldwide" (2010) (both with Wendy Russell). He has also contributed to a number of play and playwork publications including a chapter entitled "Playing in a Deleuzian playground" in the forthcoming *The Philosophy of Play* (Routledge, 2013).

L. Alison Molina-Girón was born and raised in Honduras where she completed her undergraduate studies in special education. Currently, she teaches courses on democracy and education as a part-time professor at the University of Ottawa. Her research interests lie at the intersection of citizenship, multicultural and social justice education. Dr. Molina-Girón current research examines the practice of citizenship education in urban high school classrooms in Canada with a focus on how conceptions of good citizenship, cultural diversity and socio-economic inequality are taught in classrooms, and the degree to which this prepares students to be actively engaged citizens in civic and political life.

Shauna A. Morimoto is an Assistant Professor in the Department of Sociology and Criminal Justice at the University of Arkansas. She received her PhD in sociology from the University of Wisconsin-Madison in 2008. Her research examines the dynamics of race, gender, and class as they inform organizational structures and pathways to democratic participation. Her current projects explore young people's negotiation of civic and political engagement and the gendered and raced construction of institutions of higher education.

Christopher D. O'Connor holds a PhD in Sociology from the University of Calgary and is currently an Assistant Professor of Criminal Justice at the University of Wisconsin – Superior. Dr. O'Connor teaches classes on social control, policing, community corrections, and youth delinquency. His research interests include policing, school-to-work transitions, boomtowns, youth citizenship, and youth crime/delinquency.

Kathryn M. Obenchain is currently an Assistant Professor of Social Studies Education at Purdue University in West Lafayette, Indiana. A former Fulbright Fellow to Romania, she was previously on the faculty at the University of Nevada, Reno, and the University of Texas at Austin. Her research centers on democratic citizenship education in the United States and newly emerging democracies. Her work has appeared in *Theory & Research in Social Education, Social Studies & the Young Learner, Social Studies, International Journal of Education* and *Equity & Excellence in Education*, among others. She is particularly interested in how social studies classrooms are structured to promote democratic knowledge, skills, and dispositions through curricular and instructional decisions, what informs these decisions, and students' experiences in these classrooms. Her recent work focuses specifically on the civic identities of social studies teachers and their students.

Jocelyn Solís earned her doctorate degree in Developmental Psychology from the City University of New York (CUNY) Graduate Center in 2002. Dr. Solís's research interests were in cultural psychology and the development of identity, language, literacy, and bilingualism. The title of her dissertation was *The (trans)formation of illegality as an identity: A study of the organization of undocumented Mexican immigrants and their children.* In 2003, she was an Assistant Professor in the Graduate Literacy Program of the School of Education at Brooklyn College, and subsequently a

Post-Doctoral Fellow at the University of California, Santa Cruz with Dr. Barbara Rogoff. Dr. Solís lost her life to cancer in 2004 at the age of 30. Her academic contributions and dedication to the field have led to the creation of the Jocelyn Solís Fund to help organize a Lecture Series at the Graduate Center of the City University of New York.